WEB DESIGN

Fourth Edition

INTRODUCTORY

Gary B. Shelly

Jennifer T. Campbell

COURSE TECHNOLOGY
CENGAGE Learning™

SHELLY
CASHMAN
SERIES.

Australia • Brazil • Japan • Korea • Mexico • Singapore • Spain • United Kingdom • United States

COURSE TECHNOLOGY
CENGAGE Learning™

Web Design: Introductory, Fourth Edition
Gary B. Shelly
Jennifer T. Campbell

Vice President, Publisher: Nicole Pinard

Executive Editor: Kathleen McMahon

Product Manager: Nada Jovanovic

Associate Product Manager: Caitlin Womersley

Editorial Assistant: Angela Giannopoulos

Developmental Editor: Amanda Brodkin

Director of Marketing: Elisa Roberts

Marketing Manager: Tristen Kendall

Marketing Coordinator: Adrienne Fung

Production Director: Patty Stephan

Content Project Manager: Matthew Hutchinson

Art Director: Marissa Falco

Cover designer: Joel Sadagursky

Text designer: Joel Sadagursky

Technology Project Manager: Chris Conroy

Print Buyer: Julio Esperas

Copyeditor: Karen Annett

Proofreader: Kathy Orrino

Indexer: Rich Carlson

Compositor: PreMediaGlobal

Printer: RRD Menasha

Library of Congress Control Number: 2011924478
ISBN-13: 978-0-538-48240-0
ISBN-10: 0-538-48240-0

Course Technology
20 Channel Center Street
Boston, Massachusetts 02210
USA

Cengage Learning is a leading provider of customized learning solutions with office locations around the globe, including Singapore, the United Kingdom, Australia, Mexico, Brazil, and Japan. Locate your local office at:
international.cengage.com/region

Cengage Learning products are represented in Canada by Nelson Education, Ltd.

For your course and learning solutions, visit **www.cengage.com**

Course Technology, the Course Technology logo, and the Shelly Cashman Series® are registered trademarks used under license.

To learn more about Course Technology, visit **www.cengage.com/coursetechnology**

Purchase any of our products at your local college store or at our preferred online store **www.cengagebrain.com**

Printed in the United States of America
1 2 3 4 5 6 7 17 16 15 14 13 12 11

Contents

Chapter 1

The Environment and the Tools

Chapter 2

Web Publishing Fundamentals

| # Preface

In this Shelly Cashman Series® *Web Design: Introductory, Fourth Edition* book, you will find an educationally sound and easy-to-follow pedagogy that artfully combines screen shots, drawings, and text with full color to produce a visually appealing and easy-to-understand presentation of Web design. This textbook conveys useful design concepts and techniques typically not addressed in Web authoring textbooks. It explains the connections between a detailed design plan that considers audience needs, Web site design, and various technical issues. Students learn how to balance these elements to create a successful Web site.

The book's seven chapters emphasize key written concepts and principles with numerous Design Tips boxed throughout the text. A variety of challenging written and hands-on activities both within and at the conclusion of each chapter test comprehension, build Web research skills and design awareness, and encourage critical thinking about current issues in Web design.

Objectives of This Textbook

Web Design: Introductory, Fourth Edition is intended for a one-unit introductory Web design course, or in a Web authoring course that teaches Web design techniques and also covers HTML, Adobe Dreamweaver, or Microsoft Expression Web. The objectives of this book are to:

- Present a practical approach to Web design using a blend of traditional development guidelines with current technologies and trends

- Give students an in-depth understanding of Web design concepts and techniques that are essential to planning, creating, testing, publishing, and maintaining Web sites

- Define and describe in detail the six steps in developing a solid Web design plan: define the purpose, identify the site's target audience, determine the site's general content, select the site's structure, design the look and feel of the site, and specify the site's navigation system

- Present the material in a full-color, visually appealing and exciting, easy-to-read manner with a format that invites students to learn

- Provide students with a summary of Design Tips to which they can refer quickly and easily in Appendix A

- Direct students to the World Wide Web to do additional research and allow them to evaluate and assess the design techniques and technologies discussed in the book

- Provide an ongoing case study and assignments that promote student participation in learning about Web design

Distinguishing Features

The distinguishing features of *Web Design: Introductory, Fourth Edition* include the following:

Flexibility

This text focuses on the basic concepts of good Web design rather than on a particular Web browser or Web design technology, allowing it to be used in a variety of Web design or Web authoring courses.

A Blend of Traditional Development with Current Technologies

This book goes beyond a theoretical view of Web design; every effort has been made to use procedures, tools, and solutions that parallel those used by Web designers in today's business world.

Realistic examples support definitions, concepts, and techniques, enabling students to learn in the context of solving realistic problems, much like the ones they will encounter while working in the Web design field. In this textbook, students learn to apply best practices while avoiding common pitfalls. In addition, numerous Design Tips are provided to summarize and highlight important topics.

Visually Appealing

The design of this textbook combines screen shots, drawings, marginal elements, boxes, and text into a full-color, visually appealing, and easy-to-read book. The many figures in the book clarify the narrative, reinforce important points, and show screen shots that reflect the latest trends in Web design. The marginal elements and boxes highlight features such as exploratory exercises, design topics, common questions and answers, and pointers to the Student Online Companion for this book.

Introductory Presentation of Web Design

No previous Web design experience is assumed, and no prior programming experience is required. This book is written specifically for students for whom continuity, simplicity, and practicality are essential. Numerous insights based on the authors' many years of experience in teaching, consulting, and writing are implicit throughout the book.

DESIGN TIP   More than 80 Design Tips are boxed throughout the book. The function of the Design Tips is to emphasize important Web design concepts of which students should be aware as they design a Web site.

@Source Feature

The @Source elements in the margins throughout the book encourage students to research further using the World Wide Web. The purposes of the @Source annotations are to (1) offer students additional information on a topic of importance, (2) provide currency, and (3) underscore the importance of the World Wide Web as a basic information tool that can be used in course work, for a wide range of professional purposes, and for personal use.

YOUR TURN

Your Turn Exercise

Multiple Your Turn exercises within each chapter provide hands-on activities that allow students to put concepts and skills learned in the chapter to practical, real-world use. Your Turn exercises call for critical thinking, often requiring online research.

Q&A Boxes

These marginal annotations provide answers to common questions that complement the topics covered, adding depth and perspective to the learning process.

Organization of This Textbook

Web Design: Introductory, Fourth Edition provides basic instruction on how to plan and design a successful Web site that achieves the site's intended purpose. The material comprises seven chapters, four appendices, and a glossary/index.

CHAPTER 1 — THE ENVIRONMENT AND THE TOOLS   In Chapter 1, students are introduced to the Internet, World Wide Web, Web sites, and Web pages. Topics include domain names; how the Internet and the Web are influencing society; methods and devices users use to connect to the Internet and the Web; types of Web sites; tools for creating Web sites; and Web design roles.

CHAPTER 2 — WEB PUBLISHING FUNDAMENTALS   In Chapter 2, students are introduced to the advantages of Web publishing, basic design principles, and writing techniques for the Web. Topics include publishing advantages related to connectivity, timeliness, interactivity, reduced production costs, and economical, rapid distribution; design issues related to balance and proximity; contrast and focus; unity; scannable text, and using color as a design tool; and technical, accessibility, and usability issues.

CHAPTER 3 — PLANNING A SUCCESSFUL WEB SITE: PART 1   In Chapter 3, students are introduced to the initial four steps in the six-step planning process for developing a solid Web site design plan: (1) define the site's purpose, (2) identify the site's target audience, (3) determine the site's general content, and (4) select the site's structure. Topics include identifying a specific topic for a Web site; defining target audience wants, needs, and expectations; choosing content; and using an outline, storyboard, or flowchart to plan the site's structure.

CHAPTER 4 — PLANNING A SUCCESSFUL WEB SITE: PART 2   In Chapter 4, students are introduced to the remaining two steps in the planning process for developing a design plan: (5) design the look and feel of the site, and (6) specify the site's navigation system. Topics include the relationship between page length, content placement, and usability; maintaining visual consistency across all pages at the site using color and page layout; and creating both a user-based and a user-controlled navigation system. A final design plan checklist is provided.

CHAPTER 5 — TYPOGRAPHY AND IMAGES   In Chapter 5, students are introduced to typography and images for the Web environment. Topics include typographic principles, guidelines, and tips; Web image file formats and sources; and optimization techniques for creating Web-ready images.

CHAPTER 6 — MULTIMEDIA AND INTERACTIVITY ELEMENTS   In Chapter 6, students are introduced to the basics of Web multimedia and interactivity and methods to add these elements to Web pages. Topics include guidelines and sources for using multimedia; types of Web page animation; adding and editing Web page audio and video; and Web-based forms, live chat, and other interactive page elements.

CHAPTER 7 — PROMOTING AND MAINTAINING A WEB SITE   In Chapter 7, students are introduced to basic guidelines and methods to test, publish, promote, and maintain a Web site successfully. Topics include prepublishing testing of Web pages; acquiring server space and uploading a site's files to a server; promoting a published site using search tools, affiliate programs, and online advertising networks; the importance of regular site maintenance; and using Web metrics to evaluate Web site performance.

APPENDIX A — DESIGN TIPS   This appendix lists the Design Tips developed throughout the book. It serves as a quick reference, is organized by chapter, and includes the topic of each Design Tip along with page numbers on which the Design Tips are located.

APPENDIX B — HYPERTEXT MARKUP LANGUAGE (HTML)   This appendix is a reference for HTML 4.01, a markup language used to create Web pages. Knowing the basics of HTML 4.01 allows students to troubleshoot and/or optimize the sometimes problematic code generated by WYSIWYG editors. Additionally, a fundamental knowledge of HTML 4.01 helps interpret the source code of features and functions found on other Web sites that students might want to include on their own sites.

APPENDIX C — CASCADING STYLE SHEETS (CSS)   The CSS Appendix is a brief introduction to Cascading Style Sheets in support of the discussion of CSS in various chapters in this book.

APPENDIX D — DESIGNING FOR MOBILE DEVICES   This new Appendix provides a brief introduction to the decision-making process and the technologies and considerations when creating a site for mobile devices.

End-of-Chapter Student Activities

A notable strength of the Shelly Cashman Series textbooks is the extensive student activities at the end of each chapter. Well-structured student activities can make the difference between students merely participating in a class and students retaining the information they learn. The activities in this book include the following:

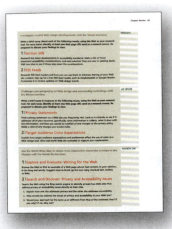

- **Chapter Review**   A review of chapter highlights is presented at the end of each chapter.
- **Terms to Know**   This list of key terms found in the chapter together with the page numbers on which the terms are defined helps students master the chapter material.
- **Test Your Knowledge**   Two pencil-and-paper activities are designed to test students' understanding of the material in the chapter: matching terms and short-answer questions.
- **Learn It Online**   Every chapter features a Learn It Online section that comprises six exercises. These exercises include true/false, multiple choice, and short answer questions, an interactive flash cards exercise using key terms, a practice test, and learning games.
- **Trends**   New to this edition, the Trends exercises encourage students to explore the latest developments in the Web design technologies and concepts introduced in the chapter.
- **@ Issue**   Web design is not without its controversial issues. At the end of each chapter, two scenarios are presented that challenge students to examine critically their perspective of Web design concepts and technologies.
- **Hands On**   To complete their introduction to Web design, these exercises require that students use the World Wide Web to gather and evaluate additional information about the concepts and techniques discussed in the chapter.
- **Team Approach**   Two Team Approach assignments engage students, getting them to work collaboratively to reinforce the concepts in the chapter.
- **Case Study**   The Case Study is an ongoing development process in Web design using the concepts, techniques, and Design Tips presented in each section. The Case Study requires students to apply their knowledge starting in Chapter 1 and continuing through Chapter 7 as they prepare, plan, create, and then publish their own Web site.

Student Online Companion

The Student Online Companion includes Learn It Online exercises for each chapter, as well as @Source links, Your Turn links, and Q&As. To access these course materials, please visit **www.cengagebrain.com**. At the CengageBrain.com home page, search for the ISBN of your title (from the back cover of your book) using the search box at the top of the page. This will take you to the product page where you can click the Access Now button.

Instructor Resources

The Shelly Cashman Series is dedicated to providing you with all of the tools you need to make your class a success. Information on all supplementary materials is available through your Course Technology representative or by calling one of the following telephone numbers: Colleges, Universities, Continuing Education Departments, Post-Secondary Vocational Schools, Career Colleges, Business, Industry, Government, Trade, Retailer, Wholesaler, Library and Resellers, 800-354-9706; K-12 Schools, Secondary Vocational Schools, Adult Education and School Districts, 800-354-9706; Canada, 800-268-2222.

The Instructor Resources include both teaching and testing aids and can be accessed via CD-ROM or at login.cengage.com.

- INSTRUCTOR'S MANUAL   Includes lecture notes summarizing the chapter sections, figures and boxed elements found in every chapter, teacher tips, classroom activities, lab activities, and quick quizzes in Microsoft Word files.

- SYLLABUS   Contains easily customizable sample syllabi that cover policies, assignments, exams, and other course information.

- FIGURE FILES   Illustrations for every figure in the textbook are available in electronic form. Figures are provided both with and without callouts.

- POWERPOINT PRESENTATIONS   A one-click-per-slide presentation system provides PowerPoint slides for every subject in each chapter. Presentations are based on chapter objectives.

- SOLUTIONS TO EXERCISES   Includes solutions for all end-of-chapter exercises, as well as Chapter Reinforcement Exercises.

- TEST BANK AND TEST ENGINE   Test Banks include 112 questions for every chapter, featuring objective-based and critical-thinking question types, and include page number references and figure references, when appropriate. Also included is the test engine, ExamView, the ultimate tool for your objective-based testing needs.

- ADDITIONAL ACTIVITIES FOR STUDENTS   Consists of Chapter Reinforcement Exercises, which are true/false, multiple-choice, and short answer questions that help students gain confidence in the material learned.

CourseNotes

Course Technology's CourseNotes are six-panel quick reference cards that reinforce the most important and widely used features of a software application or technology concept in a visual and user-friendly format. CourseNotes serve as a great reference tool for students, both during and after the course. CourseNotes are available for Adobe Dreamweaver CS5, Web 2.0: Recharged, Buyer's Guide: Tips for Purchasing a New Computer, Best Practices in Social Networking, Hot Topics in Technology and many more. Visit **www.cengagebrain.com** to learn more!

course|notes™
quick reference guide

A Guided Tour

Add excitement and interactivity to your classroom with "*A Guided Tour*" product line. Play one of the brief mini-movies to spice up your lecture and spark classroom discussion. Or, assign a movie for homework and ask students to complete the correlated assignment that accompanies each topic. "*A Guided Tour*" product line takes the prep work out of providing your students with information about new technologies and applications and helps keep students engaged with content relevant to their lives—all in under an hour!

About Our Covers

The Shelly Cashman Series is continually updating our approach and content to reflect the way today's students learn and experience new technology. This focus on student success is reflected on our covers, which feature real students from Bryant University using the Shelly Cashman Series in their courses, and reflect the varied ages and backgrounds of the students learning with our books. When you use the Shelly Cashman Series, you can be assured that you are learning computer skills using the most effective courseware available.

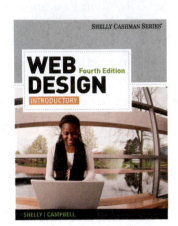

1 | The Environment and the Tools

Introduction

Designing and building a Web site is no longer a difficult, intimidating undertaking; evolving Web technologies have simplified the job. Applying Web technologies is only part of what is required to produce a successful site. A Web site that successfully communicates, educates, entertains, or provides a venue for conducting business transactions also requires good Web design. This book explains the basic elements of good Web design and shows you how to develop effective Web sites and pages for specific purposes or audiences. Chapter 1 begins the process by describing the Internet and the World Wide Web. Next, you learn about the various ways users connect to the Internet. The chapter then describes different types of Web sites and the tools for creating them. Finally, the chapter discusses the various roles, responsibilities, and skills essential to successful Web design.

Objectives

After completing this chapter, you will be able to:

1. Describe the Internet and the World Wide Web
2. Discuss ways to access the Internet and the Web
3. Categorize types of Web sites
4. Identify Web design tools
5. Explain Web design roles

The Internet and the World Wide Web

A computer **network** is composed of computers, printers, and data storage devices connected to enable the sharing of computing resources and data. Private computer networks are found everywhere — in home offices, in student computer labs, in Internet cafés, and in the offices of organizations and businesses around the world. The **Internet** is a worldwide public network (Figure 1-1) that connects millions of these private networks. For example, on a college campus, the student lab network, the faculty computer network, and the administration network can all connect to the Internet.

Figure 1-1 The Internet is a worldwide public network that connects private networks.

Q&A

What is Web 2.0?
The term **Web 2.0** defines the "next generation" Web that supports Web-based services such as online advertising models tied to search keywords, search engine optimization methods, the syndication of Web site content, and blogs.

@SOURCE

Internet Society (ISOC)
For more information about the Internet, visit the Web Design 4 Chapter 1 Student Online Companion Web page at **www.cengagebrain.com**, and then click Internet Society (ISOC) in the @Source links.

Internet2

Internet2 is a major cooperative initiative among academia, industry, and government agencies to increase the Internet's capabilities and solve some of its challenges. The nonprofit initiative has more than 200 university, corporate, government, and international members and sponsors devoted to developing and using new and emerging network technologies that facilitate research and education.

The **World Wide Web (Web)** is a part of the Internet that consists of Internet-connected computers called **Web servers** that store electronic documents called Web pages. A **Web page** is a specially formatted document that can contain images, text, interactive elements, and hyperlinks, which are links to other pages. A **Web site** is a group of related Web pages. A Web site's primary page, or **home page**, typically introduces the Web site and provides information about the site's purpose and content. Figure 1-2 illustrates the home page of Jive Software, a company that develops business collaboration software.

Figure 1-2 A Web site's primary page is its home page.

A **hyperlink,** or simply a **link,** is a word, phrase, or image (Figure 1-3) that connects Web pages. You often can identify a text link by its appearance. Text links usually are underlined or differ in color from the rest of the text. An image link might be more difficult to visually identify; however, pointing to either a text or image link with the mouse pointer changes the pointer from an arrow to a hand pointer. When you click a link with the hand pointer, you might view a picture or video, listen to a song, jump to a different Web page at the same site, or jump to a Web page at a different site. Exploring the Web by jumping from one Web page to another is sometimes called **browsing** or **surfing the Web.** To indicate visually that you have previously clicked a text link, the color of a clicked text link might change. You can see this change in color when you return to the page containing the clicked link.

Q&A

Who originally created the World Wide Web?
Tim Berners-Lee, a programmer at CERN in Switzerland, is credited with the early vision and technological developments that led to today's World Wide Web.

Whether you choose to indicate hyperlinks in text by color, bold, or underline, be consistent throughout your site.

DESIGN TIP

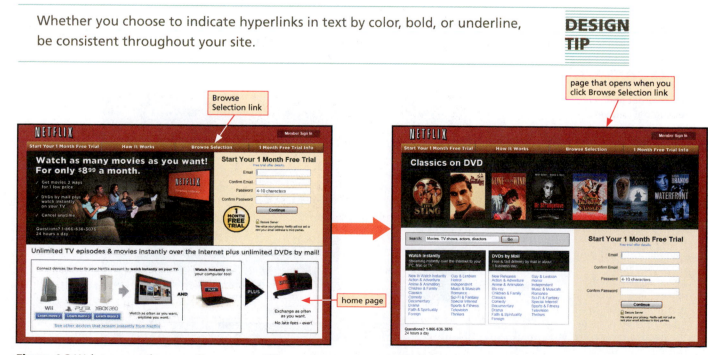

Figure 1-3 Web pages at the same site or across different sites are connected by links.

DESIGN TIP	Design your Web site so that it communicates trustworthiness, timeliness, and value.

Although the terms *Internet* and *Web* frequently are used interchangeably, remember that the Internet and the Web are not one and the same. As stated previously, the Internet is a worldwide public network that links private networks. The Internet gives users access to a variety of resources for communication, research, file sharing, and commerce. The Web, a subset of the Internet, is just one of those resources.

Influence on Society

Today, friends, families, and business professionals exchange millions of electronic messages and share information using the Internet and the Web. Students frequently turn to the Web to research topics for reports, to access podcasts or transcripts of lectures, or to collaborate on a group project. Additionally, people of all ages access the Internet and the Web for entertainment by playing interactive Web games, listening to Internet radio, and viewing television programs and movies on their computers. Consumers save money on gas and avoid crowds, parking problems, and long lines by shopping and banking online. Businesses that interact with their suppliers and customers using Internet and Web technologies can be more productive and profitable. Businesses can also use tools such as videoconferencing to avoid costs associated with business travel or to allow employees to telecommute. The Internet and the Web have significantly influenced the way the world communicates, educates, entertains, and conducts business.

COMMUNICATION   Individuals and organizations of all types use Web sites to communicate ideas and information. By effectively designing Web pages and selectively choosing content, you can ensure that your site's Web pages deliver the site's message successfully and persuasively. When a Web page's design and content communicate trustworthiness, timeliness, and value (as is the case with the site in Figure 1-4), you are more likely to save a link to the page, called a **bookmark** or **favorite**, for future reference. On the other hand, you quickly will move on from a Web site if its pages are poorly designed or the content appears unreliable, outdated, or trivial.

Figure 1-4 The MSNBC home page communicates up-to-date, accurate information.

Other communication options that rely on Internet and Web technologies include e-mail, blogging, social networking, social bookmarking, chat, instant messaging, virtual meetings and collaborative workspaces, video sharing, interactive gaming, and 3D virtual worlds.

Businesses and individuals rely heavily on electronic messages called **electronic mail** or **e-mail**. Popular e-mail software, such as Mozilla® Thunderbird®, Microsoft Outlook®, Google's Gmail™, or Windows Live Mail®, allows users to attach graphics, video, sound, and other computer files to e-mail messages. E-mail is a fast and inexpensive online communication tool.

Internet Relay Chat (IRC) and **Web-based chat** are communication technologies that provide a venue, such as a chat room, where people with common interests can exchange text, video, or multimedia messages in real time. **Instant messaging**, also called **IM chat**, is another popular way individuals can exchange one-to-one messages in real time using a chat window that is only visible to those participating in the chat. Examples of IM chat programs are AOL Instant Messenger® (AIM), Yahoo! Messenger, Windows Live Messenger®, ICQ®, and Trillian™ (Figure 1-5). The difference between IRC and IM is that IRC chats are public exchanges between two or more people in a chat room who do not necessarily know each other. With an IM program, you chat privately with people you know.

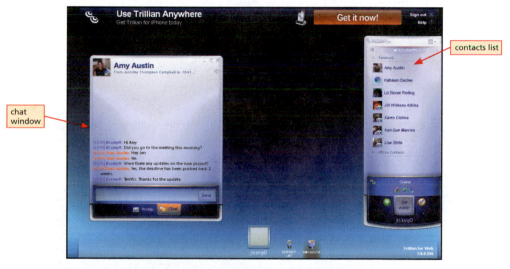

Figure 1-5 IM chat programs allow users to exchange private messages in real time.

Technology vendors, such as Microsoft, WebEx, and GoToMeeting (Figure 1-6 on the next page), provide access to **collaborative workspaces** or **virtual meeting spaces**, which are Web sites that allow users to communicate with each other using text, audio, video, whiteboard, and shared files without leaving their own desks. Collaborative workspaces are typically used in business settings. Businesses that use collaborative workspaces and virtual meeting spaces can both improve employee productivity and reduce expenses.

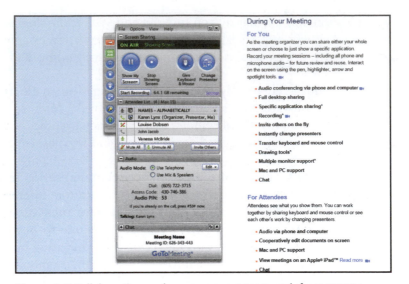

Figure 1-6 Collaborative workspaces support teamwork from remote locations.

A **blog** (short for Weblog), such as the Huffington Post or the CNET News Blog (Figure 1-7), is an online journal or diary to which readers can add their own commentary. Millions of people go online to share ideas and information by hosting and participating in blogs — a process called **blogging**. **Video sharing** Web sites, sometimes called **video blogging** sites, such as YouTube and Vimeo (Figure 1-7), allow users to share and comment on personal and professional videos.

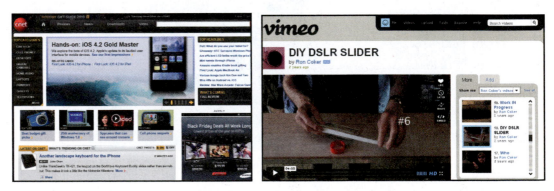

Figure 1-7 Text and video blogging sites allow Web users to share ideas, information, and video files.

Social networking is the term used to describe sites, such as Twitter, classmates.com, Facebook, and LinkedIn (Figure 1-8 on the next page), that allow participants to create a personal network of friends or business contacts. Users then use communication tools provided by the site to interact with those in their personal network. **Social bookmarking**, provided by sites such as FuzzFizz, Newsvine, Fark, StumbleUpon, and Digg (Figure 1-8), allows users to share their Web page favorites, bookmarks, and **tags** — keywords that reference specific images or documents — with others.

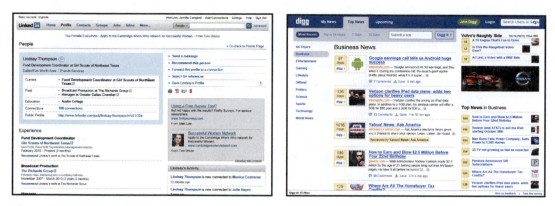

Figure 1-8 Social networking sites and social bookmarking sites allow users to share information with one another.

Gamers by the millions interact with each other by playing **massively multiplayer online games (MMOGs)**, such as Lineage® and World of Warcraft (Figure 1-9). Others create alternative personas that live their lives in **3D virtual worlds**, such as Second Life® or Entropia Universe® (Figure 1-9).

Figure 1-9 Millions of gamers enjoy MMOGs and 3D virtual worlds.

EDUCATION The Web offers exciting, challenging new avenues for formal and informal teaching and learning. If you always wanted to know exactly how airplanes fly, or dreamed of becoming a pastry chef, or wanted to learn how to protect against computer hackers, turn to the Web. The Web also can enhance traditional teaching methods. Instructors often use the Web to publish podcasts or videos of lectures, Web page links for research, syllabi and grades, and more for their students. Web sites, such as those shown in Figure 1-10 on the next page, offer a wide variety of online courses. MIT Open Courseware publishes all of the educational materials from its courses online, including homework and video lectures, so that they are free and open to everyone.

Q&A

What does it mean to "go viral"?
An article, blog entry, Web site, or video that is viewed and then shared by many users with others using social networking, blogs, and mass media is said to have "gone viral."

Q&A

What is a wiki?
A wiki is a group of related Web pages to which content can be added, edited, or deleted by its users using a Web browser. A well-known example of a wiki is Wikipedia, an online encyclopedia.

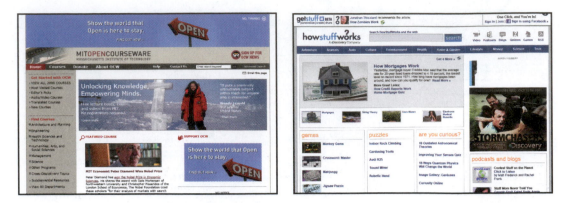

Figure 1-10 The Web offers formal and informal teaching and learning opportunities.

DESIGN TIP   Any formal or informal educational Web site should contain content that is timely, accurate, and appealing. Such sites also should include elements to provide feedback, maintain records, and assess learning.

ENTERTAINMENT AND NEWS   Millions of people turn to the Web daily for entertainment and news because of the Web's unique ability to provide interactive multimedia experiences and continually updated content. Popular entertainment sites offer music, videos, sports, games, and more. For example, you can use the Web to watch last night's episode of your favorite television program, check out entertainment news at IMDb (Figure 1-11), play fantasy baseball at mlb.com, or interact with a virtual pet at webkinz.com (Figure 1-11). Sophisticated entertainment and news Web sites often partner with other technologies. For example, NBC and MSNBC television partner their programming with the MSNBC Web site. At the MSNBC Web site, you can read news stories or watch news clips or video clips from programs that originate on NBC and MSNBC television. Additionally, the MSNBC Web site provides interactive elements, such as the ability to cast a vote about a current news topic being discussed on MSNBC television.

Figure 1-11 Entertainment and news are available with continually updated multimedia content.

DESIGN TIP   Include methods to share your site's content by providing links to send content using e-mail, post to the user's Facebook page, RSS feed, or Twitter account, as well as link to related content that site users would find interesting and relevant.

BUSINESS   **Electronic commerce** or **e-commerce** encompasses a wide variety of online business activities, including consumer shopping and investing and the exchange of business data and transactions within a company or among multiple companies. For example, a pet groomer might offer his or her services using an e-commerce Web site where a pet owner could find valuable information, such as the groomer's telephone number, location, list of services, and rates charged; the pet owner could then schedule an appointment online. At the other end of the e-commerce spectrum, a large manufacturing company could use the Internet and the Web to communicate policies and procedures to its employees, exchange business information with its vendors and other business partners, process sales transactions, and provide online support to its customers.

Business transactions that take place between an online business and an individual consumer are called **business-to-consumer (B2C) e-commerce** transactions. Today, millions of consumers rely on B2C e-commerce Web sites (Figure 1-12) to purchase an endless assortment of products and services and to conduct such financial transactions as banking and investing.

Figure 1-12 B2C e-commerce involves the sale of products and services directly to consumers.

The majority of e-commerce occurs in the corporate world and is called **business-to-business (B2B) e-commerce**. In B2B e-commerce, products, services, and business data are exchanged between businesses, such as those shown in Figure 1-13.

Figure 1-13 B2B e-commerce involves the sale of products and services and the exchange of data between businesses.

A third type of e-commerce is **consumer-to-consumer (C2C) e-commerce**. In C2C e-commerce, business transactions occur between consumers. Examples of C2C e-commerce include online auctions and person-to-person classified ads. eBay (Figure 1-14) and craigslist are examples of an online auction and classified ad site, respectively. Etsy is a C2C (Figure 1-14) site where crafters and artists can sell directly to consumers.

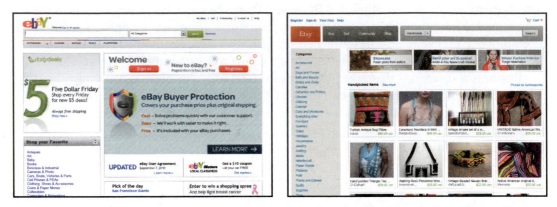

Figure 1-14 C2C e-commerce involves the sale or exchange of products and services between consumers.

Other organizations, such as nonprofit charities and government agencies, also employ B2C and B2B technologies to provide information and services to their constituencies.

DESIGN TIP

To develop an e-commerce Web site, you must determine the potential customers for your products or services. Categorize your items or provide a search feature so customers can easily find what they need. Additionally, you must decide which e-commerce technologies, such as shopping cart and credit card processing technologies, are best suited for your e-commerce site.

Ways to Access the Internet and the Web

Users access the Internet and Web using a variety of means. In the past, the most common way to access the Internet was using a dial-up telephone line. Today, faster access methods, including digital dedicated lines, cable broadband, and wireless transmissions, are increasingly the access method of choice for both individuals and organizations.

The speed at which data can travel from one device to another is called the **transfer rate**, which is expressed as bits per second (bps) — that is, the number of bits the line can transmit in one second. Transfer rates range from thousands of bits per second (called kilobits per second or **Kbps**) to millions of bits per second (called megabits per second or **Mbps**). A faster transfer rate translates into more expensive Internet access. Transfer rate has a direct impact on the user's experience with a Web site; the effect of Internet access speeds on Web design considerations is discussed in Chapter 2.

Cable Internet Access

Cable television (CATV) lines enable home or business users to connect to the Internet over the same coaxial cable that delivers television transmissions (Figure 1-15). Data can travel very rapidly through a cable modem connected to a CATV line, typically moving at speeds from 5 to 7 Mbps (download). Then, using a splitter, the line from the cable company is directed to both the television and computer. Cable Internet access is typically available only in urban and suburban areas.

data line from cable company

line splitter

computer

television

cable modem

Figure 1-15 Cable Internet access requires a line splitter and cable modem.

Fixed and Mobile Wireless Access

Fixed wireless is Internet connectivity service that uses satellite technology. Radio signals transferred between a transmitting tower and an antenna on a house or business provide a high-speed connection. People on the go can access the Internet and Web using **mobile wireless** technologies, which include radio signals, **wireless fidelity (Wi-Fi)** technologies, cellular telephones, and wireless providers' broadband networks. Wi-Fi provides wireless connectivity to devices within a certain range. A Wi-Fi network may be password protected or freely available.

Standards for mobile communications, including voice, mobile Internet access, video calls, and mobile TV, are classified by generation. **3G**, the third generation, provides mobile broadband access to devices such as laptop computers and smartphones. To be classified as 3G, a device must support speech and data services, as well as data rates of at least 200 kbps (kilobits per second). Industry analysts expect that **4G** systems will be widely available by 2013. 4G systems will support services such as gaming and streamed multimedia, and are currently being tested and offered in a few cities and countries.

Mobile devices that provide Internet access include laptop computers, smartphones, personal digital assistants (PDAs), or other handheld devices. These devices use an internal antenna or wireless card to connect to the Internet either at a **hot spot**, a location that provides public Internet access, or directly to a wireless provider's network. You can pay for mobile access on a per-Kb basis; however, most users buy a flat-rate monthly plan that allows unlimited text and data usage. Such plans typically start around $30 per month.

Telephone Lines Access

The **Public Switched Telephone Network (PSTN)** used to be the main way all users connected to the Internet; high-speed telephone access is still commonly used, in spite of developments in mobile and broadband systems. Although initially built to handle voice communications, the telephone network is also an integral part of computer communications. Data, instructions, and information can travel over the telephone network over dial-up lines or dedicated lines, which are described in the following sections.

DIAL-UP LINES   A **dial-up line** is a temporary connection that uses analog telephone lines. Because of its slow access speed, dial-up access is the least popular Internet access method and is rarely used in business. Similar to using the telephone to make a call, a modem at the sending end dials the telephone number of a modem at the receiving end. When the modem at the receiving end answers the call, a connection is established and data can be transmitted. Internet access using a dial-up line comes in two versions: regular dial-up and high-speed dial-up.

DESIGN TIP   Although large images and multimedia elements on Web pages can degrade the audience's viewing experiences at slower Internet access speeds, most sites assume users have high-speed dial-up, cable, or wireless connectivity.

DIGITAL DEDICATED LINES   Unlike a dial-up line in which the connection is reestablished each time it is used, a **dedicated line** is a constant connection between two communications devices that uses the local telephone network. This constant connection provides a higher-quality connection than a dial-up line, better suited for viewing or listening to **streaming media** — video or sound that downloads to a computer continuously to be watched or listened to in real time, and other common Internet uses. Businesses often use dedicated lines to connect geographically distant offices. Dedicated lines can be either analog or digital; however, digital lines increasingly are connecting home and business users to networks around the globe because they transmit data and information at faster rates than analog lines. Three popular types of digital dedicated lines are Integrated Services Digital Network (ISDN) lines, digital subscriber lines (DSL), and T-carrier lines.

Integrated Services Digital Network (ISDN) is a set of standards for digital transmission of data over standard copper telephone lines. With ISDN, the same telephone line that could carry only one computer signal now can carry three or more signals at once, through the same line, using a technique called **multiplexing**. Multiplexing allows for more data to be transmitted at the same time over the same line. For the small business and home user, an ISDN line provides faster data transmission than a dial-up telephone line at a modest increase in monthly cost.

DSL is another digital line alternative for the small business or home user. A **digital subscriber line (DSL)** transmits at fast speeds on existing standard copper telephone wiring. Some of the DSL installations can provide a dial tone, so you can use the line for both voice and data. An **asymmetrical digital subscriber line (ADSL)** is a type of DSL that supports faster transmissions when receiving data than when sending data. ADSL is ideal for Internet access because users generally download more data from the Internet than they upload.

A **T-carrier line** is any of several types of digital lines that carry multiple signals over a single communications line. Whereas a standard dial-up telephone line carries only one signal, digital T-carrier lines use multiplexing so that multiple signals can share the telephone line. T-carrier lines provide extremely fast data transfer rates. The most popular T-carrier line is the **T-1 line**. Businesses often use T-1 lines to connect to the Internet. A **fractional T-1** line is a less-expensive, albeit slower, connection option for home owners and small businesses. Instead of a single owner, a fractional T-1 is shared with other users. A **T-3 line** is equal in speed to 28 T-1 lines. T-3 lines are the most expensive connection method. Main users of T-3 lines include large companies, telephone companies, and service providers connecting to the Internet backbone.

Internet Service Providers

An **Internet service provider (ISP)** is a business that has a permanent Internet connection and provides temporary Internet connections to individuals and companies using one or more access methods: dial-up, high-speed dial-up, broadband, or wireless. ISPs are either regional or national. A **regional ISP**, such as NetNITCO (Figure 1-16), provides Internet access for customers (individuals or businesses) in a specific geographic area. A **national ISP** provides Internet access in most major cities and towns nationwide. National ISPs may offer more services and generally have larger technical support staffs than regional ISPs. An example of a national ISP is EarthLink (Figure 1-17). A cable company, such as Verizon, can be an ISP as well as provide cable television and telephone access; negotiating one price for all of those services can save you money and hassle, but can provide limited options if you are tied into one provider for all three because you can only choose from within the plans for each service offered by that provider.

@SOURCE

ISPs
For a comparison of Internet service providers (ISPs), visit the Web Design 4 Chapter 1 Student Online Companion Web page at **www .cengagebrain.com** and then click ISPs in the @Source links.

Figure 1-16 A regional ISP provides Internet access for homes and businesses in a specific geographical area.

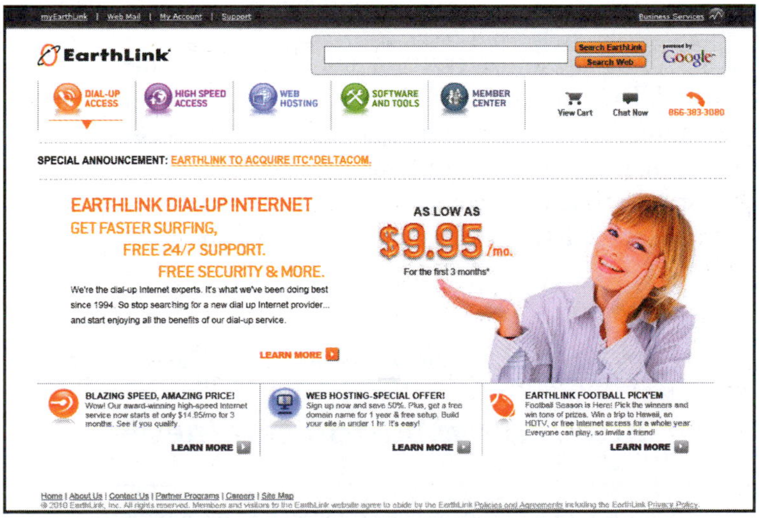

Figure 1-17 A national ISP provides Internet access for homes and businesses across the United States.

@SOURCE

Web Browsers
For more information about popular Web browsers, visit the Web Design 4 Chapter 1 Student Online Companion Web page at **www.cengagebrain.com** and then click Web Browsers in the @Source links.

Web Browsers

To view Web pages, you need a **Web browser**, also called a **browser**, which is a software program that requests, downloads, and displays Web pages stored on a Web server. Although there are many browsers available, most of them share common features, such as an Address bar, a Favorites list, a History list, tabs that open multiple pages in one browser window, and Back and Forward buttons for navigating. As of this writing, Microsoft Internet Explorer (Figure 1-18) remains the most widely used browser software, with approximately 50 percent of the browser market. The Web page illustrations in this text use Internet Explorer version 9. Mozilla Firefox (Figure 1-18) is the next-most-popular Web browser software, with approximately 27 percent of the browser market. Google released its Chrome browser in 2008; Google has about 10 percent of the market. The remaining 13 percent of the browser market is divided among other browsers, including Opera and Safari.

Figure 1-18 Mozilla Firefox and Microsoft Internet Explorer are examples of Web browsers.

DESIGN TIP

A Web page might appear differently depending on the browser type or version, so you should test your pages with different browsers as you develop your Web site. For example, features of your site that work within the Internet Explorer 9 browser might not work in earlier versions, such as Internet Explorer 6.

You can access a Web page by entering its unique address, called the **Uniform Resource Locator (URL)**, in a browser's Address bar. At a minimum, a URL consists of a domain name and a top-level domain designation. Many URLs also include folder and file designations indicating the path to a specific Web page. If included, folder and file names are separated by forward slash characters following the top-level domain designation. Figure 1-19 illustrates the URL or path to the news page on boston.com.

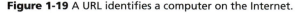

Figure 1-19 A URL identifies a computer on the Internet.

An **IP address** is the numeric address for a computer connected to the Internet. Every device in a computer network has an IP address. The Internet Assigned Numbers Authority (IANA) works with regional and local entities to assign IP addresses. A **domain name** is the text version of a computer's numeric IP address. Companies known as domain name registrars are responsible for assigning domain names. A **top-level domain (TLD)** designation (Figure 1-20) indicates the type of organization or general domain — commercial, nonprofit, network, military, and so forth — for which the domain name is registered. Some countries have their own TLDs, such as Australia (.au), France (.fr), and Canada (.ca).

Top-Level Domains

Top-Level Domain	Domain Type	Top-Level Domain	Domain Type
.aero	Air-transportation industry	.jobs	Human resources managers
.asia	Asia Pacific community	.mil	U.S. military
.biz	Businesses	.mobi	Consumers and providers of mobile products and services
.cat	Catalan linguistic community	.museum	Museums
.com	Commercial, personal	.name	Individuals
.coop	Cooperative associations	.net	Network providers
.edu	Postsecondary institutions	.org	Noncommercial community
.gov	U.S. government	.pro	Credentialed professionals
.info	General information	.tel	Business and individual contact data
.int	International treaty organization	.travel	Travel industry

Figure 1-20 Top-level domains identify the type of organization or general domain for which a domain name is registered.

In a URL, the domain name and top-level domain designation are preceded by a **protocol**, or rule, that specifies the format to be used for transmitting data. For Web pages, that protocol is the **Hypertext Transfer Protocol (HTTP)**, which is the communications standard for transmitting Web pages over the Internet. You can type the protocol when you enter the Web page domain name and top-level domain designation in the browser's Address bar; however, it is generally not necessary to do so. Most Web browsers will insert the HTTP protocol automatically as the requested Web page is downloaded into the browser.

Q&A **Who controls the registration of domain names?** The Internet Corporation for Assigned Names and Numbers (ICANN) controls the Domain Name System (DNS) and the registration of domain names through its accredited registrars, such as Network Solutions or register.com.

DESIGN TIP Select a short, easy-to-remember domain name that ties directly to a site's purpose or publisher's name or is hard to forget. Examples of effective domain names include webkinz.com (social network for kids), business.com (business-oriented search directory), and ask.com (search tool).

YOUR TURN

Exploring Domain Name Registration

1. Identify three to five possible domain names for a computer repair business.
2. Visit the Web Design 4 Chapter 1 Student Online Companion Web page at **www.cengagebrain.com** and click register.com in the Your Turn links.
3. Type each of the potential domain names in the Get a Domain Name text box; click the Get a Domain Name list box arrow, and select the top-level domain of your choice. Then click the Find It button to search existing domain names and determine if your entered domain name is available.
4. Report back to your class on the results of your domain name search. If asked to do so by your instructor, print each of the domain name search results pages.

Alternative Web Page Viewing Devices

In addition to viewing Web pages on a desktop or laptop computer, you also can view Web pages using a handheld computer. **Handheld computers**, such as Apple's iPad, shown in Figure 1-21, are wireless, portable computers designed to fit in a user's hand. A **personal digital assistant (PDA)** is a type of handheld computer used to manage personal information and access the Internet; today, most PDAs are smartphones. A **smartphone** is a mobile phone that offers other features, such as a camera, calendar, and Internet access for e-mail, music downloads, and access to Web pages in addition to cellular voice telephone service (Figure 1-22). **Netbooks** are small, lightweight, and inexpensive laptops.

Figure 1-21 Handheld computers also provide portable Internet access.

Figure 1-22 Smartphones offer mobile access to the Internet and the Web.

DESIGN TIP Some of your site visitors might be viewing your pages using a microbrowser on a handheld computer or smartphone. Limiting site graphics and keeping text brief and to the point can enhance their viewing experience. You can also create a version of your Web site specifically for smartphones or mobile devices.

Types of Web Sites

The types of sites found on the Web can be categorized as personal, organizational/topical, and commercial. A Web site's type differs from a Web site's purpose. The type is defined as the category of site, and is determined by the company or individual responsible for the site's creation. The purpose of a site is its reason for existence — often, that reason is to sell products, but it could also be to share information, collect feedback, or some other purpose. Defining purpose is discussed in detail in Chapter 3. An overview of personal, organizational/topical, and commercial Web sites follows, along with the individual design challenges they present.

Personal Web Sites

Individuals create their own **personal Web sites** for a range of communication purposes. You might use a personal Web site to promote your employment credentials, share news and photos with friends and family, or share a common interest or hobby with fellow enthusiasts. Depending on your site's purpose, you might include your résumé, blog, photo gallery, biography, e-mail address, or a description of whatever you are passionate about — from Thai food to NASCAR racing.

Creating a personal Web site is typically less complex than creating other types of sites, and you might have limited software, hardware, and other resources compared with creators of commercial sites. Working independently means you must assume all the roles necessary to build the Web site. Web roles are discussed later in this chapter. Despite these challenges, you can publish a successful Web site to promote yourself and your services, or simply tell the world what you are all about. You can also use a content management system, discussed later in the chapter, to allow you to focus on the content of your site and not its structure. The Web already offers a range of tools for creating personal sites; blogging or social networking tools are free alternatives to creating a personal Web site; Facebook can allow you to communicate and share information with your friends; LinkedIn can present your résumé, references, and business connections to potential employers.

DESIGN TIP

Do not include personally identifiable information that can be misused, such as a Social Security number, on a personal Web site. Be careful what you put online, whether it is on a personal Web site or a social networking site. Employers, college recruiters, and anyone with an Internet connection can find information, posts, or photos quite easily, even with privacy settings enabled.

Organizational and Topical Web Sites

An **organizational Web site** is one that is owned by any type of group, association, or organization, whether it is a professional or amateur group. For example, if you belong to the Advertising Photographers Association of North America, you might volunteer to create an organizational Web site to promote member accomplishments or to encourage support and participation. Conversely, as a photographer, you might choose to design a site devoted to black-and-white photography to share your knowledge with others, including tips for amateurs, photo galleries, and online resources. A site that is focused on a specific subject is called a **topical Web site**. The purpose of both types of sites is to provide a resource about a subject.

@SOURCE

Evaluating Content
For more information on critical evaluation of Web page content, visit the Web Design 4 Chapter 1 Student Online Companion Web page at **www.cengagebrain.com** and click Evaluating Content in the @Source links.

Professional, nonprofit, international, social, volunteer, and various other types of organizations abound on the Web, as do Web sites devoted to diet and nutrition, health, entertainment, arts and humanities, sports, various hobbies, and many additional topics. An organization that lacks funding might encounter the same challenges creating its site as an individual creating a Web site — specifically, limited resources, including people to create and maintain the site. As you browse the Web, you will find that some organizational and topical Web sites lack accurate, timely, objective, and authoritative content. You must always carefully evaluate a Web site's content for these four elements. Figure 1-23 shows an example of an organizational Web site.

Figure 1-23 The World Health Organization (WHO)'s organizational site.

DESIGN TIP   Take care to ensure that your Web pages contain accurate, current, objective, and authoritative content.

Commercial Web Sites

The goal of many **commercial Web sites** is to promote and sell products or services of a business, from the smallest home-based business to the largest international enterprise. The design and content of a large enterprise's Web site might be much more sophisticated and complex than that of a small business's Web site. Figure 1-24 contrasts the home page for a large B2B enterprise, SAP, which sells and supports software, with that of a small B2C business, Hometown Favorites, which offers hard-to-find food products.

In addition to sites that promote and sell products or services, commercial Web sites also include sites that generate their revenue largely from online services like advertising, such as search tool sites and portal sites.

Figure 1-24 Commercial Web sites promote and sell products and services.

SEARCH TOOLS   Search tools are Web sites that locate specific information on the Web based on a user's search requirements. Such tools include search engines, metasearch engines, and search directories.

A **search engine** is a Web-based search tool that locates a Web page using a word or phrase found in the page. To find Web pages on particular topics using a popular search engine, such as Google, Bing, or ask.com, you enter a term or phrase, called a **keyword**, in the search engine's text box and click a button usually labeled Search or Go. The search engine compares your search keywords or phrases with the contents of its database of pages and then displays a list of relevant pages. A match between a keyword search and the resulting occurrence is called a **hit**.

A search engine might use a variety of methods to create its Web site database, called its **index**. For example, most search engines use software **spiders** or **robots**, which are programs that browse the Web for new pages and then add the pages' URLs and other information to their indexes. Some search engines might also use meta tags to build their indexes. **Meta tags**, which are special codes added to Web pages, contain information such as keywords and descriptive data regarding a page. Other search engines might also use the information in a Web page title — the text that appears in the browser title bar when a Web page downloads — or keywords in the page text to index a page.

A **metasearch engine** is a search engine, such as Mamma or Dogpile, that performs a keyword search using multiple search engines' indexes. Figure 1-25 shows an example of a keyword search using the popular search engine Google. Figure 1-26 illustrates the same keyword search using the Dogpile metasearch engine.

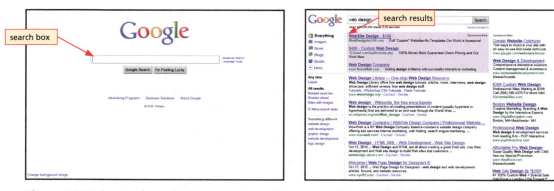

Figure 1-25 A keyword search using a search engine returns a list of Web pages related to the keyword or phrase.

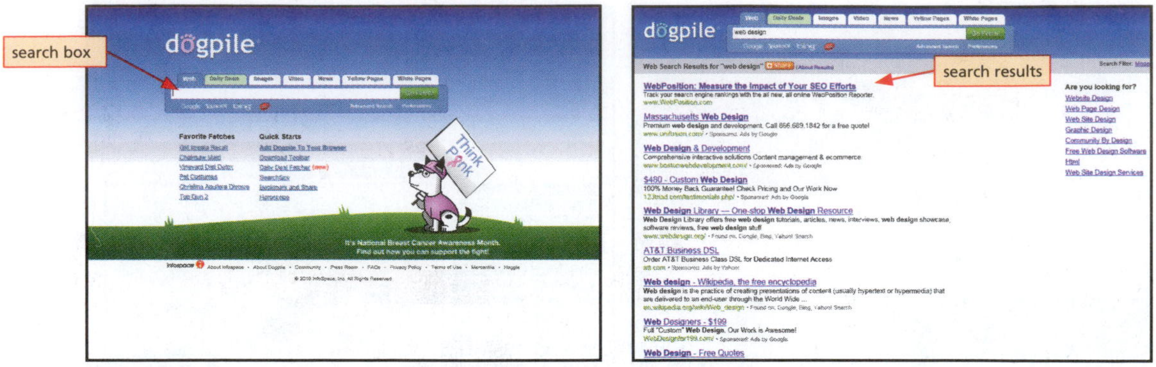

Figure 1-26 A metasearch engine searches the indexes of multiple search engines.

Search engine optimization (SEO) is the process of designing a Web page to increase the likelihood that the page will appear high in a search engine's search results list. Search engine optimization tools include meta tags, descriptive page titles, relevant inbound links from other sites, and clearly written text. You learn more about SEO in Chapter 7.

DESIGN TIP

Adding meta tags to your Web pages and carefully crafting each Web page title can increase the probability that your pages will be included in many search engines' indexes and that your pages will appear in search results lists for important keywords and phrases.

In addition to designing and writing your content for SEO, you can include paid or sponsored placements in your site marketing plan. In a paid or sponsored placement, the site publisher pays the search engine a fee to list their pages at or near the top of the search results list when a visitor uses specific keywords. Figure 1-25 illustrates a Google search results list for the phrase, Web design; paid placements are search results that are called sponsored links and are positioned prominently above and to the right of the list. You learn more about using paid or sponsored placement as a marketing tool in Chapter 7.

Unlike a search engine, a **search directory** builds its Web page index using human interaction. Site owners can submit Web site information to a search directory. The search directory's editors review pages they find or that are submitted to them, classifying them into categories such as arts and entertainment, jobs, health and fitness, travel, news, and so forth. The search directory's own Web pages present a hierarchy of links — from the most general to the most specific to the owner-submitted pages. Site directories can be general, or cover only specific topics. Site directories also can include paid links within their results.

To use a search directory, such as the Open Directory Project (Figure 1-27), you can click category and subcategory links in turn to work your way from the top of the hierarchy to eventually find Web pages with useful information about a specific topic. For example, clicking the Food link in the search directory's general Recreation category link leads to a Web page with additional links to Food subcategories, such as Spicy, which you can click to see further categories and more specific results.

Q&A

When should I use a search directory or search engine? Search directory entries are reviewed and categorized by humans, so if you are looking for information on a specific topic, a directory is a good place to start. Search engines will return a wider array of results, but might not be as accurate.

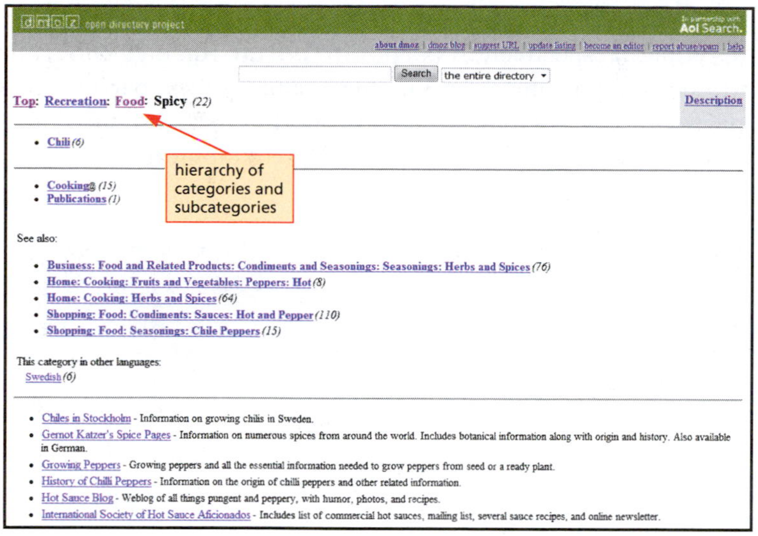

Figure 1-27 A search directory provides a hierarchy of linked categories and subcategories.

Exploring a Search Directory

1. Visit the Web Design 4 Chapter 1 Student Online Companion Web page at **www.cengagebrain.com** and click dmoz in the Your Turn links to view the Open Directory Project's home page.
2. Click the Computers link and then follow the subcategory links to drill down through the hierarchy to locate pages on basic Web design. Return to the home page and click the suggest URL link at the top of the page. Review the requirements for submitting Web page information to the directory.
3. Write two to three paragraphs that explain how you would submit a new site's pages to the Open Directory Project.

Today, many popular search tools are hybrids that combine a search engine with a search directory. Additionally, some search tools actually provide the Web page indexes used by other search tools. Because search tools' Web page indexes are created in a variety of ways, the indexes can vary substantially from search tool to search tool. For best results, you should become comfortable searching the Web for specific information using more than one search tool.

PORTALS   Portals — Web sites that offer a starting point for accessing information — can be categorized as general consumer portals, personal portals, vertical or industry portals, and corporate portals. A **general consumer portal** site offers a variety of features, including search services, e-mail, chat rooms, news and sports, maps, and online shopping. Many Web users begin their Web-based activities, including searching for specific information, from a portal, often setting a portal as a personal home page. Two early ISPs — AOL and MSN — and some of the Web's original search tools, such as Excite and Yahoo!, have evolved into general consumer portals. A **personal portal** is a version of a general consumer portal, such as MyYahoo!, which a user can customize for personal preferences. A **vertical portal**, such as usa.gov or farms.com (Figure 1-28 on the next page), provides a starting point for finding information about specific areas of interest — in these two examples, information and links to U.S. government agency Web sites and farming topics, respectively. A **corporate portal**, run on a company's intranet, provides an entry point for a company's employees and business partners into its private network. A **hyperlocal portal**, such as suzysaid.com (Figure 1-28), provides information about and is written by someone living in a specific geographical area.

Figure 1-28 Hyperlocal and vertical portals offer a variety of services, links, and information.

Exploring Consumer Portals

1. Visit the Web Design 4 Chapter 1 Student Online Companion Web page at **www.cengagebrain.com** and click Excite, AOL, MSN, and SuzySaid in the Your Turn links to view the portal pages.

2. Review the features offered by each of the portals. Identify the five features you believe are common to most portals.

3. Write a report that discusses how analyzing the features of existing portal sites can help you plan the content for a new consumer portal site.

4. Write a paragraph about how you might design a hyperlocal portal for your area. Include details such as the geographical area it will encompass, the intended audience (for example, parents, foodies, or outdoor enthusiasts), and sample content.

Web Design Tools

Web technology is constantly changing — a new browser feature or a wireless handheld device seemingly revolutionizes the way the world accesses the Internet. As soon as these new technologies surface, some Web designers charge ahead to implement these latest advances at their sites. Web sites should undoubtedly implement Web technology that represents true improvement; however, it is important to first determine the merit of new technologies. As a Web designer, you should ask the following questions:

- Does the new technology meet currently accepted standards for Web development and design?

- What specifically can the new technology do to further the purpose of my Web site?

- How will implementation of the new technology affect my Web site's visual appeal, accessibility, and usability?

- What impact will adding this technology have on security and other Web site elements?
- What are the direct and indirect costs of implementing the new technology?
- How soon will I see a return on investing in this new technology?

After evaluating the impact the new technologies will have on your Web site, you can then make an informed decision about implementing the technologies.

Make sure to integrate any new technologies with the design, features, and content of your site. Only add the new technology if it will enhance the browsing experience for site visitors.

DESIGN TIP

Various tools are available to create Web pages and add dynamic content, animation, and interactivity. These tools differ as to the skills and knowledge required to use them and the results they produce. The tools include markup languages, Cascading Style Sheets (CSS), scripting languages, text editors, HTML editors, WYSIWYG editors, and Web templates.

Markup Languages

A **markup language** is a coding system that uses tags to provide instructions about the appearance, structure, and formatting of a document. The markup languages used to create Web pages are HTML, XML, XHTML, and WML.

HTML   The **Hypertext Markup Language (HTML)** is a markup language used to create Web pages. The most current HTML standard is HTML 4.01, which specifies, among other things, that HTML tags must be in lowercase, surrounded by brackets, and inserted in pairs. You can check out Appendix B in the back of this book for more information on HTML 4.01 tags and tag modifiers, called **attributes**. A tag defines the target, such as <font>....</font>, and the attribute defines the aspect of the target, such as the color, point size, or weight of a font. Technology standards for the Web are set by the World Wide Web Consortium (W3C). The W3C, through an HTML working group, continues to pursue advancements in the HTML standard.

The HTML markup language defines how Web page elements are formatted and organized using predefined codes called **HTML tags**. For example, the <html> ....</html> tag pair indicates the beginning and the end of a Web page, respectively. The <b> ....</b> HTML tag pair indicates the text between the tags is set in bold. When a Web page is downloaded into a browser, the browser reads and interprets the HTML tags to display the page with organized and formatted text, images, and links.

Even if you are designing a Web site using a content management system or WYSIWYG editor (both described later in this chapter) that does not require the use of markup codes, it is important to understand the basic principles of markup languages to understand how Web pages are coded.

DESIGN TIP

XML   The **Extensible Markup Language (XML)** is a markup language that uses both predefined and customized tags to facilitate the consistent sharing of information, especially within large groups. Whereas HTML defines the appearance and organization of Web page content, XML defines the content itself. For example, using XML, a programmer can define the custom tag <serialnum> to indicate that the information following the tag is a product serial number.

XHTML   The HTML 4.01 standard has been rewritten to combine the features of both HTML and XML as the **Extensible Hypertext Markup Language (XHTML)**. Web pages created using XHTML display better than HTML-coded pages when viewed on smartphones and other handheld computers. Another benefit is that pages created with XHTML avoid user-access issues experienced by many users who view Web pages using assistive technologies (including screen reader software).

WML   The **Wireless Markup Language (WML)** is an XML-based markup language used to design Web pages specifically for microbrowsers on handheld computers, PDAs, and smartphones. WML uses Wireless Application Protocol (WAP) to allow Internet access by wireless devices.

YOUR TURN

Exploring a Web Page's Underlying Markup Language

1. Start your browser and type the URL of the Web page of your choice in the Address bar.
2. View the Web page's underlying markup tags in a new window. (*Hint:* right-click the page, then click View Source or View Page Source.)

3. Scroll the window to view the markup tags. If instructed to do so, print the document, then close the window.
4. If you have printed the document, use Appendix B to identify several of the markup tags.

Scripting Languages
For more information about scripting languages that can create customized, interactive Web pages, visit the Web Design 4 Chapter 1 Student Online Companion Web page at **www .cengagebrain.com** and click Scripting Languages in the @Source links.

Cascading Style Sheets

A **Cascading Style Sheet (CSS)** is a document that uses rules to standardize the appearance of Web page content by defining styles for such elements as font, margins, positioning, background colors, and more. By storing the style rules in a separate document, a Web site designer can attach the style sheet to multiple site pages; any changes made to the style sheet are automatically applied to the associated Web pages. Cascading refers to the order in which the different styles are applied. Chapter 4 discusses CSS in greater detail.

DESIGN TIP   Apply Cascading Style Sheets (CSS) to ensure that all the pages at a site have the same look.

Scripting Languages

Scripting languages are programming languages used to write short programs, called scripts, that execute in real time at the server or in the Web browser when a Web page is downloaded. **Scripts** are used to make Web pages dynamic and interactive by adding such features as multimedia, animation, and forms or by connecting Web pages to underlying databases. **JavaScript, Active Server Pages (ASP), PHP: Hypertext Preprocessor** (commonly abbreviated as **PHP**), and **MySql** are examples of scripting languages.

DESIGN TIP

A Web designer might choose to purchase ready-made scripts to perform routine or common functions, such as e-commerce shopping carts, FAQs (frequently asked questions) lists, and banner ad management. Such scripts are available on CDs or by download from commercial Web sites.

Web page content created by a scripting language such as JavaScript and ASP is also called **active content**. Unfortunately, active content can be used by hackers to transmit malware. **Malware** is malicious software, including computer viruses and Internet worms, which can infect a single computer or an entire network. From a design perspective, be aware that visitors' Web browsers might block active content by default, requiring visitors to actively instruct their browsers to display the content.

Text and HTML Editors

You can create a simple Web page by typing HTML tags and related text into a document created in a plain text editor, such as Notepad (Figure 1-29), the text editor available with the Windows operating system. A **text editor** is software used to create plain (ASCII) text files. Some Web designers or programmers prefer to use an HTML editor to create Web pages. An **HTML editor** is a text editor enhanced with special features that are used to more easily insert HTML tags and their attributes. HTML-Kit, CoffeeCup (Figure 1-29), BBEdit, and NoteTab are examples of HTML editors.

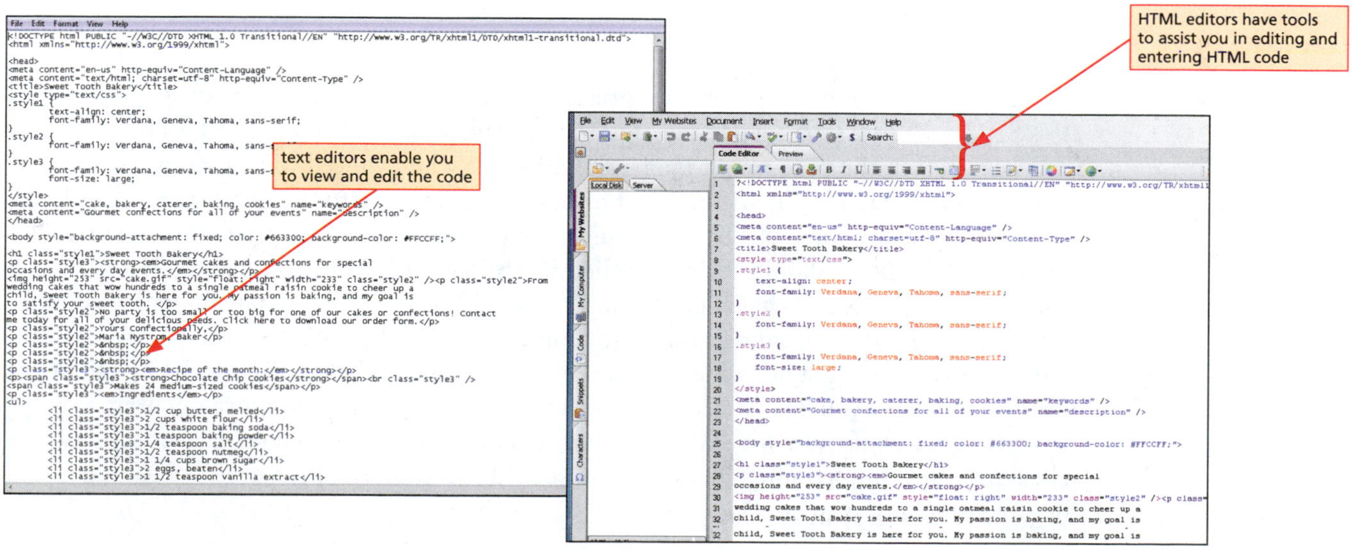

text editors enable you to view and edit the code

HTML editors have tools to assist you in editing and entering HTML code

Figure 1-29 Text and HTML editors are used to create Web pages.

WYSIWYG Editors

Many Web designers use **WYSIWYG editors**, such as Adobe® Dreamweaver®, InnovaStudio WYSIWYG Editor©, Ephox® EditLive!, and Microsoft® Expression Web®, to create Web pages. WYSIWYG stands for "what you see is what you get." Inserting and formatting text and inserting images or links in a Web page using a WYSIWYG editor is similar to creating a document in a word processor, such as Microsoft Word. Additionally, using a WYSIWYG editor to create Web pages eliminates the need to learn a markup language, which can involve complex coding procedures, because the WYSIWYG editor automatically generates the underlying markup language tags as you insert and format text, images, and links. Most WYSIWYG editors also allow you to view and manipulate the underlying HTML code, if desired. Additional benefits of using WYSIWYG editors include the capability to create Web pages rapidly and the opportunity to become familiar with HTML at a pace you choose.

If you are looking for a professional-strength WYSIWYG editor to create and manage complex, interactive, and animated Web pages, either **Microsoft Expression Web** (Figure 1-30) or **Adobe Dreamweaver** (Figure 1-30) would be a good choice. Expression Web and Dreamweaver offer sophisticated Web site design, publishing, and management capabilities. Software vendors who create WYSIWYG editors often provide additional support and resources at their sites, such as clip art and multimedia, training seminars, user forums, and newsletter subscriptions.

Figure 1-30 Microsoft Expression Web and Adobe Dreamweaver are used to create and manage complex, interactive Web pages.

Using a WYSIWYG editor does present some challenges, however. Although most WYSIWYG editors have a preview option to simulate how a Web page looks in a browser, in fact, the page might look quite different when viewed with various versions of different browsers. The inconsistent display is attributable to proprietary, nonstandard code generated by some WYSIWYG editors that has prompted some critics to claim WYSIWYG editors should really be called WYSINWYG editors — "what you see is *not* what you get." A second challenge is that some WYSIWYG editors insert unnecessary code, creating larger, slower-loading Web pages. Finally, some WYSIWYG editors — especially older versions — might not adhere to the latest markup language standards. Inconsistent display between Web browsers and browser versions is discussed in more detail in Chapter 2. Even if your WYSIWYG editor includes tools for previewing, accessibility checking, and compatibility checking, you should still perform any necessary testing before launching your site.

Web Templates and Other Design Technologies

With little or no knowledge of HTML or other Web design tools, users can quickly create a Web site and its pages using a Web template or a content management system.

A **Web template** is a predesigned model Web page that you can customize for fast Web site or Web page creation or updating. Some B2B Web hosting sites, such as Yahoo! Small Business and Homestead, provide Web templates (in addition to hosting services) that make it quick and easy for a small business owner to create his or her e-commerce site, focusing on the Web page's content rather than on the design details.

Other sites, such as DreamTemplate, TemplateWorld, and TemplateMonster, sell an enormous variety of predesigned Web templates for creating personal, organizational/topical, and commercial Web sites. Additionally, a number of sites, such as PixelMill or Expression Graphics, sell Web templates designed to be easily modified in a specific WYSIWYG editor, such as Dreamweaver. Finally, many WYSIWYG editors, such as Expression Web (Figure 1-31), also provide Web templates for fast site and page creation.

Figure 1-31 Web templates are customizable model Web pages.

In addition to creating public Web pages with templates, site designers can use Web templates to control the look and function of all the pages at internal Web sites on a company's intranet. An **intranet** is a private network within a large organization or commercial entity that uses Internet and Web technologies to share information among only its members, employees, or business partners.

For example, a company might allow employees in the Human Resources Department, who have no Web design experience or programming expertise, to add Web pages or update content on existing Web pages related to the human resources department. In this instance, employees might be required to use specific Web templates to ensure that all internal Web pages are consistent in appearance and function.

A **content management system (CMS)** is a software system that provides authoring and administrative tools that enable the management of Web content development, including authoring, reviewing, editing, and publishing. Content providers working within a CMS use Web templates and style sheets to efficiently add or update Web page content on the fly. The templates, style sheets, and other frequently used content elements, such as a logo graphic, are stored in a database called a **content repository**. Templates and other items are called up from the content repository as needed. Autonomy Interwoven Teamsite and Typo3 are two examples of robust content management system software applications.

Other Web design technologies support communication and collaboration among Web users; these include technologies for incorporating blogs, wikis, social networking, social bookmarking, and collaborative workspaces. For example, Microsoft® Office SharePoint Designer® 2010 is a professional WYSIWYG editor designed for the Microsoft® SharePoint Server® and Windows® SharePoint® services environment. You can use SharePoint Designer 2010 to create interactive Web sites that allow employees to collaborate over the Web from any location. Employees can use tools such as shared workspaces, blogs, and wikis and manage and share document libraries. Many other technology companies, such as IBM, Cisco, and Jive, also offer technologies designed to provide Web-based communication and collaboration.

Web Design Roles

From the smallest personal site devoted to a favorite hobby or special interest to the largest commercial site incorporating advanced multimedia elements, Web sites are planned and developed by people working independently, in small groups, or as part of a large team. Ongoing communication between Web development team members is crucial to the success of any Web site design project that involves multiple participants. Depending on the circumstances and the complexity of the Web development project, you might take on one or more of the following Web design roles.

@SOURCE

Web Design Training
For more information about certifications that can help you train for a career in Web Design, visit the Web Design 4 Chapter 1 Student Online Companion Web page at **www.cengagebrain .com** and click Web Design Certifications in the @Source links.

Creative Roles

If you assume a creative role, your focus primarily will be on how the site looks and feels. Jobs in the creative role category include content writer/editor, Web designer, artist/graphic designer, and multimedia producer.

As a **content writer/editor**, you create and revise the text that visitors read when they visit a Web site, and choose the links, images, video, or other media that enhances your text content. To achieve your Web site's purpose, you must write specifically for the Web environment and a targeted Web audience. Text simply cut and pasted from a print publication into an HTML document will not effectively deliver the message you want to send. Writing for the Web environment and targeting an audience are detailed in Chapters 2 and 3, respectively. To fill a content writer/editor position, an employer frequently looks for a highly creative applicant with a liberal arts background and demonstrated print and Internet writing experience.

As a **Web page designer**, your primary role is to convert text, images, and links into Web pages using tools such as markup languages; CSS; and text, HTML, and WYSIWYG editors. Your responsibilities also might include graphic design and Web site setup and maintenance. To be a marketable Web page designer, you must communicate effectively, have a thorough knowledge of Web page design technologies, have graphic design talent, and possess some programming skills. This role requires a solid understanding of how Web pages and browsers interact.

The role of a **Web artist/graphic designer** is to create original art such as logos, stylized typefaces, and avatars or props for 3D virtual worlds. You also might prepare photographs and other graphic elements and redesign print publications for the Web environment. In the workforce, this highly creative role demands experience with high-end illustration and image-editing software, such as Adobe Illustrator CS5 or

Adobe Photoshop CS5, as well as specialty hardware, such as scanners and digital cameras. Chapter 5 discusses typeface and graphics in detail.

As a **multimedia producer**, you design and produce animation, digital video and audio, 2D and 3D models, and other media elements to include in a Web site. This role demands knowledge of, and experience with, sophisticated hardware and software, as well as familiarity with art theory and graphic design principles.

High-Tech Roles

If you play a high-tech role, your focus will be primarily on a Web site's functionality and security. Examples of types of jobs in the technical role category include Web programmer/database developer and network/security administrator.

A **Web programmer** must be highly skilled in scripting languages, such as JavaScript, Active Server Pages (ASP), PHP: Hypertext Preprocessor, and MySql. These languages are used to create interactive and dynamic Web pages; they also handle form data. A **database developer** must possess the technical skills to plan, create, and maintain databases of varying complexity. Because the corporate world relies so heavily on databases to conduct day-to-day business, a database developer also needs to know how to integrate databases successfully with company Web pages.

A **network/security administrator** is responsible for ensuring the day-to-day functionality of the network and protecting it from internal and external threats. Duties and responsibilities include ongoing network inspection, maintenance, and upgrades. Regarding security, an administrator must be aware of security alerts and advisories, protect the network with intrusion-detection software, and have a fully developed plan of action if the security of the network is compromised.

Oversight Role

If you assume an oversight role, your focus is on managerial and administrative issues. Examples of types of jobs in the oversight role category include content manager and Webmaster.

The need for **content managers** has emerged in the corporate world primarily because of the growth in size and complexity of corporate sites. A content manager may determine the overall content goal; review content to assess its relevancy to the goal and ensure its accuracy and timeliness; ensure that content is published or removed expediently; and identify, implement, maintain, and provide support and training for a content management system (CMS). All sites need to go through a testing process; **testers** examine the Web site for usability across different browsers and devices.

The responsibilities of a **Webmaster** vary dramatically, depending primarily on the staffing and other resources devoted to developing and maintaining a Web site. If working independently, the Webmaster assumes all the roles. In an organizational or business setting, the Webmaster might oversee a Web development team comprising some or all of the creative and technical roles' job types. A corporate Webmaster often assumes the responsibilities for both the sites that are on the Internet and an intranet. A Webmaster, therefore, must have a broad range of skills and knowledge, including familiarity with databases, markup and scripting languages, content development, creative design, marketing, and growth and maintenance of the hardware connecting computers and users. Sometimes the Webmaster takes on the role of the system architect. A **system architect** determines the structure and technical needs required to build, maintain, and expand the Web site.

YOUR TURN

Exploring Web Design Roles

1. Visit the Web Design 4 Chapter 1 Student Online Companion Web page at **www.cengagebrain.com** and click Monster in the Your Turn links.

2. Search the Monster site for jobs related to three of the Web design roles discussed in this chapter.

3. Summarize your research in a report by listing the job description, skill requirements, salary information, and job location for at least two job postings for each of the three Web design roles you would be interested in. Compare the skills needed for the job with your own skill set; what additional training will you need?

Chapter Review

The Internet is a worldwide public network that links millions of private networks. The highly visual, dynamic, and interactive World Wide Web is a subset of the Internet. The Internet and the Web have dramatically changed the communication, education, entertainment, and business practices of millions of people worldwide.

Users can access the Internet and the Web over cable television lines or through the Public Switched Telephone Network (PSTN) over dial-up or dedicated lines. Fixed wireless connections are used where DSL or cable access is not available. Laptops and handheld devices, such as PDAs and smartphones, access the Internet using mobile wireless connectivity methods. Internet service providers (ISPs) provide Internet connections to individuals, businesses, and other organizations.

A Web browser, or browser, is a software program that requests, downloads, and displays Web pages. To view a Web page, enter its unique address, called a Uniform Resource Locator (URL) in the browser's Address bar. The two most popular Web browsers are Microsoft Internet Explorer and Mozilla Firefox. Alternatives to traditional computer-based access using desktop or laptop computers include handheld computing devices and smartphones.

Web sites can be categorized as personal, organizational/topical, or commercial. Commercial Web sites include B2C, B2B, and C2C e-commerce sites; entertainment/ news; search tools; and portal sites.

Web design technologies include markup languages, Cascading Style Sheets (CSS), scripting languages, text and HTML editors, WYSIWYG editors, and predesigned Web templates and content management systems.

Depending on resources, developing a Web site might be the job of an individual person, two or three people, or a large Web development team. Although actual titles vary and responsibilities can overlap, the primary Web design roles include creative, high-tech, and oversight.

After reading the chapter, you should know each of these key terms.

3D virtual world (7)
3G (11)
4G (11)
active content (25)
Active Server Pages (ASP) (25)
Adobe Dreamweaver (26)
asymmetrical digital subscriber line (ADSL) (12)
attributes (23)
blog (6)
blogging (6)
bookmark (4)
browser (14)
browsing the Web (3)
business-to-business (B2B) e-commerce (9)
business-to-consumer (B2C) e-commerce (9)
cable television (CATV) lines (10)
Cascading Style Sheets (CSS) (24)
cloud computing (4)
collaborative workspace (5)
commercial Web site (18)
consumer-to-consumer (C2C) e-commerce (9)
content management system (CMS) (27)
content manager (29)
content repository (27)
content writer/editor (28)
corporate portal (22)
database developer (29)
dedicated line (12)
dial-up line (12)
digital subscriber line (DSL) (12)
domain name (15)
e-commerce (9)
electronic commerce (9)
electronic mail (5)
e-mail (5)
Extensible Hypertext Markup Language (XHTML) (24)
Extensible Markup Language (XML) (24)
favorite (4)
fixed wireless (11)
fractional T-1 line (12)
general consumer portal (21)
handheld computer (16)
hit (19)
home page (2)
hot spot (11)
HTML editor (25)
HTML tags (23)
hyperlink (3)
hyperlocal portal (22)
Hypertext Markup Language (HTML) (23)
Hypertext Transfer Protocol (HTTP) (15)
IM chat (5)

index (19)
instant messaging (5)
Integrated Services Digital Network (ISDN) (12)
Internet (2)
Internet2 (2)
Internet Relay Chat (IRC) (5)
Internet service provider (ISP) (13)
intranet (27)
IP address (15)
JavaScript (25)
Kbps (10)
keyword (19)
link (2)
malware (25)
markup language (23)
massively multiplayer online game (MMOG) (7)
Mbps (10)
metasearch engine (19)
meta tag (19)
Microsoft Expression Web (26)
mobile wireless (11)
multimedia producer (29)
multiplexing (13)
MySql (25)
national ISP (13)
netbook (16)
network (2)
network/security administrator (29)
organizational Web site (17)
personal digital assistant (PDA) (16)
personal portal (21)
personal Web site (17)
PHP: Hypertext Preprocessor (PHP) (25)
protocol (15)
Public Switched Telephone Network (PSTN) (11)
regional ISP (13)
robot (19)
script (25)
scripting languages (25)
search directory (20)
search engine (19)
search engine optimization (SEO) (20)
smartphone (16)
social bookmarking (7)
social networking (6)
spider (19)
streaming media (12)
surfing the Web (3)
system architect (29)
T-1 line (12)

T-3 line (12)
T-carrier line (12)
tag (6)
tester (29)
text editor (25)
topical Web site (17)
top-level domain (TLD) (15)
transfer rate (10)
Uniform Resource Locator (URL) (14)
vertical portal (21)
video blogging (6)
video sharing (6)
virtual meeting space (5)
Web 2.0 (4)

Web artist/graphic designer (28)
Web-based chat (5)
Web browser (14)
Web page (2)
Web page designer (28)
Web programmer (29)
Web server (2)
Web site (2)
Web template (27)
Webmaster (29)
wireless fidelity (Wi-Fi) (11)
Wireless Markup Language (WML) (24)
World Wide Web (Web) (2)
WYSIWYG editor (26)

TEST YOUR KNOWLEDGE

Complete the Test Your Knowledge exercises to solidify what you have learned in the chapter.

Matching Terms

Match each term with the best description.

____ 1. Web page

____ 2. browser

____ 3. search directory

____ 4. hyperlink

____ 5. e-commerce

____ 6. HTTP

____ 7. hyperlocal portal

____ 8. XML

____ 9. content management system (CMS)

____ 10. Internet service provider (ISP)

____ 11. Uniform Resource Locator (URL)

____ 12. spider

a. The communication standard used to transmit data on the Web.

b. A Web page's unique text address.

c. The conducting of a variety of business activities online, including shopping, investing, and the exchange of data and services between business partners.

d. A Web-based tool used to locate editor-chosen Web pages based on keywords or phrases.

e. A business that has a permanent Internet connection and provides temporary connections to individuals and companies for a fee.

f. A specifically formatted electronic document that contains text, graphics, and other information and is linked to similar, related documents.

g. A markup language used to define Web site content.

h. A word, phrase, or graphical image that connects pages at the same site or pages across different sites.

i. A site that is written about, for, and by members of a specific geographical location.

j. A software program used to request, download, and display Web pages.

k. A program that searches the Web for new pages in order to create or update a search index.

l. A software program that provides Web site authoring and administrative tools.

Short Answer Questions

Write a brief answer to each question.

1. Describe the relationship between the Internet and the World Wide Web.

2. Describe the difference between a search engine and a search directory.

3. Define the following terms: CATV lines, fixed wireless, mobile wireless, dedicated lines, and dial-up Internet access.

4. Explain how the following e-commerce categories are similar and how they differ: business-to-consumer (B2C), business-to-business (B2B), and consumer-to-consumer (C2C).

5. Describe briefly the following tools for creating Web sites and Web pages: HTML, XHTML, text and HTML editors, WYSIWYG editors, Web templates, and content management systems (CMS).

6. Identify the primary responsibilities associated with each of the following Web design roles: content writer/editor, artist/graphic designer, Web page designer, Web programmer/database developer, and content manager.

7. Define the following terms: Internet Relay Chat (IRC), instant messaging (IM), blog, e-mail, and collaborative workspace.

8. Define the following terms: Uniform Resource Locator (URL), IP address, domain name, top-level domain, and Hypertext Transfer Protocol (HTTP).

LEARN IT ONLINE

Test your knowledge of chapter content and key terms.

Instructions: To complete the Learn It Online exercises, start your browser, click the Address bar, and then visit the Web Design 4 Chapter 1 Student Online Companion page at **www.cengagebrain.com**. When the Web Design Learn It Online page is displayed, click the link for the exercise you want to complete and then read the instructions.

Chapter Reinforcement TF, MC, and SA

A series of true/false, multiple-choice, and short-answer questions that test your knowledge of the chapter content.

Flash Cards

An interactive learning environment where you identify chapter key terms associated with displayed definitions.

Practice Test

A series of multiple-choice questions that test your knowledge of chapter content and key terms.

Who Wants To Be a Computer Genius?

An interactive game that challenges your knowledge of chapter content in the style of a television quiz show.

Wheel of Terms

An interactive game that challenges your knowledge of chapter key terms in the style of the television show *Wheel of Fortune*.

Crossword Puzzle Challenge

A crossword puzzle that challenges your knowledge of key terms presented in the chapter.

TRENDS

Investigate current Web design developments with the Trends exercises.

Write a brief essay about each of the following trends, using the Web as your research tool. For each trend, identify at least one Web page URL used as a research source. Be prepared to discuss your findings in class.

1 | Cloud Computing

Cloud computing affects how users store, access, and share files and software. Research the latest cloud computing trends and technologies. Use Google Docs to write your findings and submit it to your instructor.

2 | Social Networking and Bookmarking

How do social networking and bookmarking sites such as Facebook and Digg affect Internet users' personal interactions with the Internet? As a Web designer, how can you take advantage of these trends? Visit at least one social networking and social bookmarking site to see how users share information. Identify at least one site that encourages and provides opportunities for users to share content using these technologies.

AT ISSUE

Challenge your perspective of Web design and surrounding technology with the @Issue exercises.

Write a brief essay in response to the following issues, using the Web as your research tool. For each issue, identify at least one Web page URL used as a research source. Be prepared to discuss your findings in class.

1 | Impact on Lifestyle

With developments in technology such as smartphones, people are constantly able to stay connected. Whether by phone calls, text messages, alerts from Web sites about new content, or social networking sites such as Facebook and Twitter, technology provides many distractions. How do these developments enhance daily life? How have they changed daily life from five or ten years ago? What is a negative impact? Discuss the impact of technology on your lifestyle and that of those around you.

2 | Protecting Your Privacy

Social networking and blogging sites make it easy to share information, photos, links, and videos. However, you should use caution before publishing or uploading any content. Explore the privacy policies of two social networking or blogging sites. What measures would you take to protect yourself when using these sites? Discuss the advantages and disadvantages of using these sites.

Use the World Wide Web to obtain more information about the concepts in the chapter with the Hands On exercises.

1 | Explore and Evaluate: A Portal

Browse the Web to locate a portal. Follow links from the home page to view at least three related pages at the site. Then answer the following questions; be prepared to discuss your answers in class.

a. Who owns the site and what is its URL?

b. Is it a general consumer portal, a vertical portal, or a corporate portal?

c. Were the home page and related pages visually appealing? If yes, why? If no, why not?

d. Does the portal have an overall focus?

e. How easy was it to navigate to related pages using the home page links?

f. Identify the type of pages you were led to; were they related to the portal site or were they separate sites?

g. Were you able to identify any advertisements or paid promotional placements?

h. How long did it take for you to find useful information at the site?

2 | Search and Discover: E-Commerce Web Sites

Using the Google search tool, perform a keyword search to identify two commercial Web sites: a B2C site that sells sports equipment and a B2B site that sells Web design services. Follow links from each site's home page to view the specific product or service pages of your choice at each site. Then write a report that answers the following questions for each site.

a. Who owns the site and what is its URL?

b. Is the site's domain name an effective marketing tool? If yes, why? If no, why not?

c. What type of customer does the site target?

d. Was the site's home page visually appealing? If yes, why? If no, why not?

e. Was it easy to find the product or service pages using home page links?

f. Were the products or service pages visually appealing? If yes, why? If no, why not?

g. Was it easy to find useful information about a specific product or service?

h. Would you purchase a product or service from the B2C site? If yes, why? If no, why not?

i. Does the B2B site offer any type of validation, such as customer testimonials or designer certifications, that helps establish the site's authority and credibility? Is there any indication that design services offered at the site follow current Web design standards?

j. How does your personal experience at each site inform your approach to designing an e-commerce site?

Work collaboratively to reinforce the concepts in the chapter with the Team Approach exercises.

1 | Survey Search Engines

Pair up with two classmates and work as a team to conduct two different searches each using a different search engine, such as Google, ask.com, and Mamma. Assign one search engine to each team member, and decide as a group on two different keyword searches to perform.

a. Perform two keyword searches using the same keyword or phrase. Compare the search results returned by each search engine.

b. Answer the following questions:

- Are the Web pages listed in the search results lists the same or different?

- How do the search results from the Mamma metasearch engine differ from the search results returned by the other search engines?

c. How can you use a similar exercise to identify appropriate meta tag keywords and descriptive Web page titles when planning a Web site?

d. How do sponsored links affect search results? Are the sponsored links identified?

Then, as a team, create a report indicating your team's search results.

2 | Team and Client Communication Challenges

Join with four or five classmates to establish a mock Web development team. Assume the Web development team has been hired by a client to plan and create a B2C e-commerce Web site. Each team member should choose one or more of the creative, high-tech, or oversight roles discussed in this chapter. Then use the Web to research current challenges that individuals in each role might face, and identify potential resolutions to those challenges. Next, as a team, brainstorm communication issues that might arise among team members and between the team members and the client. Identify ways to resolve any potential communication issues. Finally, prepare a detailed report describing potential design and communication challenges and the team's approach to handling them. Submit the report to your instructor and be prepared to present your report to the class.

Apply the chapter concepts to the ongoing development process in Web design with the Case Study.

The Case Study is an ongoing development process using the concepts, techniques, and Design Tips presented in each chapter.

Background Information

You now will begin the process of designing your own personal, organizational/topical, or commercial Web site. As you progress through the chapters in this book, you will learn how to use design as a tool to create effective Web pages and sites. At each chapter's conclusion, you will receive instructions for completing another segment of the ongoing design process.

The following are suggestions for Web site topics. Choose one of these topics or determine your own. Select a topic that you find interesting, feel knowledgeable about, or are excited about researching.

1. Personal Web Site
   - Share a hobby or special interest: music, remote control cars, mountain biking, fantasy sports, or other
2. Organizational/Topical Web Site
   - Increase support and membership for: Habitat for Humanity, Red Cross, or a campus organization
   - Promote awareness of: health and fitness, endangered species, financial assistance for college
3. Commercial Web Site
   - Start a new business: childcare or dog walking, or expand an existing business with a Web presence
   - Sell a service: tutoring, Web design, graphic design, home maintenance
   - Sell a product: DVD labels, workout programs or gear, beauty/boutique products

The evaluation of your completed Web site, which will consist of 5 to 10 pages, will be based primarily on the application of good Web design concepts.

Chapter 1 Assignment

Follow Steps 1–6 to complete and submit a one-page report in preparation for developing your Web site.

1. Identify which type of Web site you will design — personal, organizational/topical, or commercial. Write a brief paragraph describing the site's overall purpose and its targeted audience. Create a name for your site.

2. List at least three general goals for your Web site. You will fine-tune these goals into a mission statement in a subsequent chapter.

3. List elements in addition to text — photos, music, animation, and so forth — that you could include on your Web site to support your general goals.

4. Identify the design tools you expect to use to develop your Web site.

5. Identify an available domain name and URL for your site.

6. Submit your report to your instructor and be prepared to discuss your report with the class.

Web Publishing Fundamentals

Introduction

Chapter 1 introduced you to the Internet and the Web and design tools used to create Web pages. In this chapter, you learn about the advantages of Web publishing and discover the basic design principles behind publishing a successful Web site. The chapter explains the special requirements for writing for the Web and the effective use of color as a design tool. Finally, you learn about the technical, legal, privacy, accessibility, and usability issues surrounding Web publishing.

Objectives

After completing this chapter, you will be able to:

1. Describe the advantages of Web publishing

2. Discuss basic Web design principles

3. Define the requirements for writing for the Web

4. Explain the use of color as a Web design tool

5. Identify Web publishing issues

Advantages of Web Publishing

Printed information is convenient. You can tuck a newspaper, magazine, or book under your arm, take it to your choice of reading place — an overstuffed chair, a subway seat, or a park bench — and enjoy. However, Web publishing, which is the distribution of information in a Web site, has some specific advantages for both the audience and the publisher over print publishing. Thanks to the rise in popularity of mobile devices, Web site content is just as portable as print materials. Advantages over print include currency, interactivity, reduced production costs, and rapid, economical delivery.

The Currency Advantage

Whether you are planning your next semester's classes, checking out movie times at a neighborhood theater, purchasing a new cell phone, or monitoring the weather prior to a trip, access to timely, current information is critical to making good decisions. In the past, many people made decisions about these types of activities based on information in print publications, such as class schedules, newspapers, magazines, and sales brochures. The content of print publications, however, cannot reflect more current information until the publication is updated, reprinted, and distributed; therefore, the most current information — canceled classes, special movie showings, new cell phone products, severe weather alerts — might not be available in the publication at hand. Although Web sites must be researched, edited, and laid out in ways that are similar to print publications, Web sites can be updated in minutes and the new information is immediately available. In comparison, printing and distributing revised documents can take anywhere from hours to weeks, and costs far more than updating a Web site.

The Web's **currency advantage** over print publications lies in the ability to quickly and inexpensively update Web pages. For example, suppose the chief executive officer (CEO) of a company is suddenly replaced and the company's board of directors wants to assure customers that business activities will not be affected. In just a few minutes and at a very low cost, the company's Web designer could open the source file of a currently available Web page and insert a press release explaining the change in management, along with a photograph and biography of the new CEO. The designer then could publish the revised page to the company's Web site, and submit the content through its Twitter feed, Facebook page, or RSS (Really Simple Syndication), where it is delivered to users' inboxes or news feeds. Using its Web site and connectivity tools, the company can communicate with customers long before any print publication can be prepared and distributed.

Many Web sites are updated on an hourly or daily basis, or for news sites, as stories develop. For example, newsworthy events often swiftly unfold, causing daily newspapers or weekly news magazines to very quickly lose their currency. As noted in Chapter 1, news organizations exploit the Web's currency advantage by hosting popular, high-traffic Web sites, such as washingtonpost.com or USATODAY.com (Figure 2-1), to provide continually updated weather, stock market quotes, and stories about newsworthy events — seconds after the events occur — which can be updated as the story unfolds.

news sites use a combination of videos and text

Figure 2-1 High-traffic news-oriented Web sites exploit the Web's currency advantage.

Web site visitors expect that sites providing sports, news, and weather information or e-commerce opportunities offer timely content presented in a fresh, appealing manner. If visitors do not find timely content at these types of sites, they are likely to leave, perhaps finding what they need on a competitor's site.

> Although your Web site might not need as frequent updating as a news-oriented or B2C site, you still must take care to keep the site's content up to date.
>
> **DESIGN TIP**

The Connectivity Advantage

To share information from a print publication, a user must pass along or photocopy the book or magazine. Sharing a story, press release, article, or blog post from a Web site is an instantaneous process, and the user does not have to relinquish the original copy or potentially violate copyright laws. Using aggregators such as RSS feeds, social networking tools such as Facebook pages and Twitter feeds, and social news sites such as Digg or StumbleUpon, a site's administrators can instantly alert followers to new content. In addition, the same tools can allow those users to pass links to the content to their friends and followers, allowing the word to spread quickly (Figure 2-2). The Web's **connectivity advantage**, or ability to instantaneously distribute and share content, is a benefit that print publications do not share.

The connectivity advantage can also streamline the writing process. In a print article, the writer must include any background that the reader needs to understand the topic, taking up valuable space and causing readers who are aware of the background to need to skim. A Web-published article can include links directly in the content to additional resources or background. Users can click the links to read more, or continue reading the article if they choose. Many articles contain a list of related links to other stories or articles about the same or related topics.

Q&A

Are all Web sites continually updated with timely content?
No. Some Web sites focus on content that might not change over time, for example sites that publish biographies or content based on research papers. The primary concerns of visitors to these types of sites are author credibility and content accuracy.

Figure 2-2 Web-published articles can include tools for sharing the content and links to supplemental information.

The Interactivity Advantage

In Chapter 1, you learned that the Internet is a worldwide public network that connects smaller private networks for the purpose of sharing data and other resources. The Web's **interactivity advantage** over print publications allows for data and resource sharing that enables communication with a site's Customer Service or Sales Department or that allows users to post comments on an article.

A well-designed Web site should include tools that enable its visitors to engage in interactive, two-way communication with the site's publisher. At a minimum, to encourage interactivity and communication, every site should include a page of contact information — phone numbers, mailing addresses, physical location addresses, and e-mail addresses — similar to the Ford Motor Company contact page shown in Figure 2-3.

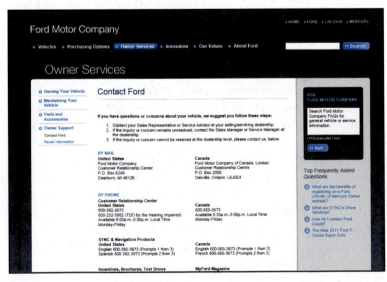

Figure 2-3 A Web site's contact page encourages communication between the site and its visitors.

Depending on the purpose of its site, a company could use other tools to promote interactivity and communication. For example, blogs have become an increasingly important internal and external tool for promoting interactivity and communication between companies and their vendors, customers, and other business partners. Companies as diverse as Eastman Kodak and The Clorox Company (Figure 2-4) host blogs that encourage interactivity and communication.

Figure 2-4 Blogs have become an increasingly important communication tool for businesses.

Another popular communication tool is a **Web-based form**. Just like a paper form, companies use Web-based forms to gather information from Web site visitors. Visitors complete forms to order products quickly and easily, participate in surveys, sign up for newsletters, request sales or customer support, register for events, or return products.

> After your Web site is published, plan to review the site's content for credibility, accuracy, and timeliness on a regular basis and update the content as necessary.   **DESIGN TIP**

As shown in Figure 2-5 (on the next page), common Web-based form elements include text boxes, check boxes, option buttons, drop-down list boxes, and a Submit or Send button. To use a Web-based form, a visitor simply types information, clicks a check box, selects an option button, or selects an item from a drop-down list and then clicks the Send or Submit button to send the information to the site. Forms can be just a few questions, or broken out into several pages to make entering and validating the data easier. Although creating a form sounds complicated, WYSIWYG editors and Web hosting services such as Homestead provide tools to create forms efficiently. Working with Web-based forms is discussed in more detail in Chapter 6.

Figure 2-5 Web-based forms gather information from site visitors.

In addition to traditional contact pages, blogs, and Web-based forms, a variety of creative methods to promote interactivity and communication are found at Web sites of all types. News-oriented sites, such as CNN.com and FOXNews.com, often promote interactivity by allowing visitors to comment on articles or by permitting visitors to submit their own breaking news stories and images. Some businesses and government agencies, such as the Small Business Administration, promote interactivity at their sites by offering chat rooms visitors can join to discuss topics in real time.

DESIGN TIP Build into your site appropriate ways to promote interactivity, such as a contact page, Web-based form, or blog.

YOUR TURN

Exploring Currency and Interactivity

1. Visit the Web Design 4 Chapter 2 Student Online Companion Web page at **www.cengagebrain.com** and then click FOX, K2 Snowboarding, and Office in the Your Turn links.

2. Explore each Web site and answer the following questions:

   a. Is the site's content current, or does it appear to be outdated? Give examples to support your answer.

   b. What tools, such as forms or comments, does the site use to promote interactivity and communication?

3. Write a report discussing your site exploration and describe how similar methods and tools could be incorporated at your Web site.

The Cost Advantage

Compared with print publishing, Web publishing is more cost effective. In the print environment, budget limitations often restrict the types of design elements you can incorporate into your piece. For example, as a print designer, to stay within a budget, you might have to opt for a two-color, rather than a four-color (or full-color), brochure to cut down on printing costs; reduce the number and size of photographs and restrict content to a limited page size or number; or eliminate design extras, such as die-cutting, to reduce design costs.

On the Web, however, the cost of publishing a piece does not vary based on its length, color composition, or design complexity; thus, the **cost advantage** allows for a very different scenario. For example, you might be able to find free downloads for photos, animations, video, and sound clips for use at your site; however, you might incur some additional cost to prepare these types of content elements for the best display and quality. You also can purchase reasonably priced photos and multimedia elements.

The technological specifications of the Web mean that it doesn't matter whether your design is a simple one-color text piece or a sophisticated piece with hundreds of colors — the cost to publish on the Web is the same. Note, however, that whenever you incorporate multimedia in your Web pages, the pages are generally larger and your site might require more storage space. You might also be limited by the amount of Web server space provided by your Web site hosting service or by budget constraints if you must lease extra Web server space to support your site's multimedia elements. For example, a Web site hosting service might limit server space for Web site files to 5 MB for a flat monthly fee; if you need more space, you might incur additional cost. Adding multimedia to a Web site is discussed in more detail in Chapter 6.

Q&A

Where can I find free photographs? Using professional photographs can enhance your Web page content. Sites such as www.flickr.com and www.morguefile.com allow photographers to post photos for use, for little or no cost. No matter where you get your photos, remember to always give credit to the artist. Cost-free does not mean copyright free — the rights to the image are still owned by the artist, even if you do not have to pay for them.

The Delivery Advantage

Delivering information over the Internet and the Web can be significantly faster and less expensive than using print media, thus the Web's **delivery advantage**. For instance, imagine that as a volunteer for your community hospital, you are asked to publicize the upcoming health fair. Because you want to get the information out quickly to as many people as possible, you use your Web site and connectivity tools to avoid costs associated with mailing 1,000 brochures overnight or first-class.

You could publish the health fair brochure on a page at the hospital's Web site and add the event to the hospital's official calendar at the site. You also could query related Web sites, such as the community Chamber of Commerce or local health and fitness clubs, to publicize the health fair. You could also send e-mail messages with a link to the health fair brochure at your Web site to last year's participants or other potentially interested individuals or organizations. Posting links to the site on your Twitter feed reaches additional interested customers. These methods cost very little, and the news about the event would be available almost immediately.

Use your Web site to expand on your printed content. For example, if you have a large event to promote, send a less-expensive postcard directing users to the Web site for the event. Provide minimal details on the postcard, but save on printing and mailing costs by having registration for the event online.

DESIGN TIP

Basic Web Design Principles

Both print publications and Web pages should be visually attractive, convey a powerful message, and leave a distinct impression. Successful publications — including Web pages — that accomplish these objectives combine creativity with the basic design principles of balance and proximity, contrast and focus, and unity and visual identity.

Balance and Proximity

From the perspective of design, **balance** is the harmonious arrangement of elements. Balance, or the absence of balance, can significantly impact the effectiveness of a Web page to express its message. A **symmetric** arrangement of Web elements is centered or even and suggests a conservative, safe, and peaceful atmosphere. The Art Institute of Chicago home page (Figure 2-6) illustrates a symmetric arrangement of Web elements. Too much symmetry, however, can lead to boring, uninteresting Web pages. To create a fun, energetic mood, position your Web elements **asymmetrically**, or off balance. The Environmental Protection Agency Kids home page (Figure 2-6) illustrates elements positioned asymmetrically.

Figure 2-6 Web pages evoke different moods by positioning Web page elements symmetrically or asymmetrically.

Proximity, or closeness, is strongly associated with balance. Proximity, as applied to Web pages, means that you place related elements close to each other. For example, position a caption near an image, an organization's name near its logo, and headings and subheadings near related body copy. Doing so visually connects elements that have a logical relationship, making your Web pages more organized. Elements on the Martha Stewart home page (Figure 2-7) illustrate proximity: the Martha Stewart logo is placed immediately to the left of the organization's name, images are positioned above or to the left of explanatory text or captions, and headings and subheadings appear above related links.

The empty space surrounding text and images, called **white space** in design, also can define proximity and help organize Web page elements, eliminate clutter, and make content more readable, as illustrated in the Martha Stewart home page.

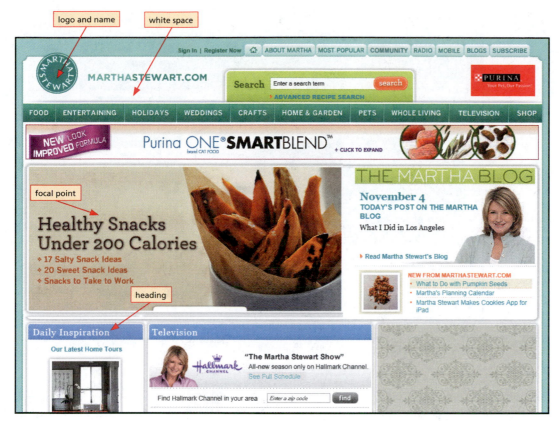

Figure 2-7 Place related Web page elements in proximity to each other and allow sufficient white space.

You can create white space by adding line breaks, paragraph returns, paragraph indents, and space around tables and images.

DESIGN TIP

Contrast and Focus

Contrast is a mix of elements to stimulate attention. Contrast also establishes a **focal point**, which is a dominating segment of the Web page that directs visitors' attention to a center of interest or activity. What do you want your Web site's visitors to focus on and to remember — a company name, a tag line or logo, a powerful photo, or some combination of these? Determine first what element on your Web page is the most important, and then use contrast to establish that dominance visually.

Using a slide show enables you to have one central focal point whose content changes automatically or as a result of user intervention. You can feature several articles at once in a small amount of space.

DESIGN TIP

Pages that lack contrast, such as those that are made up of a solid block of text or a jumble of competing elements, are uninteresting or confusing. You can create contrast by using text styles, color choices, element size, and more. For example, setting a company name in a larger typeface distinguishes it from subheads and body text, which typically are a smaller typeface. Similarly, a dark background with light, brightly colored text might draw more attention than a cream background with black text. By varying the size of Web page elements, you can establish a visual hierarchy of information that will show your visitors which elements are most important. Element size and typeface are used on The University of Chicago home page (Figure 2-8 on the next page) to create contrast and establish a focal point for the page.

Figure 2-8 Use contrast on a Web page to stimulate attention and establish the page's focal point.

DESIGN TIP   Use balance, proximity, and white space to create effective, organized Web pages. Use contrast to stimulate interest and establish a focal point for your Web pages.

Unity and Visual Identity

All the pages at a Web site must have **unity**, or a sense of oneness or belonging, to create and maintain the site's **visual identity** — the combination of design elements identified with the site and its publisher. Especially important to businesses, visual identity must be consistent, not only throughout a Web site, but also with the business's print publications, such as brochures, business cards, and letterheads.

Creating and maintaining a visual identity is an important aspect of branding a business or organization. A general definition of the term **brand** is the assurance or guarantee that a business or organization offers to its customers. Businesses and other large organizations take care to develop and reinforce their own brand over time, generally with the guidance of marketing professionals. Some brands, such as Ford Motor Company (assurance of quality vehicles), are decades old; others, such as Starbucks (guarantee of upscale coffee products) are relatively new.

An entity's brand is continually promoted by the consistent application of **branding specifications** for color, images, and text applied to all of the entity's media. Examples of design elements that promote unity, create a visual identity, and contribute to branding an entity both in print media and on Web pages include logos, fonts, colors, and tag lines. A **tag line** is a concise statement that a consumer readily associates with a business, organization, or product. An example of a tag line is Southwest Airlines' "You are now free to move about the country."

Consistent placement and repetition of elements, such as the company name, logo, and tag line, and application of the same color scheme across all pages at a site help promote unity and visual identity, as shown at the Subway Web site (Figure 2-9), and are an important aspect of branding the site. Unity, visual identity, and branding are discussed in more detail in Chapter 4.

@SOURCE

Visual Identity
For an example of visual identity and branding in action, visit the Web Design 4 Chapter 2 Student Online Companion Web page at **www .cengagebrain.com** and then click Visual Identity in the @Source links for Chapter 2.

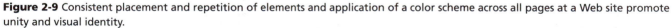

Figure 2-9 Consistent placement and repetition of elements and application of a color scheme across all pages at a Web site promote unity and visual identity.

Alignment is the placement of objects in fixed or predetermined positions, rows, or columns. Applying consistent alignment will ensure that your Web pages have a coherent, structured presentation. Visitors to a Web page expect page elements to line up; for example, the text in a photo caption should line up with the left edge of the photo beneath which it appears. If elements on a Web page are not aligned, the page will look jumbled and be perceived as inconsistent and, potentially, unprofessional. When the elements on a Web page are aligned horizontally, they are arranged consistently to the left, right, or centered. When Web page elements are aligned vertically, they are also top-justified, assisting in readability and ensuring an organized appearance, as shown on the Office Depot home page (Figure 2-10 on the next page).

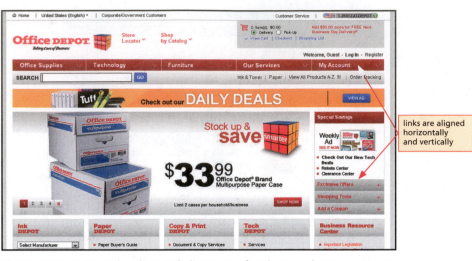

Figure 2-10 Horizontal and vertical alignment of Web page elements ensures a consistent presentation and increases readability.

Writing for the Web

In general, when writing for the Web, use language that is straightforward, contemporary, and geared toward an educated audience. Avoid overly promotional language that might not appeal to visitors and avoid the use of industry jargon or slang. Use wording in headings that clearly communicates the content of a Web page or section; avoid overly cute or clever headings that might confuse or annoy visitors. Be cautious regarding the use of humor. Small doses of humor correctly interpreted can enliven content and entertain. Remember, though, humor can be taken out of context and might be misunderstood or misinterpreted.

DESIGN TIP   To help Web users more easily find your site, carefully consider the text that you place in headings to use search engine optimization techniques to their best advantage. Search engine optimization (SEO) was introduced in Chapter 1 and is discussed in more detail in Chapter 7.

Visitors turn to the Web for a variety of reasons. Whatever the particular circumstances of a user's Web needs, distractions such as voices, ringing telephones, and time constraints most likely are present. Consequently, Web site visitors generally scan Web page text quickly to find useful information that is accurate and current, easy to read, and well organized.

DESIGN TIP   To keep Web page text succinct, place information that is not crucial, such as historical backgrounds or related topics, on linked subsidiary pages, both within the content as linked text, or as a separate link or list of links at the bottom or side of an article. For example, in a business news article about a company, you can link to the company's Web site, the NASDAQ site to show the company's current stock price, and a related story from a previous day.

Accuracy and Currency

When collecting content for your Web site, confirm its accuracy using reliable sources. Refer to respected subject experts, professional organizations, trade journals, and other resources with a proven track record. Typographical and spelling errors can embarrass you and diminish your Web site's credibility. If you publish your Web pages with such errors, your visitors might question how closely you checked your content and how committed you are to your purpose. To avoid these types of errors, write the text content for your Web pages in a word processor first so that you can perform spelling and grammar checks. Proofread your content, and then ask at least one other person to review it before you add the text to a Web page.

As noted earlier in this chapter, after you publish your Web site, you must keep the content on your Web pages current. To demonstrate the currency and freshness of your site's content, you can add the last updated date and/or time to your Web pages. Because visitors frequently print Web pages, including the last updated date also helps indicate the most current printout.

> **DESIGN TIP**
> Establish credibility for your Web site by providing accurate, verifiable content. Show content currency by including the date the content was last updated.

Scannability

Q&A **Is chunked text appropriate for all Web page text?** In some situations, a Web page might contain lengthy text articles that are intended to be printed and read offline. In these situations, you should present the text in its entirety and not chunked.

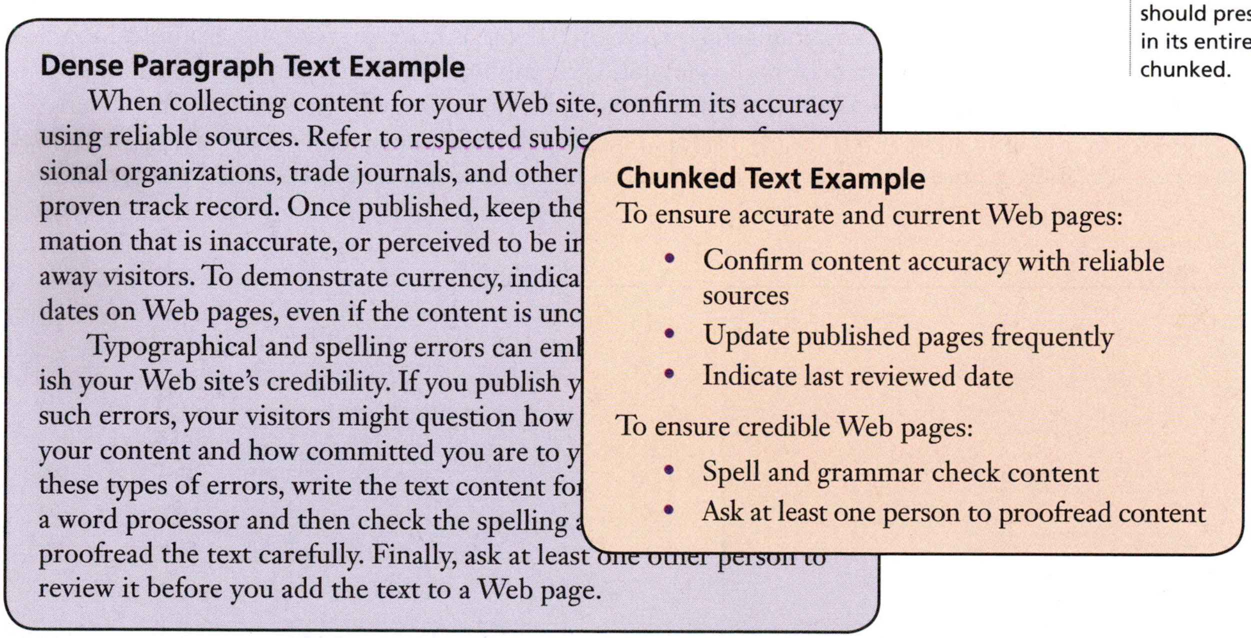

Most Web site visitors, especially those using mobile devices, prefer to quickly scan Web pages for useful information, not read long passages of on-screen text. Therefore, break Web page text into small sections with headings, subheadings, and bulleted lists that adequately but concisely cover the topic. This style of writing is called **chunked text**. For example, consider the same information presented in Figure 2-11 as dense paragraph text and then as chunked text. The chunked text is much easier to scan.

Dense Paragraph Text Example

When collecting content for your Web site, confirm its accuracy using reliable sources. Refer to respected subject experts, professional organizations, trade journals, and other resources with a proven track record. Once published, keep the information that is inaccurate, or perceived to be inaccurate, away visitors. To demonstrate currency, indicate dates on Web pages, even if the content is unchanged.

Typographical and spelling errors can embarrass your Web site's credibility. If you publish your Web pages with such errors, your visitors might question how closely you checked your content and how committed you are to your purpose. To avoid these types of errors, write the text content for your Web pages in a word processor and then check the spelling and grammar, and proofread the text carefully. Finally, ask at least one other person to review it before you add the text to a Web page.

Chunked Text Example

To ensure accurate and current Web pages:

- Confirm content accuracy with reliable sources
- Update published pages frequently
- Indicate last reviewed date

To ensure credible Web pages:

- Spell and grammar check content
- Ask at least one person to proofread content

Figure 2-11 Chunked text is much easier for readers to scan online than dense paragraph text.

> **DESIGN TIP**
> Site visitors typically scan online text looking for useful information instead of reading the text word for word. Chunking text allows your site visitors to quickly scan your Web pages and improves usability, as well as makes your page content more easily readable on a mobile device.

@SOURCE

Writing for the Web
For more information about writing easily readable Web content, visit the Web Design 4 Chapter 2 Student Online Companion Web page at **www .cengagebrain.com** and then click Writing for the Web in the @Source links for Chapter 2.

Remember that visitors to your site will likely scan your Web pages rather than taking the time to read every word. Also, be aware that many Web site users assume that blue text or underlined text represents a hyperlink. To ensure scannability, you should write your Web page content with the following guidelines in mind:

- Use chunked text, where applicable, to create short, succinct paragraphs and bulleted lists that increase the text's scannability.

- When necessary to write longer paragraphs, begin each paragraph with a topic sentence that summarizes the general idea of the whole paragraph. A visitor who scans only the first sentences of each paragraph will still get the overall picture of your Web page's purpose.

- Make certain colored text does not suggest a link. For example, because blue is traditionally the default color for an active link, you should avoid using the blue color for emphasis. Traditionally, purple indicates a visited link and also should be avoided.

- Avoid underlining text for emphasis because links are traditionally underlined.

- Use uppercase characters carefully because they can reduce scannability. Some visitors might also consider text in uppercase characters to be the equivalent of shouting.

Scannability is also affected by the choice of navigational elements, color scheme choices, and fonts. You learn more about these topics in Chapters 4 and 5.

Organization

The **inverted pyramid style** is a classic news writing style that places a summary (or conclusion) first, followed by details, and then any background information. On the Web, the spirit of the inverted pyramid style is followed by placing summary chunked text on the home page and adding links to subsidiary pages containing related details and background information.

Sometimes using chunked text for scannability is inappropriate; for example, for a press release written for both print and Web publication. In this example, it is necessary to retain the press release's dense text paragraphs; therefore, writing the text in the inverted pyramid style is particularly useful in helping visitors quickly understand the text's general idea. Figure 2-12 illustrates a press release written in the inverted pyramid style and posted to the GE Web site.

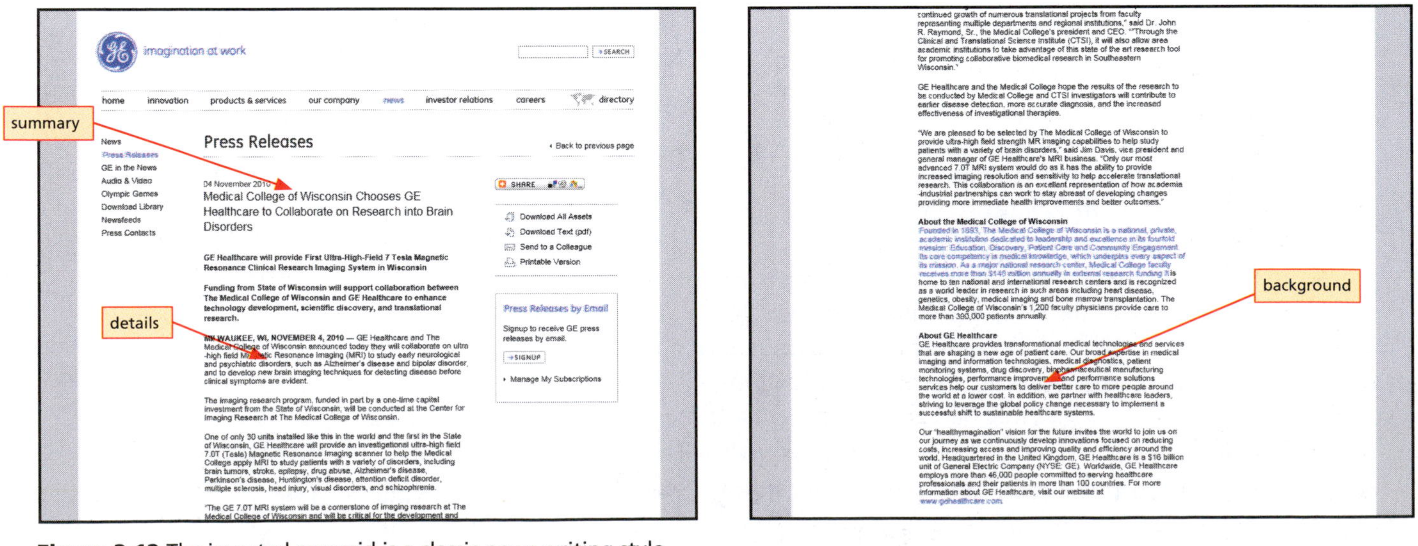

Figure 2-12 The inverted pyramid is a classic news writing style.

When writing in the inverted pyramid style, summary text should include the "who, what, when, why, where, and how" of the topic. Avoid transitional words or phrases, such as "similarly," "as a result," or "as stated previously."

DESIGN TIP

Color as a Web Design Tool

Color can be a powerful design tool for creating attractive, effective Web sites. The use of color helps to set a site's mood, as well as provide contrast between page elements. To use color as a design tool effectively, you must understand color basics: the color wheel, how monitors display colors, and visitors' expectations for color on the Web.

The Color Wheel

A basic tool for understanding color as a design tool is the **color wheel**, as shown in Figure 2-13, which can help you choose effective and appealing color combinations. The basis of the color wheel is the set of **primary colors** — red, yellow, and blue. The **secondary colors** — orange, green, and purple — result from combining two primary colors. The green, blue, and purple colors are categorized as **cool colors**, which suggest tranquility and detachment. The yellow, orange, and red colors are categorized as **warm colors**, which are associated with activity and power. **Complementary colors** are those directly opposite each other on the wheel. A combination of complementary colors creates a significant amount of contrast. Conversely, a combination of colors adjacent to each other generates significantly less contrast.

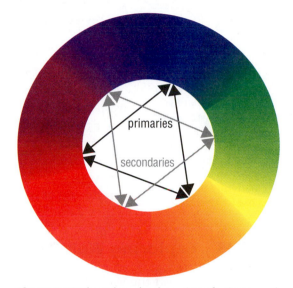

Figure 2-13 The color wheel consists of primary and secondary colors.

The RGB Color System

Computer monitors project color using the **RGB color system**, which combines channels of red, green, and blue light. The light from each channel can be emitted in various levels of intensity. These levels are called **values** and are measured from 0 to 255. When values from the channels are combined, different colors result. For example, combining values 255 (red), 102 (green), and 153 (blue) produces a dusty rose color.

Because each light channel can emit 256 levels of intensity, an RGB system can produce more than 16.7 million possible colors (256 red × 256 green × 256 blue = 16,777,216). A monitor's **color depth** is the actual number of colors that a monitor displays, and is stated in bits. For example, an 8-bit monitor can display 256 colors, a 16-bit monitor can display 65,536 colors, and a 24- or 32-bit monitor can display 16.7 million colors.

If you are using a text editor to create a Web page by manually entering markup tags, you specify a color for a Web page element by entering the color's hexadecimal code, which is the equivalent of the color's RGB values. The **hexadecimal system** uses 16 symbols, the letters A–F and digits 0–9, to signify values. For example, the hexadecimal code for the dusty rose color with the RGB values of 255:102:153 is FF6699. If you are using a WYSIWYG editor, you need not understand the hexadecimal system in detail; simply select a color and the editor will determine and enter the appropriate hexadecimal code for you.

Q&A

What is the browser- or Web-safe palette?
The Web-safe palette is a set of 216 of the available 256 colors displayed by an 8-bit monitor. Fewer and fewer Web visitors today have 8-bit monitors; therefore, many Web designers no longer restrict their color choices to the Web-safe palette.

Target Audience Expectations

Over time, certain colors have come to symbolize particular qualities. Also, color symbolization differs across various cultures. For example, in some cultures white represents good or purity, black represents negativity, red represents passion, and purple represents royalty. Keep in mind the qualities generally associated with different colors when selecting colors for your Web site. If your site's target audience is global, research color associations in various countries to ensure that you are not creating a connotation that you do not intend. For example, although white represents purity in the United States, it can mean death or mourning in some Asian countries and might be offensive to those visitors.

DESIGN TIP   Before making color choices for your Web site, it is a good idea to visit several commercial and noncommercial Web sites, including sites similar to yours, and review each site's color scheme.

@SOURCE

Color Matters
For more information about using color as a design tool, visit the Web Design 4 Chapter 2 Student Online Companion Web page at **www .cengagebrain.com** and then click Color Matters in the @Source links for Chapter 2.

When selecting colors for your Web site, do not feel there are absolute correct and absolute incorrect choices. Certain combinations produce different results and responses. Consider the intended purpose of your site, the experience you desire for your targeted audience, and their expectations. Then choose an attractive color scheme and apply colors from this scheme to Web page elements, such as the background, text headings and subheadings, and links. When designing Web pages for a commercial entity or other large organization, be sure to follow the entity's branding specifications for the use of color.

YOUR TURN

Exploring Web Page Color Schemes

1. Visit the Web Design 4 Chapter 2 Student Online Companion Web page at **www .cengagebrain.com** and click Ghirardelli, CNN.com, and Dell in the Your Turn links. Review the home page and at least two subsidiary pages at each site.
2. Analyze the color scheme at each site by answering the following questions.
   a. Is the color scheme attractive, visually appealing, and consistent across pages?
   b. Is the color scheme effective in supporting the site's overall message and main purpose? If yes, how? If no, why?
   c. How do you personally respond to the site's color scheme?
3. Write a report explaining how each of these sites uses color as a design tool. Discuss your personal response to each site's color scheme and how your response might guide you when planning a color scheme for a B2C Web site.

Web Publishing Issues

Successful Web publishing further includes recognizing certain technical, legal and ethical, accessibility, and usability issues, as well as the design techniques that can effectively manage them.

Technical Issues

Before creating your Web site, you should understand a few technical issues related to good design. These issues include bandwidth, differences among browsers, and monitor resolution.

BANDWIDTH **Bandwidth**, which is the quantity of data that can be transmitted in a specific time frame, is measured in bits per second (bps). You learned about transmitting data over a network and the data's transfer rate in Chapter 1. A larger bandwidth indicates a higher data transfer rate. In Chapter 1, you also learned that visitors can access the Internet using a variety of low transfer rate or high transfer rate methods, ranging from regular dial-up access to wireless broadband access. The bandwidth or transfer rate of the Internet connection, the amount of traffic on the Internet at a specific time, and a Web page's file size all affect how quickly the Web page downloads in a visitor's browser.

As a Web designer, you have no control over how your target audience members access the Internet and Web or the amount of traffic across the Internet. You have control only over the file size of the Web page, which includes all its elements such as text, images, and multimedia. A visitor to your site generally will wait no longer than 5 to 10 seconds for a Web page to download before moving on to another Web site; therefore, you must take bandwidth into consideration when you choose elements to include on your Web pages. With the increased usage of high-speed Internet access methods, it is less necessary to create a Web page that caters to dial-up users, but the file size of your pages should always be a concern when designing effective Web sites.

To resolve the download speed problem created by adding images to your Web pages, you could use fewer images or you could use **thumbnail** images, which are miniature versions that link to larger images. In addition to careful image choices, you can take steps to optimize images for quick download time by reducing image file sizes using image-editing programs such as Corel PaintShop Photo Pro X3© or Adobe Photoshop® CS5. Optimizing graphics is discussed in more detail in Chapter 5.

Create faster-loading Web pages by limiting the number and file size of images or using thumbnail images.

DESIGN TIP

BROWSER DIFFERENCES In Chapter 1, you learned that Microsoft Internet Explorer and Mozilla Firefox are today's most widely used browsers. These popular browsers are **graphical display browsers**, which, along with text, can display graphic elements such as photographs, clip art, animations, and video. Most visitors will view your Web site with a graphical display browser. Browsers can vary as to the support levels they offer for HTML or XHTML tags, CSS, and scripting languages. Because of these varying support levels, Web pages might appear differently when viewed with different browsers or with different versions of the same browser. Therefore, you should test your Web pages with different browsers and browser versions before publishing your site.

A visitor using a low-speed Internet access option might choose to turn images off in his or her graphical display browser to improve a Web page's download speed. **Alternative text** is language that briefly describes each image that loads in a Web page; such information appears in place of turned-off images and helps visitors better understand a page's content. Therefore, when adding images to a Web page, you should specify an alternative text description for each image. If you are using a text or HTML editor, you can add the HTML <img> </img> tag attribute alt=text to add alternative text to the image. If you are using a WYSIWYG editor, you can use an option provided by the editor to specify an alternative text description for each image. Figure 2-14 (on the next page) illustrates an example of a Web page with images turned on and with images turned off displaying the alternative text descriptions for the missing images.

Q&A

What is Lynx?
Lynx is a nongraphical display browser, which means that it displays only text. Lynx was one of the original browsers. Web developers still test their sites in Lynx to make sure that users who search the Internet with images turned off because of visual disabilities or to increase search speeds can access their site content.

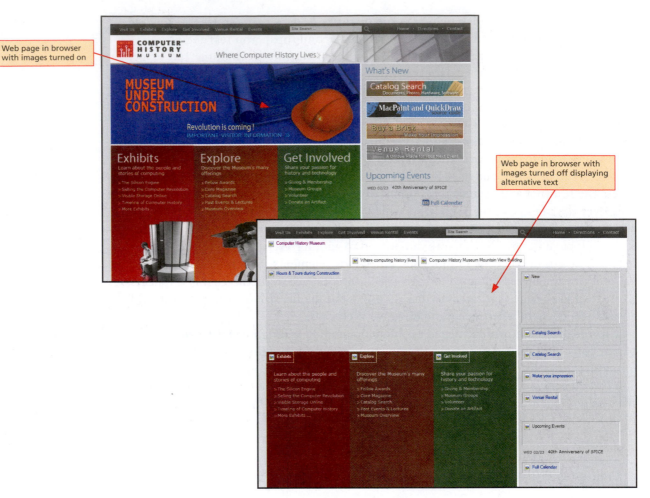

Figure 2-14 Alternative text descriptions replace turned-off images.

DESIGN TIP   Web pages might appear quite differently when viewed with different browsers and browser versions. For this reason, test your Web pages with different browsers and browser versions before publishing your site.

MONITOR RESOLUTION   A Web page also will appear differently depending on the resolution setting of the user's monitor. **Resolution** is the measure of a monitor's sharpness and clarity, related directly to the number of pixels it can display. A **pixel**, short for picture element, is a single point in an electronic image. The pixels on a monitor are so close together that they appear connected. Resolution is expressed as two numbers — the number of columns of pixels and the number of rows of pixels that a monitor can display — and represents the total number of pixels displayed on a monitor's screen.

At higher resolutions, the number of pixels increases while their size decreases. Page elements appear large at low resolutions and decrease in size as resolution settings increase. Typical modern monitor resolutions range from 800 × 600 pixels to 1280 × 1024 pixels. For some time, the recommended practice has been to design Web pages for the most commonly used resolution, which, today, is the 1024 × 768 or higher resolution. If you design Web pages to be viewed at the 1024 × 768 resolution, a visitor viewing the Web page at a higher resolution will see a blank area on one or both sides of the page. However, a visitor viewing the page at the lower 800 × 600 resolution is forced to scroll the page horizontally to see all its content. Scrolling a Web page horizontally hampers readability and is likely to frustrate visitors.

To deal with monitor resolution issues, designers use a variety of techniques. Some designers choose to design for the most commonly used resolution. Others design for a higher resolution and indicate on their Web pages the best screen resolution with which to view the Web site. Some design for a lower resolution and then add an attractive background that appears on either side of the page when viewed at a higher resolution. Many designers choose to create Web pages using liquid design. **Liquid design** or **liquid layout** techniques use HTML layout tables or CSS to create Web pages that resize as the browser window resizes for any monitor resolution. You learn more about liquid layout in Chapter 4.

MOBILE DEVICES   Creating a mobile phone version of your Web site is another way to ensure you reach visitors of your site, whether it is to check for updated information, purchase products or services, or interact with your site. Online service sites such as Mippin or Zinadoo will automatically customize your site for mobile devices. To make a mobile site, register a version of your site with the .mobi top-level domain; the mobile version of the BusinessWeek site, at www.businessweek.mobi (Figure 2-15), is an example. You also can create a separate subdomain just for mobile users. Ensure that users can easily find your mobile site by registering it with a mobile search engine.

The most important consideration when modifying a site for access by mobile devices is to simplify the navigation and content to accommodate a smaller screen size and the use of a stylus or touch screen. You can address the bandwidth differences by reducing the number of images, replacing paragraphs with lists, and removing unnecessary or duplicate HTML code. Ensure that interactive site experiences, such as shopping or commenting, are easy to do on a mobile device.

Figure 2-15 Sites optimized for mobile devices have fewer graphics and use lists instead of paragraphs.

Exploring Mobile Sites

1. Visit the Web Design 4 Chapter 2 Student Online Companion Web page at **www .cengagebrain.com** and then click Barnes & Noble or Amazon.com in the Your Turn links.

2. View the Web pages in your browser.

3. If you have a mobile device, view the sites using your mobile device. If you do not have a mobile device, click the Google Mobile Optimizer in the Your Turn links, and enter www.amazon.com and www.bn.com in separate browser tabs to view the site as it might appear in a mobile device.

4. Document the differences in how each page appears when viewed in a browser compared with mobile view.

5. Write a report that discusses differences in navigation, content, and number of images and animations.

Legal and Privacy Issues

Q&A

What are phishing and spoofing?
Phishing and spoofing are methods of misleading people into revealing personal or financial information. In a phishing scheme, a perpetrator imitates a legitimate company, such as an ISP or online bank, and sends an e-mail message requesting that the user verify account information. The message directs users to a fraudulent site, which may look legitimate but is actually a fake. The fraudulent site then collects the user's information using forms and other collection methods that appear to be legit. Spoofing is the creation of a fraudulent version of a site and masking its URL.

In addition to technical matters, you need to consider legal and privacy issues related to publishing a Web site. Legal issues include copyright infringement and content liability. Criminal activity based on identity theft is a major problem for both businesses and consumers. If you gather visitor information — names, addresses, credit card numbers — at your Web site, you must take steps to protect the privacy of that information and secure it from unauthorized access or theft.

LEGAL ISSUES   At some time, you might see a great image on a Web page that would be perfect for your Web site. To get it, all you need to do is download a copy of the image to a storage device on your computer. Although it is relatively easy to copy an image, doing so is potentially illegal and unethical. By downloading and using the image without permission, you could violate the creator's **copyright**, or ownership right to the image.

In the United States, published and unpublished intellectual property, such as Web page text or images, is protected by copyright, regardless of whether the property is registered with the U.S. Copyright Office. In general, the law states that only the owner may print, distribute, or copy the property. To reuse the property, the user must obtain permission from the owner. The owner may also request compensation for the usage.

A **copyright notice** is text that includes the word, copyright, or the © symbol, the publication year, and the copyright owner's name. You might be familiar with the copyright notice that appears on a page following the cover of a book. Most Web sites today, especially commercial Web sites, add a copyright notice at or near the bottom of the home and subsidiary pages. Figure 2-16 illustrates a copyright notice at the bottom of the Chase home page.

@SOURCE

Copyright Basics
For more information about copyright basics, visit the Web Design 4 Chapter 2 Student Online Companion Web page at **www .cengagebrain.com** and then click Copyright Basics in the @Source links for Chapter 2.

copyright notice

Figure 2-16 Web pages at commercial sites generally include a copyright notice.

Using connectivity tools to allow site visitors to share your content helps to protect you from copyright concerns. These tools direct the visitor back to your site, which allows you to share your content or connect to other sites' content while clearly crediting the source.

DESIGN TIP

Publishing a Web site might expose you to potential liabilities, such as copyright infringement, defamation, or libel, especially when your site's content is gathered from many different sources or includes links to Web pages at other sites. For protection against these potential liabilities, you can post at your site a disclaimer of liability notice prepared by an attorney, which outlines the Web site owner's or operator's limits of responsibility. Figure 2-17 illustrates the disclaimer of liability notice at the Attorney General of Nevada's Web site.

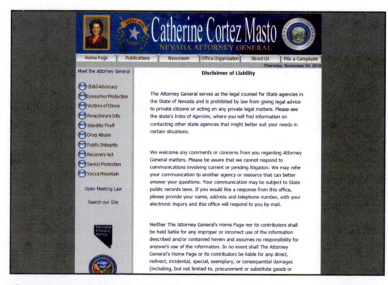

Figure 2-17 A disclaimer of liability notice can help protect Web site owners against potential liabilities.

PRIVACY ISSUES　Sensitive **personally identifiable information (PII)** — Social Security numbers, credit card numbers, names, addresses, and telephone numbers — is commonly gathered at Web sites, especially through e-commerce transactions. To provide security for transmission of personal or confidential information, such as credit card transactions, e-commerce Web sites use encryption, which prevents data from being read by an unauthorized recipient. **Encryption** is a process that encodes data into illegible content. To restore the usability of encrypted data, users apply **decryption techniques**, which remove the encryption and return data to its original format. The **Secure Sockets Layer (SSL)** protocol safeguards and encrypts confidential information as it travels over the Internet. Web pages with the https:// protocol designation instead of http:// in their URL use SSL to transmit customers' data.

Protecting sensitive information a user provides voluntarily is only part of the privacy issue. Every request for a page from a Web browser to a Web server is recorded in the server's transaction log. Many Web sites automatically collect certain information from visitors, such as domain names, browser types, and operating systems from these server transaction logs. Although the content of this information is not sensitive, sites are collecting it without a visitor's approval or control and, thus, the privacy of users is violated without their knowledge. **Cookies** are small text files stored on a visitor's hard drive. Some Web sites post cookies to a visitor's hard drive. Cookies make it more convenient for visitors to return to their favorite Web sites by storing their login data or Web page customization preferences. However, cookies can also reveal a user's information when they track pages visited and other visitor statistics. Most of the time, a visitor is not aware that a site has installed a cookie on his or her computer. Tracking visitor statistics using server logs and cookies is discussed in more detail in Chapter 7.

Web site visitors are legitimately concerned about how all their information, whether willfully submitted or automatically gathered, is being used. Additionally, visitors are concerned about the steps being taken by Web site publishers to ensure that their information remains secure and out of the hands of unauthorized parties.

To ease visitors' concerns, many sites, especially e-commerce sites, include a **privacy policy statement** that explains how any information submitted by a visitor or gathered automatically through server logs and cookies is used. For example, such a statement might explain that the information is used only to gather demographic data about site visitors and will not be released to any third party. Figure 2-18 illustrates a portion of the privacy policy statement on the Privacy and Security Policies page at the Barnes & Noble Web site.

Figure 2-18 A privacy policy statement explains how visitor information is used.

Establish privacy and data security policies for your Web site operations. Make certain everyone associated with designing, maintaining, and operating the site is aware of the policies. Then explain your policies to site visitors by publishing a privacy and security policy statement.

In addition to posted privacy and security statements, many commercial and organizational Web sites also participate in the privacy and security standards certification programs offered by entities such as TRUSTe and BBBOnline. Members in good standing of these certification programs may indicate compliance with the program's privacy and security standards by displaying program seals, or graphic symbols, on their Web pages.

Exploring Web Site Privacy and Data Security Issues

YOUR TURN

1. Visit the Web Design 4 Chapter 2 Student Online Companion Web page at **www.cengagebrain.com** and click BBBOnline, TRUSTe, Online Privacy Alliance, and National Consumers League in the Your Turn links.

2. Review the privacy and data security issues and tools discussed at each site.

3. Write a report explaining how you would use this information to ensure the privacy of visitors' information and the security of visitors' data at your Web site.

Accessibility and Usability Issues

Web site designers incorporate alternative features, called **Web accessibility**, to ensure their sites are usable by people with various types of special needs, such as lost or impaired vision or color blindness. Web accessibility is an important issue for the World Wide Web Consortium (W3C), which sets Web standards. To advance Web accessibility for people with special needs, the W3C sponsors the Web Accessibility Initiative (WAI), a consortium of government agencies, IT industry representatives, and nonprofit organizations representing people with special needs. The WAI encourages accessibility through technology, guidelines, and research. Currently, the WAI Guidelines are specifications, not regulations, which many organizations choose to adopt for their Web sites.

To further support Web accessibility, the U.S. Congress instituted Section 508 of the U.S. Rehabilitation Act. Section 508 requires that all U.S. government agencies use accessibility technologies and follow accessibility guidelines to ensure that people with special needs can acquire the public information posted to the agencies' Web sites. Many e-commerce and educational sites and most U.S. government sites now provide a statement of commitment to Web accessibility, including information describing how accessibility issues are handled at the site. Figure 2-19 (on the next page) illustrates the Web accessibility statement at the Natural Resources Conservation Service (NRCS) Web site.

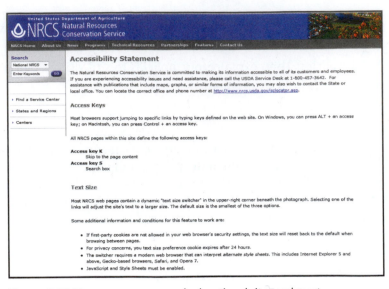

Figure 2-19 Many e-commerce and educational sites and most U.S. government sites affirm their Web accessibility compliance.

DESIGN TIP

Design your Web site to be accessible by people with various types of special needs, such as lost or impaired vision or color blindness, by following the WAI and Section 508 guidelines for Web accessibility. If using a WYSIWYG editor, use the tools provided by the program to check for potential accessibility issues.

@SOURCE

WAI and Section 508
For more information about Web accessibility standards, visit the Web Design 4 Chapter 2 Student Online Companion Web page at **www.cengagebrain .com** and then click WAI and Section 508 in the @Source links for Chapter 2.

Although the terms *Web accessibility* and *Web usability* are sometimes used interchangeably, they are related, but different, concepts. As you have learned, Web accessibility deals with ensuring access to Web-based information for people with special needs. **Web usability** involves designing a Web site and its pages so that all visitors to the site can easily and quickly satisfy their goals, such as finding information or purchasing a product or service. Web usability incorporates all elements of good Web design, including site structure, the use of text, color, and images, navigational elements, and other design guidelines discussed throughout this text.

Chapter Review

@SOURCE

Alertbox
For expert information on usability and Web design, visit the Web Design 4 Chapter 2 Student Online Companion Web page at **www.cengagebrain .com** and then click Alertbox in the @Source links for Chapter 2.

Print publishing deservedly has been a time-honored, trusted communication method. Even so, print cannot match the benefits of the Web for delivering current, interactive content and for efficient, cost-effective production and distribution of information. Web and print publications are similar in their intent to deliver a powerful message and leave a distinct impression. Achieving these objectives using Web publications requires combining creativity with the fundamental design principles of balance and proximity, contrast and focus, and visual identity and unity. Web site visitors quickly want to find accurate, easy-to-read, well-organized, and concise information that they can use. Writing content with these attributes requires applying specific techniques. Color can powerfully enhance a Web site's message and personality. Persuasive, effective color use involves being aware of established color principles and conventions. Successful Web publishing further includes recognizing certain technical, legal, privacy, accessibility, and usability issues, and applying the design techniques that can manage them effectively.

After reading the chapter, you should know each of these Key Terms.

alignment (49)
alternative text (55)
asymmetric (46)
balance (46)
bandwidth (55)
brand (48)
branding specifications (48)
chunked text (51)
color depth (53)
color wheel (53)
complementary colors (53)
connectivity advantage (41)
contrast (47)
cookies (60)
cool colors (53)
copyright (58)
copyright notice (58)
cost advantage (45)
currency advantage (40)
decryption techniques (60)
delivery advantage (45)
encryption (60)
focal point (47)
graphical display browsers (55)
hexadecimal system (53)

interactivity advantage (42)
inverted pyramid style (52)
liquid design (57)
liquid layout (57)
personally identifiable
    information (PII) (60)
pixel (56)
primary colors (53)
privacy policy statement (60)
proximity (46)
resolution (56)
RGB color system (53)
secondary colors (53)
Secure Sockets Layer (SSL) (60)
symmetric (46)
tag line (48)
thumbnail (55)
unity (48)
values (53)
visual identity (48)
warm colors (51)
Web accessibility (61)
Web-based form (43)
Web usability (62)
white space (47)

Complete the Test Your Knowledge exercises to solidify what you have learned in the chapter.

Matching Terms

Match each term with the best description.

____ 1. connectivity

____ 2. thumbnail

____ 3. asymmetric

____ 4. hexadecimal system

____ 5. cookies

____ 6. Web usability

____ 7. scannability

____ 8. contrast

____ 9. alignment

____ 10. unity

____ 11. encryption

____ 12. Web accessibility

a. Chunked text.

b. Small text files stored on a site visitor's computer.

c. Web design guidelines that ensure Web site visitors achieve their goals at the site.

d. A process that changes data, encoding it so that it cannot be understood if an unauthorized person attempts to read it.

e. Instant sharing and distribution of Web site content.

f. Uses codes for colors using RGB values.

g. A small version of an image.

h. A mix of elements to stimulate attention.

i. Off balance.

j. A sense of oneness or belonging.

k. Web design guidelines applied to sites and pages to ensure access by people with special needs.

l. Arrangement of objects in fixed or predetermined positions.

Short Answer Questions

Write a brief answer to each question.

1. Explain the Web publishing advantages that print publishing cannot match.

2. Identify the basic design principles that help Web pages deliver a powerful message and leave a distinct impression.

3. Compare the use of symmetric and asymmetric placement of Web page elements to evoke mood.

4. Discuss the role of branding in promoting unity and maintaining visual identity.

5. Define chunked text and discuss reasons for using chunked text to create scannable Web content.

6. Explain the role of color as a Web design tool.

7. Describe the color wheel and identify primary colors and secondary colors.

8. Describe the considerations unique to creating a mobile Web site.

9. Briefly discuss each of the following Web publishing issues:

    a. Bandwidth

    b. Differences among browsers

    c. Monitor resolution

    d. Legal and privacy concerns

    e. Web usability and Web accessibility

LEARN IT ONLINE

Test your knowledge of chapter content and key terms.

Instructions: To complete the Learn It Online exercises, start your browser, click the Address bar, and then visit the Web Design 4 Chapter 2 Student Online Companion page at **www.cengagebrain.com**. When the Web Design Learn It Online page is displayed, click the link for the exercise you want to complete and then read the instructions.

Chapter Reinforcement TF, MC, and SA

A series of true/false, multiple-choice, and short-answer questions that test your knowledge of the chapter content.

Flash Cards

An interactive learning environment where you identify chapter key terms associated with displayed definitions.

Practice Test

A series of multiple-choice questions that test your knowledge of chapter content and key terms.

Who Wants To Be a Computer Genius?

An interactive game that challenges your knowledge of chapter content in the style of a television quiz show.

Wheel of Terms

An interactive game that challenges your knowledge of chapter key terms in the style of the television show *Wheel of Fortune*.

Crossword Puzzle Challenge

A crossword puzzle that challenges your knowledge of key terms presented in the chapter.

Investigate current Web design developments with the Trends exercises.

Write a brief essay about each of the following trends, using the Web as your research tool. For each trend, identify at least one Web page URL used as a research source. Be prepared to discuss your findings in class.

1 | Section 508

Research the latest developments in accessibility standards. Make a list of three important accessibility considerations, and note whether they are new or existing issues. Visit two sites to see if these sites meet the considerations.

2 | RSS Feeds

Research RSS feed readers and how you can use them to enhance sharing of your Web site content. Sign up for a free RSS feed reader, such as AmphetaDesk or Google Reader. Customize it to receive updates on Web design trends.

Challenge your perspective of Web design and surrounding technology with the @Issue exercises.

Write a brief essay in response to the following issues, using the Web as your research tool. For each issue, identify at least one Web page URL used as a research source. Be prepared to discuss your findings in class.

1 | Privacy Statements

Find a privacy statement on a Web site you frequently visit. Look at it critically to see if it addresses all of your concerns, specifically: what information it collects, what it does with the information, and how you would be notified of any changes to the privacy policy. Make a note of any changes you would make.

2 | Target Audience Color Expectations

Explain how target audience expectations and preferences affect the use of color as a Web design tool. Give real-world Web site examples to support your explanation.

Use the World Wide Web to obtain more information about the concepts in the chapter with the Hands On exercises.

1 | Explore and Evaluate: Writing for the Web

Browse the Web to find an example of a Web page whose text content, in your opinion, is too long and wordy. Suggest ways to break up the text using chunked text, bullets, or links.

2 | Search and Discover: Privacy and Accessibility Issues

Search the Web using the Bing search engine to identify at least two Web sites that address privacy or accessibility issues directly at their sites.

1. Explain how one site addresses privacy and the other site addresses accessibility.

2. How would you address the issues of privacy and accessibility at your Web site?

3. Would your approach be the same as or different from that of the reviewed sites? If yes, why? If no, why not?

Work collaboratively to reinforce the concepts in the chapter with the Team Approach exercises.

1 | Rate Bookstore Web Sites

Form a team with three of your classmates. Have each team member visit the home page of four popular bookstore Web sites — Amazon, Barnes & Noble, Borders, and Books-a-Million — and then rate each site's home page plus three subsidiary pages on how well the site incorporates the basic design principles presented in this chapter:

- Balance and proximity
- Contrast and focus
- Unity and visual identity

   a. Use a rating scale of 1 through 5, where 5 is the highest rating. Meet as a team and summarize your ratings; using your summary, rank the sites from highest to lowest.

   b. Write a report explaining how you would use the design principles embodied at the highest-ranking site to plan the design for your Web site. Be prepared to discuss your report with the class.

2 | Compare Interactivity at E-Commerce Sites

Form a team of three or four classmates to evaluate how the following e-commerce Web sites use Web design to promote interactivity with their customers, potential customers, partners, and other interested parties. Which of the e-commerce sites is the most successful at promoting interactivity? Which is the least successful? Why? Suggest ways that the least successful site might better promote interactivity.

   a. ESPN

   b. Cisco Systems

   c. eBay

   d. Hometown Favorites

Write a report of your team's findings and be prepared to discuss your report in class.

Apply the chapter concepts to the ongoing development process in Web design with the Case Study.

The Case Study is an ongoing development process using the concepts, techniques, and Design Tips presented in each chapter.

Background Information

As you progress through the chapters, you will learn how to use design as a tool to create effective Web pages and sites. At each chapter's conclusion, you will receive instructions for completing each segment of the ongoing design process.

In this chapter's assignment, you are to identify methods and tools to manage currency, encourage connectivity, promote interactivity and communication at your site, create a tag line, describe how you plan to use color at your site, find resources for your site's topic, practice writing and editing scannable text, and create a plan for handling accessibility and usability issues.

Chapter 2 Assignment

1. Develop a report using word-processing software. In that report, address the following:

   a. Identify the element(s) that you could include on your Web site that would convey to its audience that the site's content is current.

   b. Identify the connectivity tools you will use to encourage users to publish or promote your content, and explain how you will use them.

   c. Identify ways you can promote interactivity at your site.

   d. Create an appropriate tag line for your site and describe how you will use it in the site's design.

   e. Describe how you plan to use color at your site.

   f. Write three paragraphs about your site's topic in inverted pyramid style. Then rewrite the paragraphs as chunked text.

   g. Describe how you plan to use basic design principles to enhance your site's usability.

   h. List ways you plan to make your site accessible.

2. Submit your report to your instructor. Also, be prepared to share your report with the class.

3 Planning a Successful Web Site: Part 1

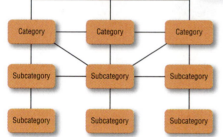

Introduction

Chapters 1 and 2 introduced you to the Internet and the World Wide Web, different types of Web sites, and the basic Web design tools and roles. You also learned about important techniques for writing text for Web pages and using color as a design tool along with privacy and security considerations.

In this chapter, you discover the important facets of the Web site development process: defining the site's goals, objectives, and purpose; identifying the site's target audience or audiences; determining the site's general content; and specifying the site's structure. Then, using what you have learned about the Web site planning process, you begin to develop a plan for your own Web site. You complete your Web site's site plan in Chapter 4.

Objectives

After completing this chapter, you will be able to:

1. Describe the Web site development planning process

2. Complete Step 1: Define the site's purpose

3. Complete Step 2: Identify the site's target audience

4. Complete Step 3: Determine the site's general content

5. Complete Step 4: Select the site's structure

The Web Site Development Planning Process

An important part of any successful endeavor is careful planning. Because you must invest significant time and other resources when creating a Web site, you should plan ahead carefully to maximize your time and resources. Before you begin to create your first Web page, you must develop a solid, detailed plan for the Web site, called a **site plan** or **design plan**, that determines the purpose, audience, content, structure, visual design, and navigation system. Following the six major steps illustrated in Figure 3-1 is a good way to approach the development of a detailed site plan.

STEP 1: Define the site's purpose

STEP 2: Identify the site's target audience

STEP 3: Determine the site's general content

STEP 4: Select the site's structure

STEP 5: Design the look and feel of the site

STEP 6: Specify the site's navigation system

Figure 3-1 Creating a successful Web site begins with developing a detailed site plan.

DESIGN TIP When creating a design plan, make sure to get the plan reviewed by colleagues, managers, or others with a stake in the outcome of your Web site. Although you might think that visual design would be the most important aspect of a Web site, you need to first determine the purpose, audience, content, and structure to come up with a visual design that meets the needs of your site.

@SOURCE

Planning
For more information about developing a design plan for a Web site, visit the Web Design 4 Chapter 3 Student Online Companion Web page at **www .cengagebrain.com** and then click Planning in the @Source links.

Because planning is critical to the development of a successful Web site, this book has two chapters devoted to a thorough discussion of the six steps illustrated in Figure 3-1. This chapter discusses Steps 1 through 4. Chapter 4 discusses Steps 5 and 6. In this and subsequent chapters, a specific Web design scenario is used to explain the concepts related to developing a detailed design plan. In this scenario, you are the head of the Web Design Department at Regifting, a new B2C e-commerce company that focuses on selling reusable and recycled products and services. You need to work with your team of Web designers to develop a site plan for the new company.

Step 1: Define the Site's Purpose

The first step when developing a solid Web site design plan is to define the site's goals and objectives and then formulate a written purpose statement for the site. **Goals** are the results you want your Web site to accomplish within a specific time frame, which can be weeks, months, or years. **Objectives** are those methods you will choose to accomplish the site's goals. A formal, written **purpose statement** summarizes your site's goals and objectives.

Web Site Goals

Although a site has a primary goal, it might also have a combination of a primary and multiple secondary goals. For example, in this chapter's scenario, your Web site's primary goal is to sell products or services. You could have a combination of secondary goals that support your site's primary goal, such as providing customer service, educating customers about new products or services, promoting communication between employees and customers, keeping customers informed about business changes in your industry, and so forth.

In the scenario, your team has identified a primary goal and multiple secondary goals for the new Web site:

- Primary goal — Increase sales of reusable and recycled goods.
- Secondary goals:
  - Promote awareness of the company and its products and mission to customers and potential customers.
  - Establish the company's credibility in the field of environmentally sound businesses.
  - Educate site visitors about tips and developments in the environment and environmentally friendly products.
  - Encourage visitors to return to the site by providing updated information in the form of a video blog and articles by industry experts.

Web Site Objectives

After identifying the Web site's goals, your next step is to determine the site's objectives, which are the methods the site developers use to accomplish the goals. For example, if the primary goal is to sell a product or service, the objectives to accomplish that goal might include posting testimonials from customers who have purchased the product or service or offering a 20 percent price discount for customers who purchase the product or service in the next 30 days.

You and your team work together to define the following objectives to accomplish the new site's primary and secondary goals:

- Develop an attractive, informative, and easy-to-use Web site to promote an online awareness of the company.
- Provide authoritative information and advice at the site to establish credibility.
- Include links to articles and quick tips to educate site visitors about the importance of using reusable and recycled products.
- Offer online tools to encourage site visitors to make changes to reduce their carbon footprint.

DESIGN TIP   You will constantly refer back to your goals and objectives as you complete the site plan. Before publishing the Web site, you should evaluate how well the site's content, structure, and design help to meet the site's goals and objectives.

Web Site Purpose Statement

After determining your Web site's goals and objectives, you should create a formal written summary of reasons the site will be published, called a purpose statement. A well-written purpose statement synthesizes into a few words the reason or reasons you are publishing your site and explains a Web site's overall goals and the specific objectives designed to achieve those goals. Figure 3-2 illustrates the approved purpose statement for the new reusable and recycled goods Web site.

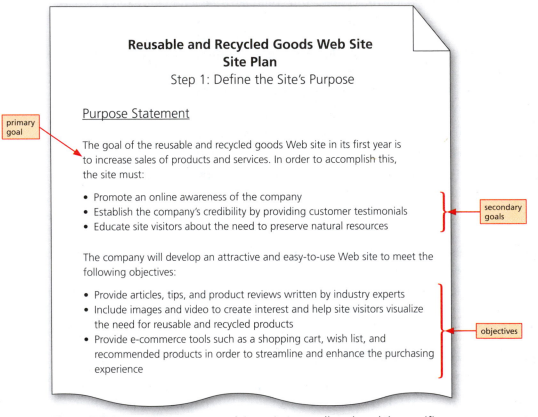

Reusable and Recycled Goods Web Site
Site Plan
Step 1: Define the Site's Purpose

Purpose Statement

primary goal

The goal of the reusable and recycled goods Web site in its first year is to increase sales of products and services. In order to accomplish this, the site must:

- Promote an online awareness of the company
- Establish the company's credibility by providing customer testimonials
- Educate site visitors about the need to preserve natural resources

secondary goals

The company will develop an attractive and easy-to-use Web site to meet the following objectives:

- Provide articles, tips, and product reviews written by industry experts
- Include images and video to create interest and help site visitors visualize the need for reusable and recycled products
- Provide e-commerce tools such as a shopping cart, wish list, and recommended products in order to streamline and enhance the purchasing experience

objectives

Figure 3-2 A purpose statement explains a site's overall goals and the specific objectives that will be used to achieve those goals.

YOUR TURN

Exploring Purpose Statements

1. Visit the Web Design 4 Chapter 3 Student Online Companion Web page at **www.cengagebrain.com** and click Dr. Gourmet, Oakland, and San Jose in the Your Turn links to review three Web site purpose statements.
2. Write down your visitor expectations for the content and design of each Web site based solely on the information contained in its purpose statement. Do not look at other site pages.
3. Next, review the home page and at least two subsidiary pages at each site. Is each site's purpose statement reflected in the site's content and design? If yes, how? If no, what is missing?

Formulating a well-written purpose statement requires a clear understanding of a site's goals and objectives.

DESIGN TIP

Step 2: Identify the Site's Target Audience

Identifying the site's target audience is the second step in a Web site design plan. Although anyone around the world who has Internet and Web access can potentially visit your Web site, you must identify the specific group of visitors to which your site is targeted, called the site's **target audience**, to create a site that provides the most value for that audience.

Target Audience Profile

To begin the process of creating a profile of your site's target audience, imagine the types of people who might visit your site. A **target audience profile** is a research-based overview that includes information about potential site visitors' demographic and psychographic characteristics. **Demographic characteristics** include gender, age group, educational level, income, location, and other characteristics that define who your site visitors are. **Psychographic characteristics** include social group affiliations, lifestyle choices, purchasing preferences, political affiliations, and other characteristics that explain why visitors might want to access your site.

Using research developed from sources such as the U.S. Department of Labor, the U.S. Census Bureau, the Small Business Administration, and reports prepared by and sold by companies who specialize in demographic and psychographic research, you can ask and answer questions similar to the following to develop a formal target audience profile for your site:

- What is the age range for your likely audience members?
- What are audience members' gender, educational background, and marital status?
- What are the typical careers and income levels of audience members?
- Where do audience members live?
- What are audience members' social group affiliations, lifestyle choices, interests, and purchasing preferences?

Your team has developed the target audience profile for the new site for the scenario, as shown in Figure 3-3.

Q&A Can a Web site have more than one target audience?
Yes, many Web sites have multiple target audiences. For example, the Office Depot e-commerce Web site promotes its brick-and-mortar stores for walk-in customers, sells office equipment and supplies online to individual consumers, and offers specialized services directed to business customers.

Q&A What are other considerations when defining a target audience?
You should also consider how the audience will access your site: primarily through a PC, primarily using a mobile or handheld device, or both? This information will help you determine whether you need to design a separate mobile site, or make changes to your site to make it accessible by mobile devices.

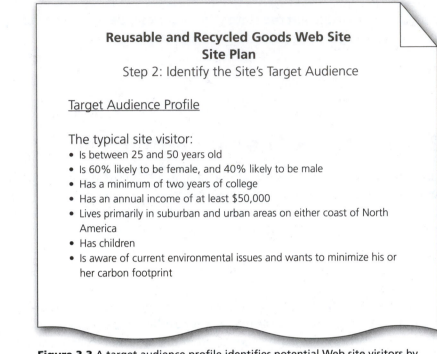

**Reusable and Recycled Goods Web Site
Site Plan**
Step 2: Identify the Site's Target Audience

Target Audience Profile

The typical site visitor:
- Is between 25 and 50 years old
- Is 60% likely to be female, and 40% likely to be male
- Has a minimum of two years of college
- Has an annual income of at least $50,000
- Lives primarily in suburban and urban areas on either coast of North America
- Has children
- Is aware of current environmental issues and wants to minimize his or her carbon footprint

Figure 3-3 A target audience profile identifies potential Web site visitors by defining *who* they are and *why* they are likely to visit your site.

@SOURCE

Audience Profile
For more information about developing a target audience profile, visit the Web Design 4 Chapter 3 Student Online Companion Web page at **www .cengagebrain.com** and then click Audience Profile in the @Source links.

After identifying the members of your target audience, your next step is to determine the audience members' wants, needs, and expectations to be fulfilled by a visit to your Web site.

Target Audience Wants, Needs, and Expectations

Successful Web sites fulfill their audience's wants, needs, and expectations in both general and specific ways. In general, all audiences expect an attractive, interesting, and well-organized site that conveys useful information and is easy to use. An audience's specific expectations for a site will vary based on the site's purpose. For example, a B2C site must offer the products or services that visitors want to purchase to meet its audience's specific expectations. If a site does not meet its target audience's various expectations, visitors will take their business elsewhere.

After you identify your site's target audience, conduct a **needs assessment** by answering questions such as the following to determine your target audience's wants, needs, and expectations:

- What do audience members expect to gain from a visit to your Web site?
- What usability or accessibility issues are important to audience members?
- Are audience members generally experienced or inexperienced Web users?
- Will audience members have any cultural biases, norms, or customs that must be accommodated in the site's design and organization?

Your team has performed a needs assessment and identified the target audience's major wants, needs, and expectations for the new site for the site scenario, as shown in Figure 3-4.

**Reusable and Recycled Goods Web Site
Site Plan**
Step 2: Identify the Site's Target Audience

<u>Target Audience Wants, Needs, and Expectations</u>

The typical site visitor:
- Prefers attractive, professional-looking sites containing credible content
- Is likely to share articles and products with others using social media
- Chooses sites that have easy-to-use site navigation
- Favors sites that meet Web accessibility standards
- Is likely to return frequently to Web sites that include current content, articles, and product tips
- Responds to advice on how to make environmentally friendly choices
- Expects to pay a little more for quality products that are environmentally friendly

Figure 3-4 A successful Web site meets its target audience's expectations by creating a content-rich, attractive, and usable site.

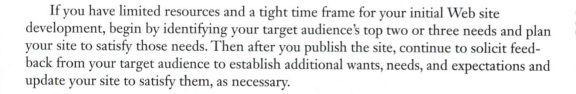

To create a successful Web site, you should assess your target audience's wants, needs, and expectations and then design your site to satisfy them.   **DESIGN TIP**

If you have limited resources and a tight time frame for your initial Web site development, begin by identifying your target audience's top two or three needs and plan your site to satisfy those needs. Then after you publish the site, continue to solicit feedback from your target audience to establish additional wants, needs, and expectations and update your site to satisfy them, as necessary.

Step 3: Determine the Site's General Content

A Web site's general content likely will include multiple Web pages using a combination of text, images, audio, video, animations, and multimedia elements. This section provides an overview of three types of Web pages: the home page, underlying pages, and a splash or entry page. Additionally, this section introduces the different kinds of Web content that might appear on these pages.

Q&A

Is determining target audience wants, needs, and expectations a one-time process? No. After creating your Web site, you should continually gather feedback from your target audience to update your target audience profile and fine-tune the site's content.

The content elements you choose for your Web site must support the site's purpose and satisfy your target audience's needs and expectations.   **DESIGN TIP**

Home, Underlying, and Splash Pages

Most Web sites consist of two types of Web pages: a home page and underlying pages. The home page is the anchor for the entire site, and the **underlying pages** provide detailed content and interest. Some sites also have an entry or splash page that you see before moving to the home page, although the popularity of splash pages is diminishing.

HOME PAGES   As you learned in Chapters 1 and 2, a Web site's primary page is called its home page. Generally, a home page is the first Web page visitors see. A home page should indicate clearly *who* owns or publishes the site, *what* visitors can expect to find at the site, and *where* specific information or site features are located, as shown on the Hallmark home page in Figure 3-5. In designing a home page, you should include the following elements:

- Who: Company name in text format, graphic logo, tag line, copyright notation, and similar elements that clearly identify *who* owns and publishes the site
- What: Summary text and images that show visitors *what* content is available at the site
- Where: Easily identifiable navigational links to other pages at the site to indicate *where* specific information or features are found

The answer to the Who? question should be evident throughout the site through use of corporate logos, a contact link, and copyright notices. An e-commerce site's home page could answer the What? question using a slide show or tabbed window to show a variety of the types of products or services sold at the site, whereas a blog site home page could indicate the topics discussed in the various blogs. The home page of a B2B site that sells Web hosting services could have links to pages that detail the types of hosting services provided, fees, customer support information, privacy and security policy information, and so forth to answer the Where? question. A home page for a large site often includes a **search feature**, which is a text box into which users enter a search term; the search tool then searches the site for that term. Search features use similar technologies as search engines, but only search within the site for matching results.

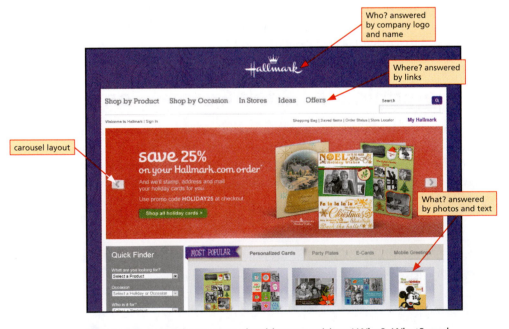

Figure 3-5 A site's home page should answer visitors' Who?, What?, and Where? questions.

A Web site's home page should contain elements that draw the visitor in and encourage further exploration. The home page should also be different enough to stand out as the primary page, but still connect visually with other pages at the site.

DESIGN TIP

Additionally, a site's home page should contain elements that establish the site's visual identity. Chapter 2 introduced the concepts of branding and using design elements to create and maintain visual identity. Organizations and companies spend a large amount of time and money defining, creating, and maintaining a positive, recognizable brand. Often, branding is so successful that the company then becomes synonymous with or symbolizes a specific product or service. For example, through successful branding, McDonald's is synonymous with fast food and the American Red Cross symbolizes disaster relief. As you learned in Chapter 2, you can exploit the power of branding on a home page using design elements — images, logo, typeface, and color scheme — alone or in combination to establish and maintain visual identity.

One way to add content to a home page without creating clutter is to use a tabbed window, or a slide show or carousel to provide access to several articles, videos, or other content at once. On most pages, these elements display a rotation of articles or images and automatically advance to the next tab or screen, as well as provide user controls to navigate to or pause at a certain screen (Figure 3-6). Clicking a screen in the tabbed window, slide show, or carousel opens the complete content page in the browser.

@SOURCE

Home Page
For more information about strategies for creating home pages, visit the Web Design 4 Chapter 3 Student Online Companion Web page at **www .cengagebrain.com** and then click Home Page in the @Source links.

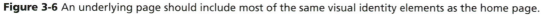

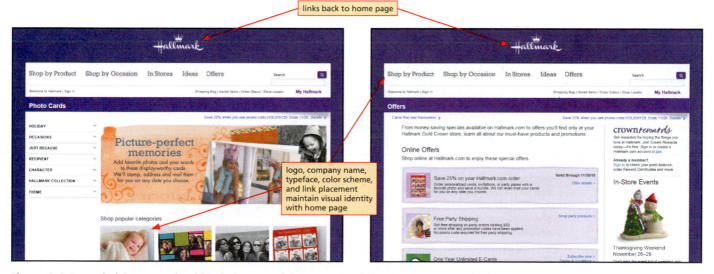

Figure 3-6 An underlying page should include most of the same visual identity elements as the home page.

Exploring Home Page Content

1. Visit the Web Design 4 Chapter 3 Student Online Companion Web page at **www.cengagebrain.com** and click Art Institute, NAPA, and Uvault in the Your Turn links to review three Web site home pages.

2. Review each home page and determine how well each page's content answers the Who? What? and Where? questions site visitors have when visiting these sites.

3. Write a report for your instructor that summarizes your home page review. Discuss the content employed at each site to address these three questions. Note the site that, in your opinion, does the best job of answering these three questions and the one that does the poorest job. What design recommendations would you make to improve the home page that does the poorest job of answering these questions?

UNDERLYING PAGES   In Chapter 2, you also learned that a Web site generally includes multiple subsidiary or underlying pages that provide details to the summary information shown on the site's home page. Links connect the home page with an underlying page and, where necessary, connect one underlying page to another underlying page. For example, typical underlying pages found at an e-commerce site include pages that provide the following:

- Product catalogs
- Checkout information
- Customer account information
- Customer service information
- Contact information
- Privacy policy and security information
- A business blog

Each underlying page at a site should include the same elements — name, logo, typeface, color scheme — as its home page to provide unity and promote visual identity. Figure 3-6 (on the previous page) depicts two underlying pages at the Hallmark site — comparing these pages with the home page shown in Figure 3-5 illustrates how Hallmark has implemented visual unity throughout its site. Additionally, like the two Hallmark underlying pages, each underlying page at a site should provide a link back to the site's home page.

Q&A

What is a landing page?
A *landing page* is a page that appears when a visitor reaches a site by clicking on an advertisement. They are used as marketing tools to measure the effectiveness of the advertisement by evaluating the number of times the page is visited and whether the visitor completes any transactions on the site.

Exploring Types of Underlying Pages

1. Browse the Web or use a search tool to locate at least five commercial Web sites. Include two each B2C and B2B sites and one C2C site.

2. Review the types of underlying pages offered at each site.

3. Write a report for your instructor that summarizes the typical underlying pages found at each type of commercial site. Be prepared to discuss your report in class.

SPLASH AND ENTRY PAGES   A **splash page** uses images, animation, and sound to capture visitors' attention and draw them into the site for further exploration. Visitors generally can click a link on the splash page to move on to the home page or, in some instances, wait until the home page automatically appears. A traditional splash page has little or no content beyond visual or sound elements. However, some sites use a splash page to help the visitor make choices about how to view the site, such as language or Flash versions. *Warning! Many visitors strongly dislike dealing with splash pages.* Decide whether to include an entry or splash page in context with your site's purpose and the needs and expectations of its target audience.

If you must include a splash page, be sure to add a link that jumps to the site's home page for those visitors who do not want to view the splash page.

DESIGN TIP

In the reusable and recycled goods Web site scenario, you and the team agree that a splash page is not appropriate for the new site, which will consist of a home page and multiple underlying pages, as shown in Figure 3-7.

@SOURCE

Splash Pages
For more information about the pros and cons of splash pages, visit the Web Design 4 Chapter 3 Student Online Companion Web page at **www .cengagebrain.com** and then click Splash Pages in the @Source links.

**Reusable and Recycled Goods Web Site
Site Plan**
Step 3: Determine the Site's General Content

Web Site Pages

The site will contain the following page types:
- Home page with slide show layout; no splash page
- About Us summary page, plus Annual Report, Management Team, and History detail pages
- Customer Testimonials page
- Products pages, including categories for Lunch Boxes, Bedding, Cleaning Products, and Clothing
- Contact Us page with customer service links

Figure 3-7 The reusable and recycled goods site will consist of a home page and multiple underlying pages.

Value-Added Content

Although it is tempting to fill your Web site with content, you should be selective, basing your choice of elements on how effectively they will contribute to your site's message and purpose. Content that furthers a Web site's purpose adds value, not merely volume. **Value-added content** is information that is relative, informative, and timely; accurate and of high quality; and usable.

In general, you should create original content elements prepared specifically for the Web instead of choosing existing content elements designed for print. For example, when including a written purpose statement, incorporate a short video clip of the CEO explaining the site's purpose.

If you must use an existing content element from another medium, you should **repurpose**, or modify, the element for the Web. Repurposing content frequently involves abbreviating and rewriting text, adding hyperlinks to background or additional information, rescanning or altering photos, and editing or segmenting video and audio. Most important, it requires creative thinking and keeping the Web environment and audience needs and expectations as a foremost consideration.

DESIGN TIP   Do not reuse content created for print on Web pages. Repurpose the content so that it will add value.

The following questions help you determine if the content you plan to add is truly worthwhile, regardless of whether you are considering images, animation, multimedia, or dynamically generated content at your site. Does the content element:

- Add value to the site?
- Further the site's purpose?
- Enhance visitors' experiences at the site?

If you answer no to any of these questions, do not include the content element. The availability of cutting-edge technology alone is never a valid reason to use it.

You might use different types of value-added content on your Web site, including the elements briefly discussed here and covered in more detail in later chapters: text, images, video, audio, animation, multimedia, and dynamically generated content.

Q&A

What are public domain materials? The rights to these materials belong to the public at large. Examples of public domain material include material on which the copyright has expired and U.S. government work, such as publications or photographs that are not covered by copyright protection. Copyrights or patents do not protect public domain materials.

TEXT   Remember, visitors typically scan Web page text for information rather than read the text word for word. Avoid long paragraphs, and break up text with images, links, and multimedia. When writing original text, follow the guidelines for writing for the Web introduced in Chapter 2. You can also follow similar guidelines to repurpose print publication text for the Web:

- Chunk text for scannability.
- Place explanatory or detailed information on linked, underlying pages.
- Use active voice and a friendly tone.
- Remove transitional words and phrases like *as stated previously*, *similarly*, and *as a result*, which might not be relevant for the chunked text.

YOUR TURN

Exploring How to Repurpose Text for the Web

1. Review the public domain Q&A and then visit the Web Design 4 Chapter 3 Student Online Companion Web page at **www.cengagebrain.com** and click FTC in the Your Turn links.

2. Locate the Key Publications section on the FTC Identity Theft page and open a copy of a PDF publication on identity theft in your browser; print the publication.

3. Using the guidelines for repurposing text from print publications, repurpose at least four paragraphs from the printed publication for your own Web site. As an acknowledgment, cite the source of the repurposed text in a line below the text.

4. Submit your repurposed text to your instructor. Be prepared to compare your repurposed text with the original printed publication text in class.

IMAGES   Images, which are files including graphic elements such as clip art, illustrations, diagrams, and photographs, are the most commonly used content element on Web pages, after text. Photographs on a Web page can familiarize the unknown and aid in decision making. For example, imagine that you want to buy a house in a new city. Visiting Web sites that display photographs of available houses in your price range (Figure 3-8) shows you options in your price range, enabling you to narrow your list before you contact a realtor.

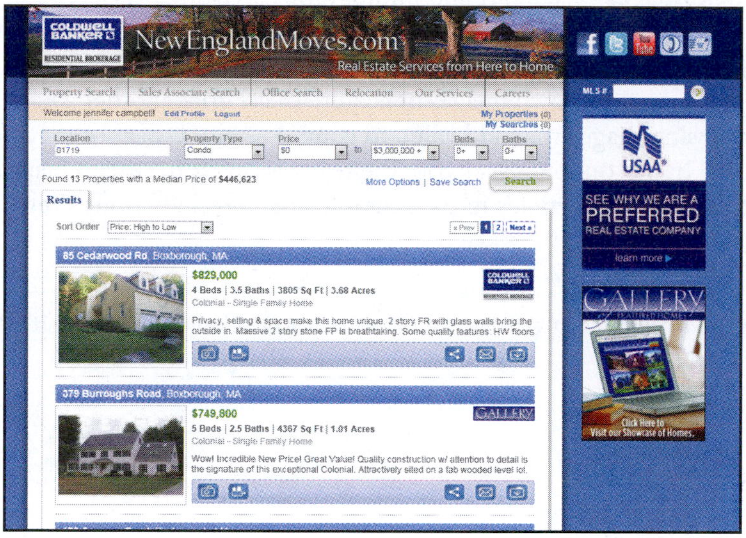

Figure 3-8 Web site images can familiarize the unknown.

You can deliver a message and/or prompt an action beyond the capabilities of text alone using images, such as clip art or photographs. Suppose you are an avid rock climber and need to lease a four-wheel drive vehicle that can handle difficult terrain. Before you visit a dealership, you decide to shop online and visit the Jeep Web site. As you click through to view the photos of different Jeep models, the photo of the sporty new yellow Jeep Wrangler poised atop a snowy mountain (Figure 3-9) captures your interest. The image prompts you to read the vehicle specifications on the Web site, determine that it fits your needs, and contact your local dealership to set up a test drive.

Figure 3-9 Powerful imagery can contribute to a site visitor purchasing or inquiring about your products.

DESIGN TIP   Web page images can powerfully communicate and motivate. Select relevant, high-quality images that can support the Web site's purpose.

You can draw your own illustrations and diagrams using illustration software or you can shoot your own photographs using a digital camera. Alternatively, you can find free or low-cost **stock images** — clip art and photographs — from a variety of online sources. In Chapter 5, you learn more about Web page images and the tools you can use to create and/or edit them.

Whether you create your own images or acquire them from another source, preselecting high-quality, relevant images that add value to your Web site is part of the Web site planning process. In our ongoing scenario, the team asks you to research appropriate photographs to accompany articles in the reusable and recycled goods Web site.

DESIGN TIP   Remember to ensure that content elements you use at your Web site are free of copyright restrictions.

YOUR TURN

Exploring Stock Photographs

1. Search the Web using keywords similar to *stock photos* or *stock images* to locate at least six sources of stock photographs. Include sources of royalty-free and low-royalty photographs as well as those for which you must pay a standard licensing or royalty fee.

2. Research the selected sources' offerings for eco-friendly or recycling-related images and identify four photographs in total from the six sources suitable for the reusable and recycled goods Web site in our ongoing scenario.

3. Create a report containing a table that compares all stock photograph sources. Include the following columns of information in the table: source name, type of photographs offered, and typical cost. Add a second table that lists the four photographs selected for the reusable and recycled goods Web site. Include the photograph name or other identifying reference, description, source name, and cost.

4. Submit your report to your instructor. Be prepared to discuss the results of your research in class.

AUDIO AND VIDEO   **Audio**, or sound, is frequently used as an extremely effective, low-bandwidth alternative to video. Audio can vary in both form and intensity — from a child's whisper to the president's State of the Union address, or from a heavy metal band to the U.S. Navy Choir. Audio can persuade, inspire, personalize, motivate, or soothe.

Audio also enhances recall. Does a lyric that keeps playing in your head remind you of a significant life event? Does a stirring speech bring to mind images of the time in which the powerful words were spoken? Think of the ways that audio — with its capability of evoking emotion, prompting action, and triggering memory — can benefit your Web site. Imagine, for example, the persuasive effect of a glowing testimonial about your product from a satisfied customer, or recall the possibilities of a catchy jingle.

Inform visitors when a site link launches an audio file so that they can use a headset or turn off their speakers so as not to disturb those around them. Repetitive sounds can be irritating to frequent site visitors, so use sound sparingly.

Typically, **video clips**, or moving imagery, incorporate the powerful components of movement and sound to express and communicate ideas. Delivering quality video over the Web efficiently can present challenges. The primary problem is the extremely large size of video files, resulting from the enormous amounts of data required to depict the audio and video. When presenting video, Web designers must decide whether to limit the size of downloadable video files or to generate streaming video. As you learned in Chapter 1, streaming media, such as audio or video, begins to play as soon as the data begins to stream, or transfer, to the browser. **Downloadable media**, on the other hand, must be downloaded in its entirety to the user's computer before it can be heard or seen.

Consider how your target audience will be accessing your site when adding video clips to your site. Most Internet connections can present video without causing delays or problems, but if a large portion of your audience uses lower bandwidth connection methods, think about reducing the size or number of video files.

ANIMATION AND MULTIMEDIA   **Animated images** are often used by Web sites to attract attention and enliven Web pages. A popular format is the **animated GIF** format, which adds movement to otherwise static images. Another type of popular animation, called **Flash animation**, is an animated movie created using Adobe Flash CS5 software. If your site uses Flash movies, visitors must download the free Flash player plug-in if their browser does not already have it.

Animated GIFs and Flash movies can add interest and appeal to your Web pages; however, you must use them sparingly and only in support of your Web site's purpose and only when doing so meets your target audience's expectations for content at your site. For example, a topical Web site promoting sports activities to a young target audience might benefit from the use of animated GIFs or Flash movies that encourage them to participate. However, the target audience for a B2B e-commerce site offering consulting services might find animated GIFs and Flash movies distracting and annoying.

Simple animated GIFs and Flash movies are not difficult to create, as you will learn in Chapter 6. Additionally, many online vendors offer free or low-cost animated GIFs and Flash movies. As with any element, excessive use of animation at your site can shift your audience's focus away from the other content and mask your site's purpose. Overuse of rotating objects, scrolling text, animated advertising banners, or Flash movies could annoy site visitors to the extent that they might exit your site and not return.

Q&A

Can multimedia elements play in all Web browsers?
Multimedia elements might require that your visitors install Web browser plug-ins, software that allows multimedia elements to play in the visitors' Web browsers. Adobe's Flash media player, Apple's QuickTime media player, and RealNetwork's RealPlayer media player are popular, free Web browser plug-ins. Many, if not most, of your site visitors will have already downloaded and installed browser media players.

Although definitions vary, **multimedia** is typically regarded as any combination of text, images, animation, audio, or video. Multimedia elements are popular because they can add action, excitement, and interactivity to Web pages. Web page multimedia elements can also be interactive; the Web site visitor participates as the multimedia plays instead of simply watching it. For example, the Disney Web site (Figure 3-10) offers its visitors both a multimedia and an **interactive multimedia** experience. Multimedia elements such as animation, video, and music invite visitors to play at the site by entering a product sweepstakes, listen to music from popular performers, check out cool fashions, play games and more — all while promoting the Disney brand.

Figure 3-10 Multimedia elements can add action, excitement, and interactivity to a Web site.

DESIGN TIP   Limit the use of animation and multimedia on your Web pages. Animation and multimedia elements should be used only when doing so supports your site's purpose and satisfies your target audience's expectations for content at your site.

Although viewers might find your site's multimedia elements intriguing and entertaining, developing multimedia elements for your Web site internally can require considerable expertise, time, and money. Therefore, it might be more cost effective to purchase appropriate multimedia elements from a professional multimedia developer.

Additionally, like animated GIFs and Flash movies, you should use multimedia elements *only* in support of a site's purpose and *only* when such elements enhance visitors' experiences at the site.

DESIGN TIP   Web designers without the necessary programming resources and expertise can purchase ready-made multimedia elements from professional multimedia developers.

Exploring Web Page Animation and Multimedia

1. Visit the Web Design 4 Chapter 3 Student Online Companion Web page at **www.cengagebrain.com** and click Disney, Wendy's, Warner Bros. Studios, and Extreme Sports Channel in the Your Turn links to review the home page and three of the underlying pages at each site.

2. Evaluate each site to determine how, in your opinion, the:

   a. Home page content makes clear the site's purpose

   b. Home page content satisfactorily answers the Who?, What?, and Where? visitor questions

   c. Animation or multimedia elements on the home and underlying pages support the site's purpose and meet target audience needs and expectations

3. Write a report for your instructor that identifies each site and its purpose and describes the animation and/or multimedia elements used. Discuss whether these elements contribute to the site's purpose and enhance visitors' experiences at the sites. Be prepared to discuss your report in class.

Dynamically Generated Content

Dynamically generated content, unlike static information, updates periodically and can appear on a site's pages when triggered by a specific event, such as the time of day or by visitor request. Web pages that display dynamically generated content typically acquire the information from a database. A **database** is a file that stores data, such as a store's inventory or a library's card catalog, so that the contents are searchable and easily updated. Sites that use databases to generate dynamic content are called **database-driven Web sites**. Figure 3-11 illustrates the result of a request for dynamically generated content — course and schedule information — from a Portland Community College database.

Figure 3-11 Dynamic content is generated when requested from a database.

Q&A

What is a gadget?
A *gadget* or *widget* is a fragment of code that creates dynamic content. Examples of gadgets include dynamic calendars, live weather, clocks, "to-do" lists, interactive games, virtual animals, and more. Some sites allow you to copy gadget code and then paste the code into your Web page to add the gadget. Most WYSIWYG editors include widgets or gadgets.

Continuing with the Regifting scenario, you and the team agree that the value-added content for your site will include text articles and tips, appropriate photos and a logo image, product information, and video clips of client testimonials. Animated GIFs and multimedia are not appropriate for the site's purpose and target audience expectations, but dynamically generated content is necessary to populate the product catalog. Figure 3-12 illustrates further development of the planning document for the reusable and recycled goods Web site.

Reusable and Recycled Goods Web Site
Site Plan
Step 3: Determine the Site's General Content

Value-Added Content

The site's value-added content will include the following:
• Company logo
• Photos of products
• Video clips of customer testimonials and video blogs
• Current news pages with articles and columns
• Environmental tips and tricks on most pages

Figure 3-12 Value-added content for the reusable and recycled goods Web site includes text, images, video clips, and dynamically generated content.

Organizing Web Site Files

As you develop your Web site, you should organize the resulting files, including HTML, image, animation, and multimedia files, to make it easier to maintain them and to ultimately publish your site. If your Web site is small — fewer than 5–10 total files — consider creating a single folder on your computer's local drive for all the files. If your Web site will exceed 10 files, consider creating separate, logical subfolders; for example, include subfolders for HTML code, photographs, audio, video, animation, and multimedia files. Remember that a single Web page can comprise many files, because each graphical element and article or document is its own file. For both small and large Web sites, create a subfolder in which you can place original files, such as word-processing files or image files that you later will convert into Web-usable formats.

To protect the system of folders and subfolders that you create, you should regularly back up your files and store the backups at a location separate from your local hard drive. For example, back up to a removable flash drive or online file storage service.

Plan an organized file system for your Web site files. You will work more effectively, minimize the risk of losing or misplacing content elements, and facilitate the publishing of your Web site if you are organized. Back up your files on a regular basis.

**DESIGN
TIP**

Step 4: Select the Site's Structure

After you define a site's purpose and identify its target audience, you are ready to plan the structure of the Web site — the linked arrangement of the site's pages from the home page. The Web site's structure should support the site's purpose and make it easy for visitors to find what they want at the site in as few clicks as possible. Planning the site's structure before you begin creating its pages has several benefits, such as the ability to do the following:

- Visualize the organization of the site's pages and linking relationships.
- Organize the pages by level of detail.
- Follow the links between pages to make certain visitors can quickly click through the site to find useful information — fewer clicks mean satisfied site visitors.
- Detect **dead-end pages**, pages that currently do not fit into the linking arrangement.
- Rearrange pages and revise linking relationships, and then visualize the changes before you create the site.

An outline of a Web site's structure can serve as a blueprint and illustrate how visitors can follow links from page to page. Some designers use a text outline to plan a site's structure, whereas others follow the storyboard process to create a visual representation of the site's structure. A **storyboard** is a series of pages originally developed to graphically present scenes for a movie or television program. To create a simple Web site storyboard, arrange sticky notes or index cards — each note or card representing a Web page — on a wall or corkboard to visualize a site's proposed structure. Figure 3-13 is an example of a storyboard used to plan a Web site's structure.

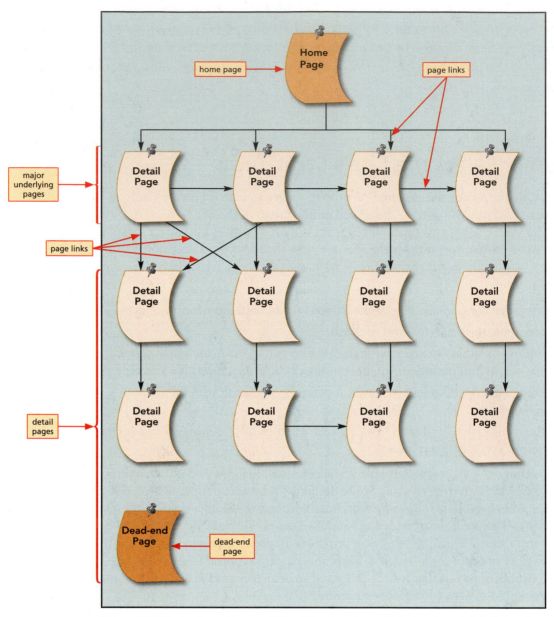

Figure 3-13 A storyboard is a useful tool for planning a site's structure and defining the links between pages.

Q&A
Can I use Microsoft Office® to create a flowchart?
Yes. Microsoft Word, Microsoft Excel, and Microsoft PowerPoint provide SmartArt objects, which allow you to create hierarchical or graphical representations of linked pages.

A **flowchart** is a diagram that shows steps or processes; flowcharts are another useful way to outline a site's structures. To create a flowchart, draw an arrangement of shapes and lines where each shape indicates a page and each line indicates a link from page to page. You can manually draw the structure flowchart, use the SmartArt objects available in Microsoft Word, Excel, or PowerPoint, or use drawing software, such as Microsoft Office Visio Professional 2010®.

As a Web designer, you should choose the method that you find most flexible to outline your site's structure. Regardless of the tool you use, your site's structure will likely follow one of three structural themes: linear/tutorial, random, or hierarchical.

Linear/Tutorial Structure

A **linear/tutorial site structure** organizes and presents Web pages in a specific order, as shown in Figure 3-14. A training Web site could use this structure to ensure that steps will not be missed or performed out of sequence. For example, a Web site that illustrates how to serve a tennis ball properly would use this structure to demonstrate the necessary range of motions in the correct order. The linear/tutorial structure controls the navigation of users by progressing them from one Web page to the next. Linear/tutorial structure is also appropriate for information that needs to be viewed in a historical or chronological order; for example, a Web site that details the explosive growth of e-commerce might benefit from this structure.

Home Page → Step 1 → Step 2 → Step 3 → Step 4

Figure 3-14 A linear/tutorial site structure organizes Web pages in a specific order.

Random Structure

A **random site structure**, also called a **webbed site structure**, does not arrange its pages in a specific order. From the home page of a site organized around a random structure, visitors can choose any other Web page according to their interests or inclinations. Figure 3-15 illustrates a random site structure and shows how a visitor to this type of Web site could navigate to different Web pages as he or she sees fit. The random structure might be appropriate for a simple Web site with few pages. However, visitors to a larger, complex Web site organized in this manner might be confused and frustrated trying to find useful information.

Q&A

Do all Web sites have multiple pages?
No. A current trend is to create one-page Web sites, where information is presented in one scrollable page, or all of the information is presented within a standard screen view. This is not appropriate for any content-heavy sites such as e-commerce or news sites, but can be effective to provide information about an event, or for a musician or artist wanting to provide links to a blog or to his or her work on other sites, such as Flickr or YouTube.

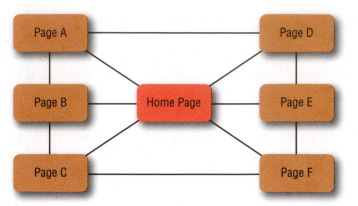

Figure 3-15 A random site structure does not arrange its pages in a specific order.

Hierarchical Structure

A **hierarchical site structure** organizes Web pages into categories and subcategories by an increasing level of detail, as shown in Figure 3-13 (the storyboard illustration) and in Figure 3-16. Organizational and topical Web sites are usually well suited to a hierarchical structure. A university Web site, for example, might structure its Web pages in three categories with multiple subcategories:

- Academics category with majors and departments subcategories
- Athletics category with teams and schedules subcategories
- Students category with current and prospective students and alumni subcategories

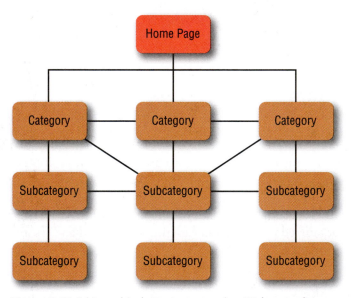

Figure 3-16 A hierarchical structure organizes Web pages into categories and subcategories by increasing level of detail.

Site Structure
For more information about planning Web site structure, visit the Web Design 4 Chapter 3 Student Online Companion Web page at **www .cengagebrain.com** and then click Site Structure in the @Source links.

Web sites with many pages and multiple objectives, such as an e-commerce site, might use a combination of the three primary Web site structures rather than adhering to a single site structure to organize its pages. Returning to the reusable and recycled goods Web site scenario, you and your team agree on a site structure that combines the hierarchical and linear structures. Figure 3-17 illustrates the update to the design plan to include the structure flowchart.

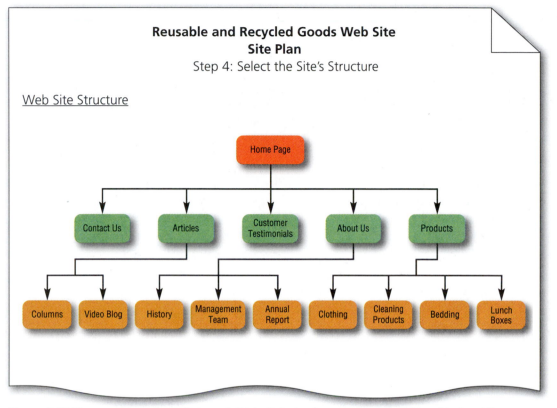

Reusable and Recycled Goods Web Site
Site Plan
Step 4: Select the Site's Structure

Web Site Structure

Figure 3-17 The reusable and recycled goods Web site's structure combines the hierarchical and linear structures.

> Plan the structure of your Web site to support the site's purpose and make it easy for visitors to meet their needs and expectations at the site. Formalize the structure plan using a text outline, storyboard, or flowchart.

DESIGN TIP

Chapter Review

Creating a Web site demands a considerable investment of time and other important resources. To ensure a Web site's success, a detailed site plan is essential. Planning Step 1 defines the purpose of the Web site, which entails determining goals and objectives. Planning Step 2 identifies the site's target audience, including developing a target audience profile and needs assessment. Planning Step 3 identifies the general content of the site, including Web page selection and types of value-added content to be used. Content types include text, images, video, audio, animation, multimedia, and dynamically generated content. As you develop a Web site, having an organized electronic filing system for files and folders will help you work more effectively, minimize the risk of losing or misplacing elements, and smooth the process of publishing your Web site. Finally, Planning Step 4 involves planning the site's structure: linear/tutorial, random, or hierarchical.

TERMS TO KNOW

After reading the chapter, you should know each of these key terms.

animated GIF (83)
animated images (83)
audio (82)
database (85)
database-driven Web sites (85)
dead-end pages (87)
demographic characteristics (73)
design plan (70)
downloadable media (83)
dynamically generated content (85)
Flash animation (83)
flowchart (88)
goals (71)
hierarchical site structure (90)
interactive multimedia (84)
linear/tutorial site structure (89)
multimedia (84)

needs assessment (74)
objectives (71)
psychographic characteristics (73)
purpose statement (71)
random site structure (89)
repurpose (80)
search feature (76)
site plan (70)
splash page (79)
stock images (82)
storyboard (87)
target audience (73)
target audience profile (73)
underlying pages (76)
value-added content (79)
video (83)
webbed site structure (89)

TEST YOUR KNOWLEDGE

Complete the Test Your Knowledge exercises to solidify what you have learned in the chapter.

Matching Terms

Match each term with the best description.

____ 1. site plan

____ 2. widget

____ 3. interactive multimedia

____ 4. database-driven Web site

____ 5. purpose statement

____ 6. linear/tutorial site structure

____ 7. psychographic characteristics

____ 8. plug-in

____ 9. random site structure

____ 10. splash page

____ 11. dead-end page

____ 12. animated GIF

____ 13. hierarchical site structure

a. A site that delivers content from a collection of data based on user input, such as a library card catalog.

b. A page that appears before the home page is visible.

c. Web pages organized by categories and subcategories.

d. Social group affiliations, lifestyle choices, purchasing preferences, political affiliations, and other characteristics that explain why visitors might want to access your site.

e. A page that currently does not fit into the linking arrangement.

f. A format that adds movement to otherwise static images.

g. Software that allows certain content to function in a browser window.

h. Web pages organized in no specific order.

i. An experience involving a combination of media, such as images, audio, video, and animations, in which the viewer participates.

j. A fragment of code that creates dynamic content.

k. A formal written explanation of a Web site's overall goals and the specific objectives related to those goals.

l. A formal document that states a Web site's purpose, goals, objectives, general content, and structure.

m. Web pages that must be viewed in a specific order.

Short Answer Questions

Write a brief answer to each question.

1. Differentiate between goals and objectives when planning a site. Describe a purpose statement.

2. Identify the first four steps in developing the site plan for a Web site.

3. Discuss how to develop a target audience profile and target audience needs assessment.

4. Define the three primary questions visitors want answered by home page content and identify the types of content on a commercial Web site's home page that can answer visitors' questions.

5. Define demographic characteristics and explain their role in creating a target audience profile.

6. Discuss the functions of a home page, splash page, and underlying pages.

7. What is value-added content? Discuss how the following content types can add value to a Web site: text, images, animation, Flash movies, video and audio, multimedia, and dynamically generated content.

8. Explain what a database-driven Web site is, and give two examples of such sites.

9. Define the term, storyboard, and explain its importance in the Web site development process.

10. Describe three basic Web site structures and give examples that illustrate when each type of structure is appropriate.

Test your knowledge of chapter content and key terms.

Instructions: To complete the Learn It Online exercises, start your browser, click the Address bar, and then visit the Web Design 4 Chapter 3 Student Online Companion Web page at **www.cengagebrain.com.** When the Web Design Learn It Online page is displayed, click the link for the exercise you want to complete and then read the instructions.

Chapter Reinforcement TF, MC, and SA
A series of true/false, multiple-choice, and short-answer questions that test your knowledge of the chapter content.

Flash Cards
An interactive learning environment where you identify chapter key terms associated with displayed definitions.

Practice Test
A series of multiple-choice questions that test your knowledge of chapter content and key terms.

Who Wants To Be a Computer Genius?
An interactive game that challenges your knowledge of chapter content in the style of a television quiz show.

Wheel of Terms
An interactive game that challenges your knowledge of chapter key terms in the style of the television show *Wheel of Fortune*.

Crossword Puzzle Challenge
A crossword puzzle that challenges your knowledge of key terms presented in the chapter.

Investigate current Web design developments with the Trends exercises.

Write a brief essay about each of the following trends, using the Web as your research tool. For each trend, identify at least one Web page URL used as a research source. Be prepared to discuss your findings in class.

1 | Carousels, Slide Shows, and Tabbed Windows

Find examples of carousels, slide shows, and tabbed windows. What navigation or user control features do they have in common? How many screens does each show? How do they add value to the Web page?

2 | One-Page Web Sites

The Web sites with which you are familiar typically consist of several linked pages with a clear organization and an easy-to-use navigation system. However, some Web sites consist of only one page. Research the trend of creating one-page Web sites. Find an article that reviews or advises how to use one-page Web sites. View a few one-page Web sites. Are they effective or too long? How much scrolling do you have to do to view the entire page? As a Web designer, what type of client would you advise to have a one-page Web site?

Challenge your perspective of Web design and surrounding technology with the @Issue exercises.

Write a brief essay in response to the following issues, using the Web as your research tool. For each issue, identify at least one Web page URL used as a research source. Be prepared to discuss your findings in class.

1 | Web Site Purpose Statements vs. Web Site Mission Statements

A commercial or noncommercial organization often develops an organizational mission statement to succinctly explain to its constituencies (members, customers, employees, business partners, government agencies, and so forth) why the organization exists. The use of succinctly worded Web site mission statements is an outgrowth of the use of these organizational mission statements. However, some business and Web critics consider formal organizational or Web site mission statements to be useless "bizspeak." After researching the arguments for and against Web site mission statements, create a report that accomplishes the following:

a. Compares Web site *purpose* statements as described in this chapter with examples of Web site *mission* statements. How are they alike? How are they different?

b. Describes how, as a Web designer, you would advise a client on the inclusion of a Web site purpose and/or Web site mission statement at a B2B site.

2 | Using Multimedia

Find an example of video, animated GIFs, audio, or other multimedia elements that are used as value-added content where text could be used instead. Do you agree with the site designer's choice? Alternatively, find a site that is text-heavy, and think about how multimedia could be used to enhance the site. In both instances, does the use of multimedia fit with your assumptions of the site's target audience?

HANDS ON

Use the World Wide Web to obtain more information about the concepts in the chapter with the Hands On exercises.

1 | Explore and Evaluate: Web Site Structure

Browse the Web to locate a variety of personal, organizational/topical, and commercial Web sites. Select four of these sites, and identify what you think the site's primary structure is. Can you find examples of all three structures discussed in the chapter? For one of these sites, draw a flow chart for the primary site pages. You may use paper or Microsoft Office SmartArt tools to create your flowchart.

2 | Search and Discover: Free or Inexpensive Animated Images

Use the Ask.com search tool to identify at least five sources of free or inexpensive animated images for use on Web pages. Then write a brief description identifying each source, the types of animated images offered, and, if not free, the typical cost. List any restrictions imposed on the use of free animated images. Select one animated image from each site and describe a situation in which you, as a Web designer, might include it on a Web page.

TEAM APPROACH

Work collaboratively to reinforce the concepts in the chapter with the Team Approach exercises.

1 | Target Audience

Businesses and other large organizations spend considerable amounts of time and money determining the target audience of their site. Good Web design involves using value-added content that attracts, informs, and entices site visitors. Team up with two other students to identify characteristics of the following sites' target audiences and the design and content choices that the site owners made to meet the audience's expectations.

 a. Shutterfly

 b. Avon

 c. Cool Running

 d. food52

 e. Intuit

Create a report summarizing your research explaining how each site uses value-added content to maintain visual identity. Cite examples that support the teams' decision on how well each site uses value-added content in support of the site publisher's branding efforts.

2 | Web Site Goals, Objectives, and Purpose Statement

Join with two other classmates to create a team for this activity. Select two of the team members to form a Web design team. The third team member will assume the role of the client who hires the Web design team to develop his or her Web site.

 a. The client develops an idea for a B2C Web site of his or her choice, for example, a bike shop or a used CD store.

 b. The design team works with the client to develop a list of site goals and objectives, write a formal purpose statement, and develop the target audience profile and needs assessment for the site.

c. As a team, search for two sites that are similar to the one you have planned. Create a presentation for the instructor and other classmates that compares the team's site plan with the sample sites. Include in the presentation an evaluation of how the sample sites met their objectives and what changes you would make to their site or your site plan after doing the comparison.

CASE STUDY

Apply the chapter concepts to the ongoing development process in Web design with the Case Study.

The Case Study is an ongoing development process using the concepts, techniques, and Design Tips presented in each chapter.

Background Information

The four steps described in this chapter covered a lot of material — from defining the Web site's goals and objectives to planning a site's structure. If you have carefully explored the information in each step and have worked your way through the end-of-chapter materials for this chapter, you are ready to tackle this chapter's assignment.

Chapter 3 Assignment

In this assignment, you will begin to create your own formal Web site plan by defining the site's goals and objectives, writing a formal purpose statement, and creating a target audience profile and needs assessment. You will also plan its general content and structure.

1. Using the report you created in the Chapter 2 Case Study as your starting point, create a formal site plan.

    a. Determine your site's goals and objectives and draft the site's purpose statement.

    b. Identify your site's target audience(s) and determine the wants, needs, and likely expectations that your site's design and content can satisfy for that audience.

    c. Identify the pages you initially plan to include at your site.

    d. Add to your site plan a list of value-added content that will help achieve your Web site's purpose and satisfy target audience needs. Identify possible sources for the content, keeping in mind the copyright issues discussed in Chapter 2.

    e. Determine which of the three Web site structures — linear/tutorial, random, or hierarchical (or a combination of structures) — will best meet your site's purpose. Use a text outline, or manually draw the structure, create a storyboard, or use flowcharting software to illustrate your site's structure as part of your design plan.

2. Submit your partial design plan to your instructor. Be prepared to discuss the elements of your partial design plan in class.

4 | Planning a Successful Web Site: Part 2

Introduction

In Chapter 3, you completed the first four of the six steps required to develop a solid Web site design plan: you defined the site's goals and objectives and stated its purpose, identified the site's target audience, planned the site's general content, and specified the site's structure. In this chapter, you continue the development of your site plan by discovering how appropriately using two variables—page length and content placement—can enhance page usability; then you complete Step 5 and Step 6. Finally, you use a checklist to review your completed site plan.

Objectives

After completing this chapter, you will be able to:

1. Discuss the relationship between page length, content placement, and usability

2. Complete Step 5: Design the look and feel of the site

3. Complete Step 6: Specify the site's navigation system

4. Use a checklist to review your design plan

Page Length, Content Placement, and Usability

The initial, visible screen area of a Web page is extremely important space because it provides the first glimpse of a page's content and the first opportunity to satisfy visitors' content needs and usability expectations. As you learned in Chapter 2, the monitor resolution setting for visitors' browsers can determine just how much of a page is visible. Most Web users today set their monitor resolutions to 1024 × 768 or higher; at lower resolutions, a visitor likely will need to scroll vertically and perhaps horizontally to view the entire Web page. You also learned in Chapter 2 that visitors typically dislike unnecessary scrolling and often avoid doing so; therefore, any page content below and to the right of the visible screen area is less likely to be seen.

Because you cannot control visitors' monitor resolution or scrolling habits, you should take care to position visual identity content, such as logos and names, and important links above and to the left of the potential scroll lines or the **scroll zone**, which is the area beyond the initial visible screen. Positioning page content that identifies the site and allows visitors to move from page to page above and to the left of the scroll zone is especially important for your site's home page. As you learned in Chapter 3, your home page introduces your site by informing visitors who you are, what you offer at the site, and where they can find specific information or site features. One way to maximize the initial visual content is to employ carousels or slide shows, as previously mentioned; doing so gives readers quick access to three to five articles or images in the space of one.

The entire Real Simple home page (Figure 4-1) is visible at the 1024 × 768 monitor resolution with no vertical or horizontal scrolling, which is an ideal situation for site visitors who dislike scrolling. To accommodate visitors who are viewing at a lower resolution, the Web site designers of the Real Simple home page positioned content important for visual identity and links to major areas of the site above and to the left of the potential scroll lines.

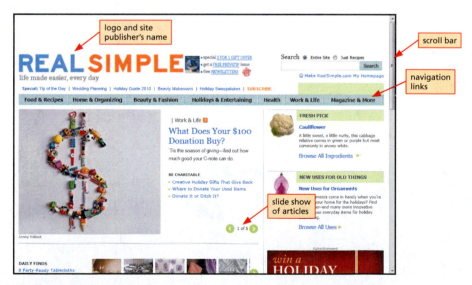

Figure 4-1 Place content important for visual identity and navigation above and to the left of the scroll zone.

DESIGN TIP   You have no control over visitors' monitor resolution or scrolling habits. To increase usability, take care to place important content, such as logos, names, and major links, above and to the left of potential scroll lines.

To increase usability and promote unity, you should also position visual identity and navigation content above and to the left of the potential scroll lines on underlying pages. By their nature, underlying pages provide greater detail in support of a specific topic or Web site feature and might not lend themselves to a single page of text, graphics, and other content. When it is necessary to extend Web page content beyond a single visible screen, consider limiting the page length to two screens of content. If you follow the two-screen guideline, your visitors will not need to scroll excessively to view the page's entirety. If you cannot limit a Web page to two screens, provide "top of page" links at logical positions within the page so that your visitors can quickly return to the top of the Web page, as shown in Figure 4-2. Web pages intended to be printed and read offline provide an exception to the two-screen guideline. Pages intended to be printed should be left full length without "top of page" links.

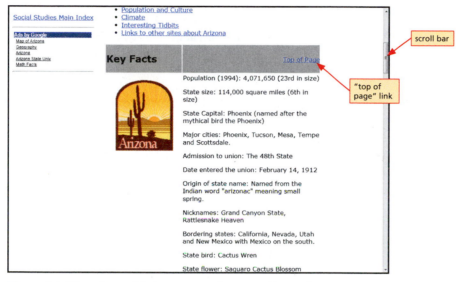

Figure 4-2 "Top of page" links on pages that extend beyond one screen allow visitors to quickly return to the top of the page.

DESIGN TIP

If vertical scrolling is necessary, ensure a logical flow of information. Avoid horizontal scrolling on all pages. Add "top of page" links at logical positions within a page that flows beyond two screens and is not intended to be printed and read offline.

Another issue to consider in content positioning is *where* visitors typically look first when viewing a Web page. **Eye-tracking studies** use various technologies to produce **heat maps** in which data is represented by color. Eye-tracking heat maps are created by analyzing the movement of a visitor's eyes as he or she views a Web page. Over the past several years, eye-tracking studies suggest that a site's visitors typically first look at the top and left areas of a page, and then look down and to the right. These eye-tracking studies add support to the concept of placing visual identity content and major links at or near the top and left side of a page to improve usability. Figure 4-3 illustrates the Johnson & Johnson home page with visual identity content and major links positioned at or near the top and on the left side of the page. Eye-tracking studies are also used in Web site marketing. You learn more about Web site marketing in Chapter 7.

Figure 4-3 Visitors typically look first at the top and left areas of a Web page.

When designing a Web page, you can choose to set your page width in two ways. A **fixed-width page layout** sets a specific pixel width for the page. The benefit of fixed-width pages is that the layout is consistent no matter the resolution; the downside is that on monitors displaying lower resolution visitors may need to scroll horizontally. A **liquid** or **flexible page layout** sets the width of the page as a percentage of the browser window. The benefit of liquid layouts is that the page expands to fill the entire window, maximizing the viewable content; however, liquid layouts allow for less control over size or placement of images and text, which can result in awkward or unreadable placement or content.

DESIGN TIP   Consider the needs of your likely site visitors when deciding on a fixed-width or liquid layout, and make sure to test your pages at different resolutions.

YOUR TURN   ## Exploring Liquid and Fixed-Width Web Page Design

1. Using the search tool of your choice and the keywords *liquid v. fixed-width Web page design* or similar keywords, locate and review several articles that compare the benefits and downsides of each.

2. Write a report for your instructor that summarizes your research. Discuss how you might apply what you learned about Web page width to the design of a site, taking into consideration audience needs and how the page will look at different resolutions.

Step 5: Design the Look and Feel of the Site

At this point, you have determined the Web site's purpose and audience, you have developed a plan for the site's general content and structure, and you have an understanding of the roles of page length and content placement in usability. Now you are ready to tackle the next step, which is planning the look and feel of your site. Chapter 2 introduced you to the concepts of unity and visual identity and the importance of following an entity's branding specifications when planning the look and feel of a site. To promote unity and maintain visual identity across pages at your site, use visual consistency when choosing color and typeface and when positioning content across all pages at your site.

Visual Consistency

When a Web site's underlying pages fail to include common content and design features found on the home page, site visitors might feel confused; they might even believe an underlying page belongs to an entirely different Web site. To avoid confusing visitors, all of the pages at a site must share a visual consistency that reassures visitors as they move from page to page.

You can create **visual consistency** by repeating design features — typeface, content position, color scheme — and actual content — name, logo, major links — across all pages at a site. Repeating design features and content, as shown at the UFood Grill Web site in Figure 4-4, unifies a site's pages, strengthens a Web site's visual identity and brand, and maintains visual consistency.

Figure 4-4 Repetition of design and content elements promotes unity, maintains visual identity, and creates visual consistency across a site's pages.

> Repeating design features, such as the color scheme, and content, such as a logo, name, and major links, across all pages at a site is one technique for creating visual consistency.

DESIGN TIP

Color and Visual Contrast

In Chapter 2, you learned about the principles of color as a design tool and that a well-chosen color scheme creates unity among pages at a Web site. As you consider color options for a Web site's pages, remember the power of color to influence moods, the cultural implications of color, and your target audience's expectations for the use of color at your site.

Apply the same color scheme to the background, graphic art and illustrations, and text across all pages to build visual consistency throughout your Web site. Figure 4-5 illustrates a red, white, and blue color scheme across pages at the University of Kansas's Web site. The red, white, and blue text and graphics stand out against the contrasting backgrounds, creating an effective visual contrast. The colors in the photographs add additional visual appeal. Observe that on both pages in Figure 4-5 the logo graphic, publisher's name, and major links are positioned above and to the left of the scroll zone and at or near the top and on the left side of the page. Page length, content positioning, and use of color come together at the University of Kansas Web site to create attractive and usable pages.

Figure 4-5 Standard use of color, page length, and content positioning applied to all pages maintains visual consistency within a site.

You should choose background and text colors that provide sufficient contrast to enhance readability and that permit print legibility. For example, studies have shown that, in general, the greater the contrast, the greater the readability. Thus, Web designers commonly use white, gray, and cream as background colors contrasted with black or dark blue or red text colors. Alternatively, some sites use darker background colors, such as black or dark blue or dark red, and create contrast with light-colored text, although these combinations can be less readable depending on how well they are executed. Figures 4-4 and 4-5 illustrate good examples of effective contrast between background and text colors.

YOUR TURN   Exploring the Use of Color: Visual Consistency and Visual Contrast

1. Visit the Web Design 4 Chapter 4 Student Online Companion Web page at **www.cengagebrain.com**, and then click links in the Your Turn section to review the home page and at least three underlying pages at the following Web sites to determine how successfully each site uses color:
   a. 1-800-PetMeds
   b. Hotels.com
   c. Sundrops Soap
   d. USA Today

2. Create a report for your instructor that summarizes your review. Describe how each site uses color — including overall color scheme and individual background, graphic element, text, and image colors. Does the color scheme offer sufficient contrast between the background, foreground, and text? Does the site use its color scheme to create visual consistency across pages? Discuss how you would modify the color, if necessary, to improve readability and visual consistency.

Color is used on Web pages for more than just text readability. As you learned in Chapter 2, Web page color is also used to evoke mood, stimulate interest, support a site's purpose, and meet audience expectations for the type of content found at a site. With this in mind, you might choose to use background, graphic art, and text color combinations beyond the simple, but effective color combinations illustrated in Figures 4-4 and 4-5. One way to select an appropriate color scheme and then make certain it is applied across all pages is to use a template to create your pages. In Chapter 1, you learned that some WYSIWYG editors, such as Expression Web and Dreamweaver, offer Web templates to which a color scheme has already been applied, as shown in Figure 4-6. Using templates with a predefined color scheme can help ensure visual consistency among all pages at your site.

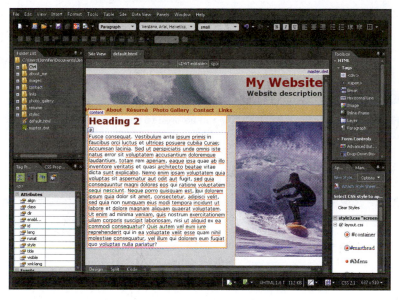

Figure 4-6 Using a WYSIWYG editor Web template with a predefined color scheme ensures visual consistency across pages at a site.

Q&A

What are the Web Accessibility Initiative (WAI) guidelines for color usage?
The WAI specifies that color alone should not indicate information, for example, a text link. A common practice is to combine color and underlining for a link. The contrast between background and foreground colors should be sufficient for visitors with vision problems or those using a monochrome monitor. However, many Web site designers rely on color and bolding alone to indicate links.

Limit your Web site color scheme to three major colors. Choose a text color for titles, headlines, and so forth to attract the appropriate amount of attention. Test the background and text colors in your color scheme to ensure both on-screen readability and print legibility.

DESIGN TIP

Another way to choose an effective color scheme with appropriate contrast between background and text colors is to use inexpensive color matching software, such as Color Scheme Designer®, Color Wheel Pro®, ColorShade®, or ColorCache®. **Color matching software** contains tools you can use to create sample Web site color schemes based on color theory, preview the color schemes in a browser, and then apply the colors in the selected scheme to your Web pages.

In Chapter 3, you were introduced to an ongoing scenario, in which you manage a team of Web designers developing a Web site for the Regifting reusable and recyclable goods e-commerce business. Continuing this scenario, your team meets to discuss potential color schemes that promote professionalism and the educational tone of the site's content. To assist in the discussion, your team reviews the company's print media — for example, letterhead, business cards, brochures — that illustrate the company's branding specifications for the use of color. Based on this material and your discussions with your team, you use color matching software to create several sample Web site color schemes for management review and approval, including the sample shown in Figure 4-7.

What is the current W3C standard for CSS and do all browsers support it?

The current W3C style sheet standard is CSS Level 2.1. Microsoft Internet Explorer and Mozilla Firefox have improved support for CSS; some browsers or older browser versions do not fully support CSS. The development of CSS standards is ongoing; CSS Level 3 (CSS3) is in various draft stages.

Figure 4-7 Color matching software can be used to develop a Web site's color scheme based on color theory.

DESIGN TIP

Images that you include on Web pages, such as clip art, illustrations, and photos, will add more color to your pages. Choose images with colors that match or complement your site's color scheme.

CSS

For more information about the W3C standards for CSS, visit the Web Design 4 Chapter 4 Student Online Companion Web page at **www.cengagebrain.com**, and then click CSS in the @Source links.

CSS and Formatting

As you learned in Chapter 1, Web designers use the CSS specification to create a text document, called a **style sheet**, to control the appearance of one or more pages at a site.

In word-processing software, a **style** is a group of formatting properties, such as bold, italic, font type, font size, or font color, applied as a group to selected text. Similarly, when you use CSS, you create a style sheet containing **style rules**, which are specifications that allow you to define one or more formatting properties (declarations) and their values for specific HTML tags (selectors). For example, suppose you want all the top-level heading text surrounded by the <h1> </h1> HTML heading style tag pair to be a blue color. You could create a style rule for the <h1> heading tag consisting of the heading tag itself, called the style rule's selector and the CSS property: value combination {color: blue}, called the style rule's declaration. You can add this style rule to your pages in one of three ways:

- As an **inline style** inserted within the <h1> HTML tag on a page
- As part of an **internal style sheet** inserted within a page's HTML heading tags
- As part of an **external style sheet** saved in the folder with the site's pages and linked to them with an HTML tag

---

DESIGN TIP

Because no current browser supports all CSS specifications, be sure to test how the Web pages you format using CSS appear in different browsers.

Style sheets centralize formatting, which saves time and simplifies the process of creating and modifying Web pages. Using style sheets helps you avoid inserting HTML tag formatting attributes and values for individual tags. If you make a style change, such as changing the font color for all headings, the Web pages are automatically updated to reflect the change to the style sheet. Using style sheets also helps you maintain visual consistency across all pages at your site. Modern WYSIWYG editors, such as Expression Web, provide CSS tools you can use to create and edit style sheets and link style sheets to your pages. These tools also include templates with style sheets already linked to them (Figure 4-8). You can also create style sheets using **CSS editor software**, such as JustStyle CSS Editor® (Figure 4-8) or Rapid CSS Editor 2010®. To learn more about using CSS, check out Appendix C at the back of this text.

Q&A

What does *cascading* mean for style sheets? CSS prioritizes style rules to determine precedence in case of conflicting rules. The first priority is for specifications set by the author in the form of inline or embedded styles, or external style sheets. The second priority includes local CSS files a user specifies. The last priority are styles specified by the browser. Style rules are applied in cascading order based on priority.

Figure 4-8 WYSIWYG and CSS editors provide support for inline, internal, and external style sheets.

Page Layout

Earlier in this chapter, you learned about the important relationship between usability and page length and content placement. With page length, content placement, and usability in mind, you should create a logical, standardized **page layout**, or arrangement of content elements, that ensures visual consistency across your site's Web pages. A logical, standardized page layout fosters a sense of balance and order that Web site visitors find appealing and reassuring — and that sophisticated Web users have come to expect. Figure 4-9 on the next page shows the consistent layout of pages at the Medline Web site:

- Logo and name in upper-left corner of each page
- Search feature at the top of each page
- Main navigation links at the top of each page
- One- or two-column content area in the middle of the page

Not shown in Figure 4-9 are a standard copyright notation, contact phone number, and links to Legal Info and Contact Us pages at the bottom of each page. These types of links often appear below the scroll zone on a page that cannot be viewed in its entirety without scrolling. Observe that the visual identity content and major navigation links on the Medline pages are above and to the left of the scroll zone.

Figure 4-9 A logical, standard page layout provides visual consistency across all pages at a site.

A layout grid, layout tables, and Cascading Style Sheets are all used to create attractive page layouts.

LAYOUT GRIDS   Many designers use an underlying structure of rows and columns, called a **layout grid**, to position content on a page. You can precisely position and align content, set margin width, and make more adjustments using a layout grid. A layout grid serves only as a visual guide for positioning content and does not appear when a Web page is actually viewed with a browser.

You can draw a layout grid on paper. Alternatively, you can use the layout grid provided by a WYSIWYG editor, such as Expression Web or Dreamweaver. Using a WYSIWYG editor layout grid (Figure 4-10) has several advantages over drawing a layout grid on paper. For example, it is easy to add and reposition content on a WYSIWYG grid. Additionally, you can change grid line color, spacing (pixels, inches, or centimeters), and style (dotted, solid, dashed). You can also set a command to have content automatically "snap to," or align precisely with, the closest grid line.

Figure 4-10 Using a WYSIWYG editor layout grid makes it easy to position content precisely.

Use a layout grid to position page content that consistently appears on all pages, for example, the logo, site publisher's name, images, and major links. Then carefully add other page content that generates interest and variety while maintaining visual consistency.

CSS AND PAGE LAYOUT   Earlier in the chapter, you learned how style sheets are used to control formatting across pages, thus creating visual consistency. Style sheets can also be used to control page layout by dividing a page into sections, such as a header section or a navigation section. The <div> tag within a page's code specifies a section identified by the style sheet (Figure 4-11). Within each <div></div> tag pair reside the other content tags for that section. Figure 4-12 illustrates the external style sheet for a WYSIWYG template that establishes page sections and a portion of the page code for a section established by the style sheet.

Figure 4-11 <div> tags are used to specify sections on a Web page.

Figure 4-12 Style sheets are also used to control page layout.

HTML Tables

For more information about using HTML Tables, visit the Web Design 4 Chapter 4 Student Online Companion Web page at **www .cengagebrain.com**, and then click HTML Tables in the @Source links.

What are frames?

Frames are a method for dividing the screen into multiple areas, with each area containing a separate Web page. Frames were commonly used so that page elements could be scrolled individually and for easy site maintenance. Frames are no longer considered an acceptable method for page layout due to accessibility issues and difficulty with setting bookmarks or direct page URLs. CSS has replaced many of the reasons people used frames.

TABLES A table is an arrangement of columns and rows; the intersection of a table column and a row is called a cell. You might be familiar with using tables in word-processing software, such as Microsoft Word, or spreadsheet software, such as Microsoft Excel. A Web page **HTML table** can be used in the same way as a table in a word-processing document or in a spreadsheet — as a **data table** that organizes text or numbers. Figure 4-13 illustrates a formatted HTML data table on a Web page.

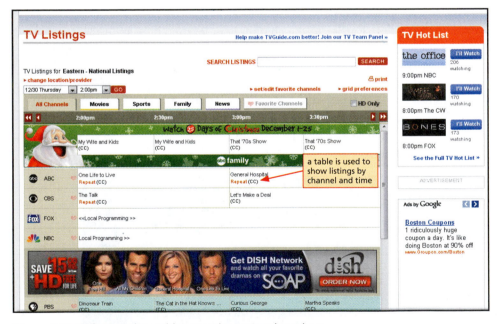

Figure 4-13 Web page data tables organize text and numbers.

HTML data tables are easy to format by modifying table properties. Three data or layout table properties specific to HTML tables are the float, cell padding, and cell spacing properties. The **float property** sets the left or right position of an element, such as text, positioned outside the table. The **cell padding property** sets the amount of space between table cells; the **cell spacing property** sets the amount of space inside the cell between its contents and its borders. In addition to modifying table properties, you can also modify the height, width, alignment, and so forth of individual table cells.

Exploring CSS Editor Software

1. Using the search tool of your choice and the keywords *CSS editor software* or similar keywords, research the different options for CSS editor programs used to create CSS style sheets.
2. Write a report for your instructor that compares the features and costs of three different programs. Find and read reviews on each if possible. Describe which you, as a Web designer, might use to create style sheets for your Web pages, and why. Include whether you might prefer to use this type of software program as opposed to other methods of creating style sheets, such as text editors and WYSIWYG programs.

Continuing with the Regifting scenario, your team agrees on a color scheme, based on the company's branding specifications, and a page layout for the visual identity content and major links on each page. You also agree on pursuing a liquid layout for the pages and using CSS for both formatting and layout. Figures 4-14 and 4-15 illustrate the update to your formal site plan for Step 5.

Figure 4-14 An appropriate color scheme applied across all pages at a site contributes to the site's look and feel.

Q&A

Can tables be used for Web page layout?
An HTML tool known as layout tables were a feature of many WYSIWYG programs and were used to position Web page content. This capability has been removed from many WYSIWYG programs and is less commonly used than CSS to control page layout due to issues with accessibility and to meet WAI standards.

@SOURCE

Accessible Tables
For more information about tables and accessibility, visit the Web Design 4 Chapter 4 Student Online Companion Web page at **www .cengagebrain.com**, and then click Accessible Tables in the @Source links.

**Reusable and Recycled Goods Web Site
Site Plan**
Step 5: Design the Look and Feel of the Site

Page Layout
The reusable and recycled goods site's page layout:
• Pages will use a liquid layout controlled by CSS
• Header at top of each page containing logo, tag line, company name, search tool, and Contact Us link
• Major navigational links down left side of page
• Content area in center of the page
• Contact Us page link, privacy and security policy statement page link, and copyright notation at the bottom of each page

Figure 4-15 A consistent and logical page layout across all pages at a site contributes to the site's look and feel.

Step 6: Specify the Site's Navigation System

After the color scheme and page layout are determined, the final step in developing your site plan is to specify the navigation system you will use. A navigation system that is easy for visitors to understand and follow will draw them deeper into your site to view detail pages with content that can satisfy their needs and expectations. A Web site navigation system consists of different types of links: text links; image links; related link groups presented as menus, bars, or tabs; breadcrumb trails; and site maps. Sites often use a combination of these link types as part of a navigation system. A large site with many pages may also include a search capability, which is another popular navigation tool. No matter what combination of link types you use for your site's navigation system, the links should be both user based and user controlled.

User-Based and User-Controlled Navigation

In Chapter 3, you learned about the three common structures used to organize the pages at a site: a linear/tutorial site structure, a random site structure, or a hierarchical site structure. In our ongoing scenario, the site team has selected a combination of the hierarchical site structure and the linear site structure for the reusable and recyclable goods Web site. In Chapter 3, you also created a flowchart (see Figure 3-17) that illustrated the organization of site pages and the major links between pages. With this structure in mind, you are ready to select the link types for your pages.

A **user-based navigation system** provides a linking relationship between pages based on the site *visitors*' needs rather than the site *publisher's* needs. To develop a user-based navigation system, you can combine the target audience profile information you developed in your site plan's Step 2 and the basic site structure developed in Step 4 with an understanding of exactly how visitors will use your site. One way to get a better understanding of how visitors will actually use your site — and to ensure that your site's navigation system is user based — is to perform usability tests as you develop the system.

A formal Web site **usability test** is an evaluation that generally takes place in a structured environment, such as a testing laboratory, and is conducted by usability and design professionals who observe exactly how visitors use a Web site and formulate their research in a report containing design recommendations. Formal Web site usability tests can be very expensive, costing perhaps several thousand dollars, and might be well beyond your budget. An informal usability test, however, involves using a team of friends, family members, coworkers, or other interested parties to test a site's navigation system or other site features and then report on their experiences. Informal usability testing is generally very inexpensive, perhaps even free, but the feedback you gain can be invaluable.

You do not have to wait until your site is published to perform usability testing on the site's navigation system. You can begin by having a testing team evaluate your proposed navigation system as part of the planning process. Continue frequent testing as you develop the site. Testing does not end with site development; you must continue to ensure that your navigation system works as intended through periodic testing after the site is published. In Chapter 7, you learn more about testing your site before and after publishing it.

User-controlled navigation allows visitors to move around a site in a manner *they* choose — and not be restricted to the site publisher's opinion of how visitors should move from page to page. For example, some visitors to a B2C site might go straight to the product catalog, whereas others might prefer to first learn more about the company publishing the B2C site before going to the product catalog. Still others might prefer to search for a specific product rather than peruse the entire catalog. A **user-controlled navigation system** provides a variety of ways visitors can move around a site beyond the major links from the home page. For example, you can include a link back to the home page on all underlying pages and include Next Page and Previous Page links on pages to be visited sequentially, such as multiple pages in a catalog. Offering different types of links in your navigation system allows site visitors the freedom to choose how they want to move from page to page at your site.

Q&A

Does navigation system testing end when the site is published?
No. It is important to ensure that the links on your site's pages continue to work as intended. You should plan to conduct periodic testing of the site's navigation system throughout the life of your site.

@SOURCE

Usability Testing
For more information about navigation and usability, visit the Web Design 4 Chapter 4 Student Online Companion Web page at **www.cengagebrain.com**, and then click Usability Testing in the @Source links.

Create a user-based navigation system to match the way visitors actually move from page to page at your site. Consider conducting usability testing as you develop your site's navigation system to ensure navigation is user based.

DESIGN TIP

Link Types

To create a well-designed, user-controlled navigation system for your site, consider combining different types of links: text links; image links; groups of related links presented as menus, bars, or tabs; a breadcrumb trail; and a site map. You should also consider adding a search capability to your site.

TEXT LINKS   **Text links** are hyperlinks based on a word or words in an HTML document; text links are a common way to navigate from section to section on the same page, from page to page at the same site, or from a page at one site to a page at another site. A text link should clearly identify its **target**, the page to which the link points. Avoid using ambiguous text, such as *click here*, to indicate a text link; instead, use text that clearly identifies the target page, such as the page's title.

As you learned in Chapter 2, the traditional formatting for a fresh, unclicked text link is blue, underlined text. After a text link is clicked, the text remains underlined, but the color traditionally changes to purple to indicate a followed link. Over time, Web page visitors have learned to recognize the traditional formatting for a fresh or followed link. Because of visitors' expectations, using traditional formatting for the text links on your pages can enhance the pages' usability. Additionally, you should add both underlining and color to indicate a text link to meet accessibility standards. Conversely, avoid using underlining for emphasis in body text, as underlining implies a link. Instead, use bold or italic formatting for emphasis.

DESIGN TIP   Consider using the traditional blue text link color for fresh links and purple text link color for followed links. Avoid using color alone to specify a text link; add underlining in addition to color to meet accessibility standards.

Q&A

What are the WAI guidelines for links (navigation mechanisms)?
WAI guidelines specify that the target for a link should be clearly identified and that color alone should not be used to identify information, such as a link. Related links should be grouped together in navigation bars that are used in a consistent way across all pages at a site.

Today, advances in technology and the increased sophistication of Web users combine to encourage designers to add variety to text link formatting. When you browse the Web or review Web page illustrations in this text, you might find text links in almost any color, sometimes underlined and sometimes not. When visiting Web pages, you might also find text links that look like body text until you hover the hand pointer over the text, at which time it changes color and/or is underlined indicating a link. This type of hidden link is called a **mouseover link** or **rollover link**. Although it might be tempting, as a designer, to create interesting and fun rollover links or use different color scheme colors for your text links, use caution. Remember that you are designing your Web pages for your site's target audience, not for yourself. User-based navigation requires that you first consider the effect of hidden or differently formatted fresh and followed text links on the usability and accessibility of your site's pages.

If you decide that including hidden text links serves a purpose or adds interest to your pages while still accommodating visitors' navigation needs and expectations, you can create the rollover effects with scripts or CSS.

DESIGN TIP   Avoid hidden mouseover or rollover text links unless their inclusion satisfies your target audiences' expectations for text links and there is no adverse effect on the usability and accessibility of your site's pages.

YOUR TURN

Exploring Text Link Formatting

1. Browse the Web or use a search tool to locate six Web sites: two commercial sites, two topical sites of interest to senior citizens, and two organizational sites. Follow text links at each site.
2. Write a report for your instructor that discusses how each site presents text links. Does the link text clearly identify the link's target page? Are traditional fresh and followed link colors and underlining used to define text links? Are hidden or rollover text links used? Is there any difference in the approach to text links among the different types of sites: commercial, topical, or organizational? How easy or difficult was it for you to identify and follow the text links? Will the results of your research determine how you format text links at your site? If yes, how? If no, why not?

IMAGE LINKS   You can create an **image link** by assigning a link to an image, including clip art, an illustration, or a photograph. A common use of an image link is an image map. An **image map**, sometimes referred to as a clickable map, is an image that contains **hot spots**, areas on the image to which a link is assigned. A common use of an image map is a clickable geographic map, such as the NOAA climate map shown in Figure 4-16. Figure 4-17 illustrates an image map with hot spot links to underlying pages. An image map does not have to be a geographic map.

@SOURCE

WAI Guidelines
For more information about WAI guidelines for links and other Web page elements, visit the Web Design 4 Chapter 4 Student Online Companion Web page at **www .cengagebrain.com**, and then click WAI Guidelines in the @Source links.

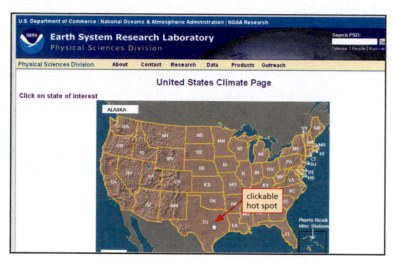

Figure 4-16 A common use of an image map is a clickable geographic map.

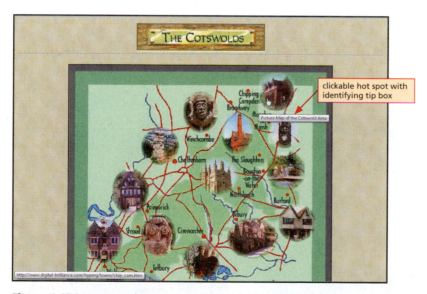

Figure 4-17 Image map hot spots can also link to a site's featured underlying pages.

Image maps can be either client-side or server-side image maps. The hot spot link information in a **client-side image map** resides in the HTML coding of the page and is processed by the visitor's browser. With a **server-side image map**, the x- and y-coordinates of the clicked hot spot are sent back to the server, where a script processes the hot spot link information and returns the link's target page. Although all

Q&A

What are the WAI guidelines for image maps?
WAI guidelines specify that you should provide a text equivalent for a graphic element, such as an image map, use client-side image maps when possible, and provide redundant text links for server-side image map hot spots.

Web browsers can process server-side image maps, they are more complicated to create than client-side image maps, increase demands on a server, and typically have slower response times than client-side image maps. If you decide to use an image map, choose a photograph or illustration that accurately represents the target pages and meets design guidelines for visual consistency.

@SOURCE

Image Maps
For more information about client-side and server-side image maps, visit the Web Design 4 Chapter 4 Student Online Companion Web page at **www .cengagebrain.com**, and then click Image Maps in the @Source links.

MENUS, BARS, AND TABS　Related links grouped into navigation menus, bars, and tabs create an eye-catching design element and help visitors quickly identify links to a site's major underlying pages.

- A **navigation menu** (Figure 4-18) is a list of related links. A navigation menu might contain multiple levels of links displayed as vertical **pop-out menus**.

- A **navigation bar** (Figure 4-19) generally uses graphic buttons to present links. Pointing to some navigation bar buttons displays **drop-down menus**. Some sites add navigation bars with text links instead of button links at the bottom of each page.

- **Navigation tabs** (Figure 4-20) present links as small tabs; navigation tabs work best when linking to alternative views of the content.

DESIGN TIP　Follow WAI guidelines for image maps. Remember to choose an image that accurately represents the target pages and follows design guidelines for visual consistency.

@SOURCE

Navigation and Usability
For more information about navigation and usability, visit the Web Design 4 Chapter 4 Student Online Companion Web page at **www .cengagebrain.com**, and then click Navigation and Usability in the @Source links.

No matter which of these navigation elements you include at your site, basic design rules still apply. Navigation elements should be used consistently across all pages at your site. Also, navigation element colors should follow the site's overall color scheme to maintain visual identity. Finally, the text for a menu, button, or tab link should clearly indicate its target page.

Figure 4-18 A navigation menu is a list of related links; some menu links also display pop-out or drop-down menus of additional links.

Figure 4-19 A navigation bar uses graphic buttons to present links; some navigation bar buttons also display drop-down menus of additional links.

Figure 4-20 Navigation tab with drop-down menu that is displayed upon hovering.

Basic design rules apply to navigation menus, bars, and tabs. Use these design elements consistently across all pages at a site, use color scheme colors, and make certain the target page is clearly indicated.

DESIGN TIP

BREADCRUMB TRAIL   A **breadcrumb trail** is a hierarchical outline or horizontal list that shows a visitor the path he or she has taken from the home page to the page currently being viewed. A breadcrumb trail (Figure 4-21) not only provides a visitor with a visual understanding of the linking relationship between pages, it also offers additional navigation tools. A visitor can click a link in the breadcrumb trail to move back to that link's target page. Although breadcrumb trails are very useful, they do not replace navigation elements, such as menus or bars, but should be used to help a user find his or her way back to pages previously viewed in the site.

Figure 4-21 A breadcrumb trail shows the path between the home page and the current page.

DESIGN TIP   A breadcrumb trail displays the relationship between the home page and the current page. Use a breadcrumb trail in combination with other navigation elements, such as navigation menus or bars.

SITE MAP   A site with a large number of pages and a complex structure often provides a **site map**, also called a **site index**, which is a summary page of links to major pages at the site. Figure 4-22 illustrates the site map at the Apple Web site. Although in the past some site maps were illustrations or image maps, most site maps today consist of text links arranged alphabetically or by topic to meet the WAI standard for conveying information using text. With the use of search features, multiple navigation structures, and breadcrumbs, a site map might seem like an outdated or unnecessary feature. However, it can be helpful to visitors at a large site, and is an easy page to create and add to your Web site.

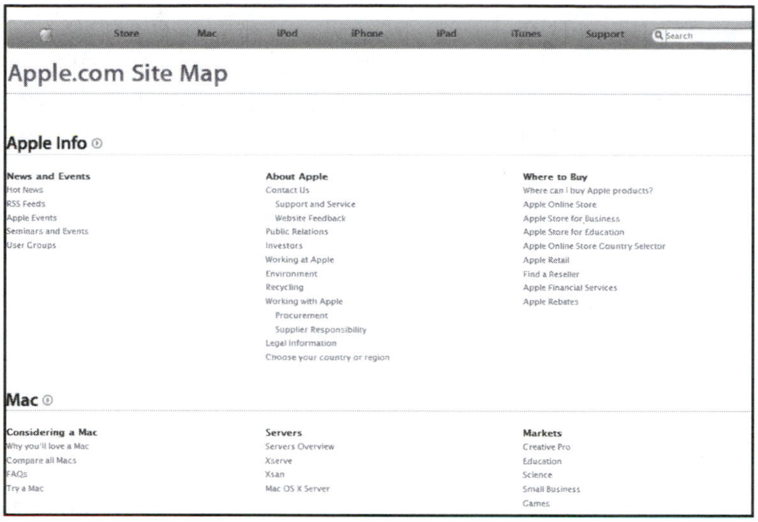

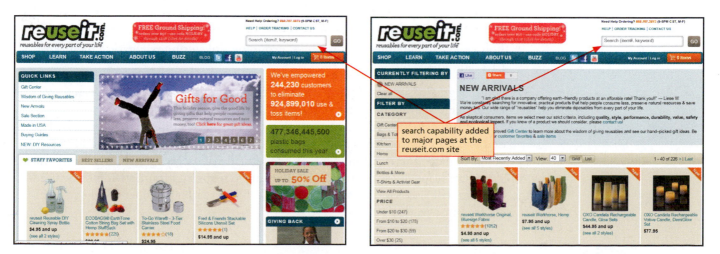

Figure 4-22 A site map provides summary links to a site's major pages.

Provide a text link-based site map for large Web sites with many pages. Organize a site map's text links in a logical way, such as alphabetically or by topic.

SEARCH CAPABILITY   Adding a keyword search capability and a search box (Figure 4-23) to all of your site's major pages allows visitors to quickly locate pages at your site that contain specific keywords without browsing your site page by page — and maintains visual consistency across pages. Like a site map, a **Web site search feature** is another popular navigation tool for sites with a large number of pages. A large business or organization that manages its own Web servers can use server-side scripts to create and maintain a searchable site index on its servers. If you do not manage your own Web servers, you can contract with a hosted Web site search provider to provide search services. A **hosted Web site search provider** is a third-party company that uses spiders or other tools to build a searchable index of your site's pages and then hosts the index on their servers. You use templates and tools provided by the search provider to add a search box to your pages. Another tool you can add to your search features is AutoComplete. **AutoComplete** provides suggestions to site visitors as they type in the search box.

@SOURCE

Search Capability
For more information about incorporating search capability at your site, visit the Web Design 4 Chapter 4 Student Online Companion Web page at **www.cengagebrain.com**, and then click Search Capability in the @Source links.

Figure 4-23 Adding search capability to all major pages at your site allows visitors to quickly locate specific information without browsing page by page.

YOUR TURN

Exploring Hosted Web Site Search Providers

1. Using the search tool of your choice and the keywords *hosted Web site search* or similar keywords, identify five B2B companies that offer hosted Web site search services.
2. Write a report for your instructor that compares the services offered by each company. Include a summary of special features and cost for each company's service. Then choose a hosted Web site search service you could recommend to a client for whom you are developing a B2C e-commerce site. Give the reasons for your recommendation.

DESIGN TIP

Create a user-controlled navigation system by combining in your navigation system text links; image links; navigation menus, bars, and tabs; a breadcrumb trail; a site map; and search capability as appropriate for your target audiences.

Navigation Design Tips

Remember that if your Web site's navigation is poorly designed, visitors might become confused and frustrated as they attempt to find information or site features. In the virtual world, dissatisfied customers typically respond as dissatisfied customers in the real world do: they quickly leave, don't return, take their business elsewhere, and frequently voice their criticism. As you plan your navigation system, remember to do the following:

- Create both a user-based and a user-controlled navigation system. If possible, test your navigation system for usability as you develop it.
- Place major links at the top and/or down the left side on all pages at your site to promote unity, visual consistency, and usability.
- Avoid ambiguous text in text links. Consider usability and visitors' expectations before varying from traditional text link colors and underlining.
- Ensure that links clearly identify their target pages.
- Include a link back to the home page on underlying pages. Include Next Page and Previous Page links on pages to be visited sequentially.
- Follow WAI guidelines for text links, grouping links using navigation menus or bars, and image maps.

A well-designed, user-based navigation system ensures that your visitors can move from page to page at your Web site with ease.

Your Regifting site design team agrees that the site's navigation system must be both user based and user controlled. The navigation system will consist of a navigation bar at the top of each page, a navigation menu on the left side of each page, a site map organized by topic, and traditionally formatted text links. Image maps and frames will not be used at the site. You will also contract with a hosted Web site search provider to add a search feature to the site's pages.

To ensure a focus on user-based and user-controlled navigation, your team conducts usability testing with a group of participants consisting of two employees, two representatives from the product vendors, and two longtime customers. They will test the navigation system's usability on a regular basis during both site development and prepublishing testing. Figure 4-24 illustrates the update to the site plan.

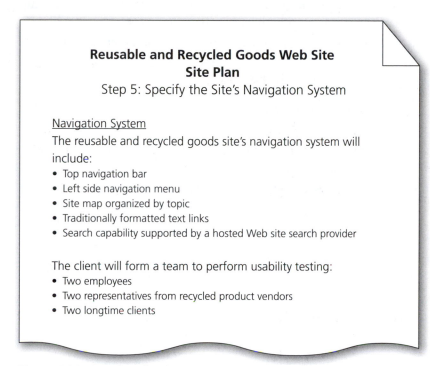

Reusable and Recycled Goods Web Site
Site Plan
Step 5: Specify the Site's Navigation System

Navigation System
The reusable and recycled goods site's navigation system will include:
- Top navigation bar
- Left side navigation menu
- Site map organized by topic
- Traditionally formatted text links
- Search capability supported by a hosted Web site search provider

The client will form a team to perform usability testing:
- Two employees
- Two representatives from recycled product vendors
- Two longtime clients

Figure 4-24 A user-based and user-controlled navigation system enhances your Web site usability.

Site Plan Checklist

Detailed planning is vital not only in the development of a Web site, but also in any other similar investment to which time and other significant resources are dedicated. To ensure a successful Web site, use the following checklist to develop your formal design plan.

Step 1: Define the Site's Purpose

- Identify the primary and secondary goals for your Web site.
- Determine the objectives necessary to meet the site's goals.
- Write a formal purpose statement for the site.

Step 2: Identify the Site's Target Audience

- Develop a target audience profile that identifies the demographic and psychographic characteristics of audience members.
- Perform a needs assessment to determine the target audiences' wants, needs, and expectations that can be satisfied by your site.

Step 3: Determine the Site's General Content

- Determine your site's pages: home, underlying, and splash or entry pages.
- Ensure that the content on your site's home page answers visitors' *who*, *what*, and *where* questions.
- Determine the visual identity content to be added to all pages that will brand your site.
- Determine the value-added content for your pages: text, images, audio, video, animation, multimedia, and dynamically generated content.
- Plan a file folder organization for your HTML and content files.

Step 4: Select the Site's Structure

- Consider the best way to structure your site to achieve its purpose: linear/tutorial, random, hierarchical, or some combination of structures.
- Create an outline of your site's structure: text outline, storyboard, or flowchart.

Step 5: Design the Look and Feel of the Site

- Position visual identity and vital page content above and to the left of potential scroll lines.
- Maintain visual consistency across pages with a color scheme and page layout.
- Follow WAI accessibility guidelines for the use of color.

Step 6: Specify the Site's Navigation System

- Create a navigation system that is both user based and user controlled, offering a combination of text links; image links; navigation menus, bars, and tabs; a breadcrumb trail; a site map; and a search feature.
- Maintain visual consistency with the color and page placement of navigation elements.
- Perform usability testing on the navigation system during the planning and development phases.
- Follow WAI accessibility guidelines for links and image maps.

Chapter Review

Critical visual identity and navigation elements should be placed above and to the left of the scroll zone to reduce visitors' Web page scrolling. Additionally, the typical visitor looks first at the top of a Web page, then to the left, and then down and to the right. The content you want your visitors to see first should be placed at or near the top and on the left side of a Web page. Also consider the visible screen area when designing underlying pages. Ensure that visitors never have to scroll horizontally to view pages and that the information on underlying pages flows smoothly and logically.

Using color and page layout to maintain visual consistency across all pages at a site promotes unity, strengthens visual identity, and reassures visitors. Apply a uniform color scheme and a consistent page layout created with tools such as grids and CSS to create visual consistency.

A user-based navigation system creates links between pages based on how visitors actually move from page to page at a site. A user-controlled navigation system allows visitors to move between pages in the manner of their choosing and offers both major navigation links as well as other options, such as a breadcrumb trail, site map, and search capability. Common types of navigation links include text links; image links; groups of related links presented as menus, bars, or tabs; breadcrumb trails; and site maps. After completing planning Steps 1 through 6, use the design plan checklist to review your design plan.

After reading the chapter, you should know each of these Key Terms.

AutoComplete (117)	liquid page layout (100)
breadcrumb trail (116)	mouseover link (112)
cell padding property (109)	navigation bar (114)
cell spacing property (109)	navigation menu (114)
client-side image map (113)	navigation tab (114)
color matching software (103)	page layout (105)
CSS editor software (105)	pop-out menu (114)
data table (108)	rollover link (112)
drop-down menu (114)	scroll zone (98)
external style sheet (104)	server-side image map (113)
eye-tracking studies (99)	site index (116)
fixed-width page layout (100)	site map (116)
flexible page layout (100)	style (104)
float property (109)	style rule (104)
heat maps (99)	style sheet (104)
hosted Web site search provider (117)	target (111)
hot spot (113)	text link (111)
HTML table (108)	usability test (111)
image link (113)	user-based navigation system (110)
image map (113)	user-controlled navigation system (111)
inline style (104)	visual consistency (101)
internal style sheet (104)	Web site search feature (117)
layout grid (106)	

Complete the Test Your Knowledge exercises to solidify what you have learned in the chapter.

Matching Terms

Match each term with the best description.

___ 1. scroll zone

___ 2. external style sheet

___ 3. client-side image map

___ 4. breadcrumb trail

___ 5. rollover

___ 6. user-based

___ 7. target

___ 8. hot spot

___ 9. inline style

___ 10. AutoComplete

___ 11. navigation bar

___ 12. heat map

___ 13. usability test

___ 14. liquid layout

___ 15. fixed-width

a. A navigation system that bases linking relationships on the way site visitors actually move from page to page.

b. A way to evaluate exactly how site visitors will access site information and move from page to page at a site.

c. A text file containing formatting instructions saved in the folder with the site's pages and linked to them with an HTML tag.

d. The area beyond the initial visible screen.

e. The page to which a link points.

f. A clickable area on an image map.

g. A(n) _____ specifies a page's width specified as a percentage of the browser window.

h. A group of related links.

i. A hidden link that appears when you point to it.

j. A hierarchical outline that shows the visitor the path between the home page and current page.

k. A(n) _____ layout specifies a page's width specified in pixels.

l. The colored data results of an analysis of site visitors' eye movements.

m. An image map in which the hot spot link information resides in the HTML document and is processed by the browser.

n. Provides suggestions to visitors as they type in a search box.

o. Inserted within the <h1> HTML tag on a page.

Short Answer Questions

Write a brief answer to each question.

1. Describe the effect of page length and content placement on usability.

2. What is the value of maintaining visual consistency across all pages at a site?

3. Discuss the differences between fixed-width and liquid page layouts.

4. Discuss the WAI guidelines for the use of color and links.

5. Explain the different ways styles and style sheets can be used to format content.

6. Define different methods of user-based and user-controlled navigation.

7. Define five common types of links used in a navigation system.

8. Describe an image map, and explain the difference between client- and server-side image maps.

9. Describe a hosted Web site search.

10. Describe mouseover or rollover links.

LEARN IT
ONLINE

Test your knowledge of chapter content and key terms.

Instructions: To complete the Learn It Online exercises, start your browser, click the Address bar, and then visit the Web Design 4 Chapter 4 Student Online Companion Web page at **www.cengagebrain.com**. When the Web Design Learn It Online page is displayed, click the link for the exercise you want to complete and then read the instructions.

Chapter Reinforcement TF, MC, and SA

A series of true/false, multiple-choice, and short-answer questions that test your knowledge of the chapter content.

Flash Cards

An interactive learning environment where you identify chapter key terms associated with displayed definitions.

Practice Test

A series of multiple-choice questions that test your knowledge of chapter content and key terms.

Who Wants To Be a Computer Genius?

An interactive game that challenges your knowledge of chapter content in the style of a television quiz show.

Wheel of Terms

An interactive game that challenges your knowledge of chapter key terms in the style of the television show *Wheel of Fortune*.

Crossword Puzzle Challenge

A crossword puzzle that challenges your knowledge of key terms presented in the chapter.

TRENDS

Investigate current Web design developments with the Trends exercises.

Write a brief essay about each of the following trends, using the Web as your research tool. For each trend, identify at least one Web page URL used as a research source. Be prepared to discuss your findings in class.

1 | AutoComplete

Find at least one search engine or a Web site with its own search feature that uses AutoComplete (suggested sites: google.com, amazon.com, netflix.com). In the site's search box, enter a search term relative to the site's content. Your essay should discuss how the use of AutoComplete helped or hindered your search.

2 | Breadcrumb Trails

Using the Google search engine and the keywords *breadcrumb trail* or similar keywords, locate an article that expresses an opinion — positive or negative — about their use. Summarize the article, and discuss whether you agree with it. Include any personal response you have based on your use of breadcrumb trails as a navigation tool.

AT ISSUE

Challenge your perspective of Web design and surrounding technology with the @Issue exercises.

Write a brief essay in response to the following issues, using the Web as your research tool. For each issue, identify at least one Web page URL used as a research source. Be prepared to discuss your findings in class.

1 | Cascading Style Sheets (CSS)

Cascading Style Sheets (CSS), a multifeatured specification for HTML, offers designers an expedient, powerful method to control the formatting and layout of Web pages. Research the current level of support for style sheets by leading browsers and the current W3C recommendations for style sheet usage. Create a report summarizing your research. Explain why you will or will not use Cascading Style Sheets to design your Web site.

2 | Fixed-Width and Liquid Page Layouts

Fixed-width and liquid page layouts each have their pros and cons. Using the Bing! search engine and the keywords *fixed-width versus liquid page layouts*, or something similar, find two articles with opposite viewpoints or that are neutral on the topic. Create a report summarizing the reasons given, and why you would or would not use one or the other as a Web designer.

HANDS ON

Use the World Wide Web to obtain more information about the concepts in the chapter with the Hands On exercises.

1 | Explore and Evaluate: Page Length, Content Placement, and Usability

Browse the Web to identify a Web site that effectively uses page length and content placement to enhance the site's usability and a Web site that, in your opinion, does not. Write a report comparing and contrasting the two sites. Include your recommendation for ways the latter site could use page length and content placement to improve usability.

2 | Search and Discover: Web Sites and Visual Identity

Using the Google search engine and the keywords *Web site visual identity* or similar keywords, locate visual identity topic pages posted at three Web sites. Then write an outline for a presentation to your class on the results of your research. Include in your outline a discussion of how you would use visual identity elements at your Web site and whether you think it is necessary to address visual identity on a page at your site.

Work collaboratively to reinforce the concepts in the chapter with the Team Approach exercises.

1 | Web Site Search Features

Join with two other students to research how to add a Web site search feature to a Web site. Find examples of free and hosted solutions and reviews of each. Compile the team's findings and examples in a report for your instructor. Be prepared to present your report to the class.

2 | User-Based and User-Controlled Navigation Systems

Join with another student to create a two-person research team. Then identify six Web sites — two commercial, two topical, and two organizational sites — and review their navigation systems. Create a presentation for the class in which you describe the navigation system for each site. Use examples of each site's navigation system elements to illustrate whether the site's navigation system is both user based and user controlled.

Apply the chapter concepts to the ongoing development process in Web design with the Case Study.

The Case Study is an ongoing development process using the concepts, techniques, and Design Tips presented in each chapter.

Background Information

Continuing with the development of your site plan that you began in Chapter 3, complete Step 5: Design the look and feel of the site and Step 6: Specify the site's navigation system. Then use your design plan checklist to evaluate your complete plan.

Chapter 4 Assignment

In this assignment, you will finalize your Web site's site plan by completing the remaining two steps discussed in this chapter: planning the look and feel of your site and planning its navigation system.

1. Review the related chapter material on page length, content placement, and usability.

2. Define your site's color scheme by using a WYSIWYG template or color matching software.

3. Plan the page layout for your home page and underlying pages. Explain how you will control page layout with tables or CSS.

4. Review the guidelines for user-based and user-controlled navigation systems, and then specify the individual elements of a user-based and user-controlled navigation system for your site.

5. After completing the final two steps of your design plan, review your design plan using the design plan checklist. After your review, make any necessary additions or edits to your design plan.

6. If time permits, meet with three classmates to compare and evaluate each other's design plans and offer constructive suggestions as applicable.

5 Typography and Images

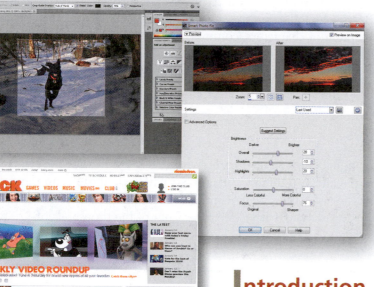

Introduction

After your research is complete and you have developed a solid site plan, you are prepared to create your Web site. As you learned in Chapters 2 and 4, Web designers primarily use text and image content elements to effectively communicate. In this chapter, you learn more about the standards for applying good typography to text. You also learn how to select appropriate images, such as photographs, diagrams, illustrations, clip art, and more, which add value to your Web site and support your Web site's message. Then, you learn how to prepare your selected images for the Web.

Objectives

After completing this chapter, you will be able to:

1. Explain Web page typography issues

2. Discuss effective use of Web page images

3. Describe image file formats

4. Discuss how to prepare Web-ready images

Web Page Typography Issues

In Chapter 2, you learned the importance of composing text that is accurate, easy to read, understandable, and comprehensive. You also learned that such text must be concisely written specifically for the Web. Composing your text, however, is just the first step. You can make your text more effective by following the rules of good typography. **Typography** is the appearance and arrangement of characters, commonly referred to as **type**, used to create printed and on-screen material. The characteristics that define type are typeface, style, and size. Selecting the appropriate type for your Web pages' text is part of the design process.

Font Sizes and Styles

A **typeface** is a group of alphabetic characters, numbers, and symbols with the same design, such as the slant and thickness. You might be familiar with two of the commonly used typefaces in word processing — Times New Roman and Arial. Figure 5-1 illustrates these two commonly used typefaces along with three others out of the thousands of typefaces that exist.

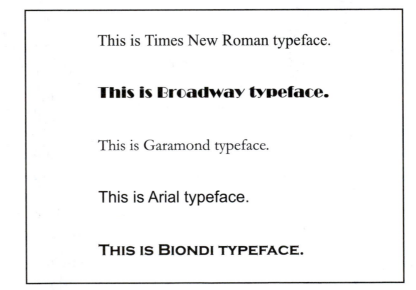

This is Times New Roman typeface.

This is Broadway typeface.

This is Garamond typeface.

This is Arial typeface.

THIS IS BIONDI TYPEFACE.

Figure 5-1 A typeface is a group of characters with a common design.

Type style refers to the variations in form such as roman (regular), italic, or bold. In desktop publishing, **type size** is measured in points, where 72 points = 1 inch. In digital publishing, font size is sometimes measured in pixels, where 16 pixels equals approximately a 12-point font. Your experience with word-processing software has likely made you familiar with setting the style and point size of text. In typography, a specific combination of typeface, style, and size is called a **font**. For example, the general name *Times New Roman* refers to a typeface, and the more specific *Times New Roman, 12-point bold* indicates a font. Figure 5-2 illustrates three fonts.

@SOURCE

Typography
For more information about the rules of good typography, visit the Web Design 4 Chapter 5 Student Online Companion Web page at **www .cengagebrain. com**, and then click Typography in the @Source links.

Q&A

What are leading, tracking, and kerning?
Leading refers to line spacing, or the amount of vertical space between lines of text; more line spacing generally means greater readability. Tracking is a spacing technique that allows designers to squeeze or stretch text, as necessary, to fit in a specific amount of space. Kerning adds or removes space between two individual characters.

This is the Times New Roman 12-point (regular) font.

THIS IS THE BIONDI 14-POINT BOLD FONT.

This is the Arial 16-point italic font.

Figure 5-2 In typography, a font is a specific combination of typeface, style, and size.

Font Selection and Web Design

In Web design, the term *font* is generally used interchangeably with *typeface*, to identify a group of characters with the same design. Identifying the best font for your Web pages requires considering how your font selection will affect visitors' reading speed and comprehension. You also need to consider whether your site's visitors will be able to view a specific font because a browser can only display fonts that are installed on the visitor's computer. In addition, your font selection can help establish the mood of your site — from lighthearted and fun to serious and professional. As a designer, you should evaluate potential fonts based on readability, availability, and the mood you want to promote.

READABILITY   Fonts can be grouped into five generic font types: serif, sans serif, cursive, fantasy, and monospace fonts. Cursive, or script, fonts replicate handwriting; fantasy fonts are used for decoration; and monospace fonts, which have equal spacing between characters, simulate characters created on a manual typewriter. Cursive, fantasy, and monospace fonts might not be appropriate for most Web page text because it can be difficult to read them online. Another reason to avoid cursive or fantasy fonts is that specific examples of these fonts are not widely available across different operating systems. The most common fonts used in Web design are serif or sans serif.

Some fonts, like Times New Roman, have a short line extending from the top or bottom of a character called a **serif**; research indicates that the serif helps the reader's eyes move across a line of text being read word for word. Fonts that do not have serifs, such as Arial, are called **sans serif** fonts. Some Web designers consider a serif font more difficult for visitors to scan and prefer to use sans serif fonts for Web page text. Figure 5-3 illustrates characters in the Times New Roman serif font and the Arial sans serif font.

Q&A

What are the Web Accessibility Initiative (WAI) guidelines for font selection?
The WAI guidelines state that you should use CSS and the font-family, font-style, font-weight, and font-size properties to specify fonts instead of the HTML <font> tag and its attributes. When you specify a font, such as Verdana, you should also specify an alternative generic font, such as sans serif.

@SOURCE

Serifs and Readability
For more information about research on the sans serif and serif readability debate, visit the Web Design 4 Chapter 5 Student Online Companion Web page at **www .cengagebrain.com**, and then click Serifs and Readability in the @Source links.

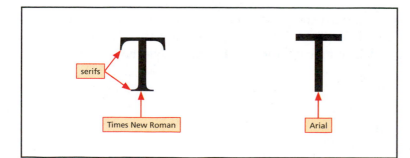

Figure 5-3 A serif is a short line extending from the top or bottom of a character.

Web-Safe Fonts
For more information about Web-safe fonts, visit the Web Design 4 Chapter 5 Student Online Companion Web page at **www.cengagebrain.com**, and then click Web-Safe Fonts in the @Source links.

Many site designers ensure the readability of their site's content by using a Web-safe font. A **Web-safe font** is a commonly available font that most site visitors' browsers will be able to display. Examples include Arial, Times New Roman, Impact, Tahoma, and Verdana. WYSIWYG editors allow you to specify a **font family** (Figure 5-4), which includes a default Web-safe font and backup font types, including a generic serif or sans serif font, to ensure that browsers can recognize the font used in your page or replace it with one of the backups if your page's font is not available on the user's browser.

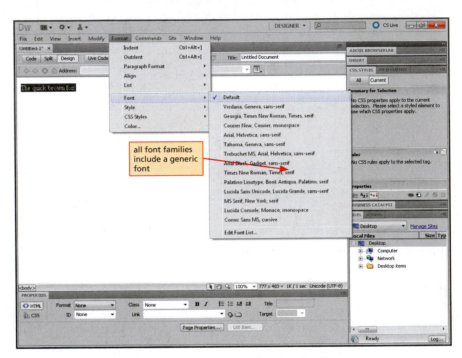

Figure 5-4 WYSIWYG editors allow you to specify a font family.

What are TrueType, PostScript, and OpenType fonts?
TrueType is a font standard used by Windows and Macintosh operating systems. PostScript is a font standard developed by Adobe Systems for PostScript printers. OpenType is a newer font standard that incorporates TrueType and PostScript fonts for Windows and Macintosh operating systems.

Sans serif fonts are a popular choice of many Web designers; however, the use of sans serif fonts to enhance the readability of Web pages is not universal. As you browse the Web, you will find pages using both serif and sans serif fonts. Despite a number of research studies, no clear direction exists regarding serifs and online readability. Although some early studies point to sans serif fonts as more readable for online text, more recent studies suggest that style, size, spacing between characters, contrast, white space, line length, readers' familiarity with the font, and other characteristics might play a larger role in readability than the presence or absence of serifs.

Web browsers have both a default font and a default font size setting. If you do not specify a font or font size using an HTML tag and attributes or CSS properties and values, browsers will use their default font to display text. Times New Roman is the default font for both Microsoft Internet Explorer and Mozilla Firefox, as shown in Figure 5-5. The default font size for both Internet Explorer and Firefox is 16 pixels.

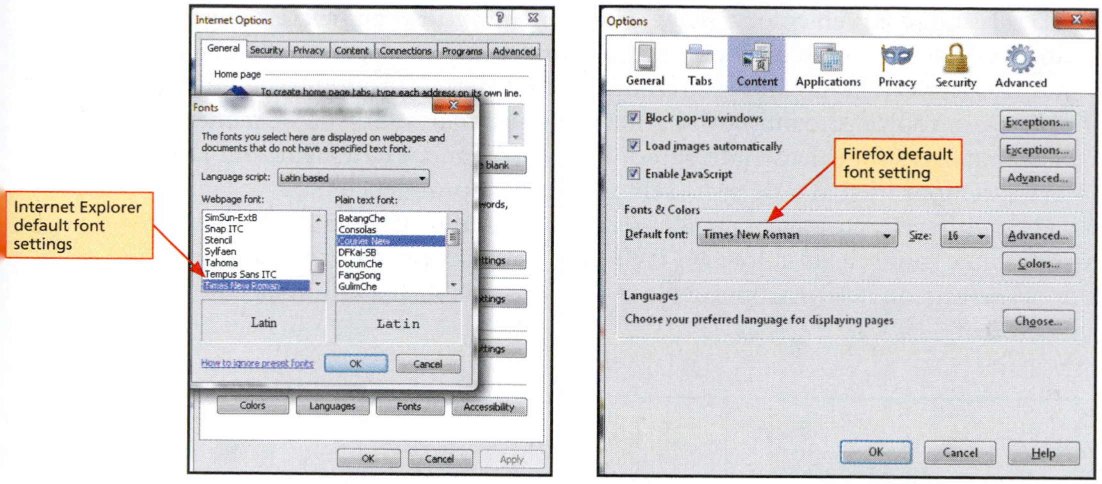

Figure 5-5 Times New Roman is the default font for both Internet Explorer and Firefox.

Font size also plays an important role in your selection of a font. A Web page's font size can be expressed as an absolute size or a relative size. **Absolute font sizes**, which might not change when visitors change their browser font size settings, are measured in inches, points, centimeters, millimeters, and picas. Absolute font sizes are used by designers who want to maintain control over the size of page text. **Relative font sizes** are specified in pixels (relative to the viewing screen) or as a percentage in relation to the font size of surrounding text, a percentage of an em unit, where one **em unit** equals the font size. You also can specify relative font size with a keyword, such as medium or large. Using relative font sizes allows visitors to control font size by changing their browsers' font size settings. Absolute or relative font sizes specified in a Web page's markup overrides the Web browser default size setting.

Use bold and italic font styles for emphasis. For example, apply the bold font style to paragraph headings or important words in paragraph text. Take care, however, not to overuse the bold and italic font styles. Recall from Chapter 2 that you should never use underlining for emphasis, as underlining typically indicates a link. Additionally, avoid using all uppercase characters for words or phrases, as this can reduce scannability.

AVAILABILITY   Computer operating systems, such as Windows, Macintosh, or Linux, provide sets of installed fonts; however, these font sets often differ across operating systems. For example, one survey of commonly used fonts by operating system indicates that the Arial font was available on 96 percent of the surveyed computers running the Windows or Macintosh operating systems but available on only 64 percent of surveyed computers running Linux. In the same survey, the Verdana Web font was available on 96 percent of surveyed computers running Windows, 93 percent running Macintosh, and only 53 percent running Linux. Therefore, when specifying a font for your pages, choose a Web-safe font to reduce the instances of browser font substitution. If a specific font effect is absolutely necessary, for example as part of a logo, consider saving the font as an image using image-editing software.

@SOURCE

Font Size
For more information about absolute and relative font sizing, visit the Web Design 4 Chapter 5 Student Online Companion Web page at **www .cengagebrain.com**, and then click Font Size in the @Source links.

@SOURCE

Font Survey
To learn more about commonly used fonts by operating system, visit the Web Design 4 Chapter 5 Student Online Companion Web page at **www .cengagebrain.com**, and then click Font Survey in the @Source links.

Specify commonly used fonts for your Web pages to increase your chances of overriding default browser font settings. Before publishing your Web pages, test your font and font sizes in different browsers and on different operating systems.

DESIGN TIP

@SOURCE

Fonts and Accessibility

For more information about fonts and Web accessibility, visit the Web Design 4 Chapter 5 Student Online Companion Web page at **www.cengagebrain.com**, and then click Fonts and Accessibility in the @Source links.

MOOD Just like a Web color scheme, your font selection can help establish an emotional connection with your visitors by contributing to a specific mood or state of mind. A site's mood should always promote and not detract from the site's message. For example, a topical site on snowboarding or a site that offers online games for preteens requires a font that contributes to a mood of fun, excitement, and challenge. However, the font used at a B2B site selling technical products or services must send a very different message — one of seriousness and professionalism. Figure 5-6 illustrates how font selection for two Web sites — an investment company and the children's television network Nickelodeon — helps establish a different state of mind for site visitors.

font choices contribute to a serious mood at an investment site

font choices contribute to a fun mood at a kids' entertainment site

Figure 5-6 Fonts can help set the mood for a visitor's Web site experience.

YOUR TURN

Exploring Fonts

1. Visit the Web Design 4 Chapter 5 Student Online Companion Web page at **www.cengagebrain.com**, and then click links in the Your Turn section to the following sites to review how fonts and font sizes are used at each site:

   a. Vitabot.com

   b. Toshiba Direct

   c. Yahoo! Kids

2. Review the home page and two underlying pages at each site. How are fonts and font sizes used to set the mood for site visitors?

3. Create a report that explains how the site's choice of fonts, font styles, and font sizes does or does not set a mood that matches the site's content and message.

Image Text

Some image-editing software packages, such as Adobe Photoshop CS5, contain features that allow you to create and edit horizontal or vertical text as part of an image. For example, you can add headlines or larger text paragraphs to an image and then use editing tools to give the text shape, color, fade effects, or opacity to make the image more interesting.

Adding text to an image is much like working with Web page body text or text in a word-processing document. First, you select an editing tool that allows you to type the text. Then, you select the font, font size, font style, and font color options you want for your text, click an area of the image where you want the text to appear, and type your text. The text appears in a box, called a **bounding box**; the shape of the bounding box can also be altered to add interest. Figure 5-7 illustrates image text created in Adobe Photoshop CS5. Although text can add excitement and interest to an image, remember that images alone should not be used to convey information on a Web page. Make certain that the information you are trying to convey with image text is also present as body text and as alternative text that can be read and interpreted by assistive technologies, such as screen readers.

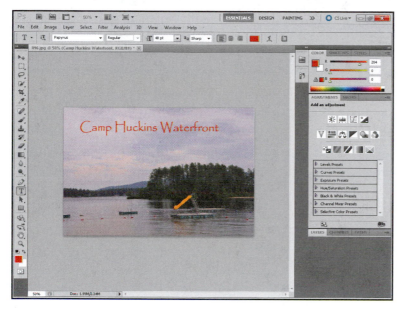

Figure 5-7 Text can add interest to an image.

Web Page Images

In Chapter 3, you learned how Web page images — clip art, illustrations, diagrams, and photographs — can personalize and familiarize the unknown, deliver a message, and prompt visitors' actions. When you select images, be sure you select high-quality, relevant images that achieve the following:

- Add value to your Web site.
- Match or complement your Web site's color scheme.
- Accurately represent the content to which they link, if used for image mapping.
- Contribute to the overall mood you want to set and support the site's message.

Be creative in the use of images on your Web pages. For example, tilt a photograph slightly in image-editing software to add visual interest to a page. Besides enlivening a page, a tilted photograph creates welcome white space between it and the text. Similarly, removing a photograph's background will produce an eye-catching silhouette that can serve as a focal point.

Keep Web accessibility in mind as you select images for your Web pages. Include redundant text links for image maps and add an alternative text description for each image.

DESIGN TIP

Remember to follow best practices for images and Web usability and accessibility: include redundant text links for image map links, add an alternative text description for each image, and avoid background images that obscure text. Also make sure to use images to which you own the copyrights, or, if necessary, secure the copyrights and give proper credit to the image owner or creator.

YOUR TURN

Exploring the Effective Use of Web Page Images

1. Visit the Web Design 4 Chapter 5 Student Online Companion Web page at **www.cengagebrain.com,** and then click links in the Your Turn section to the following sites to review the home page and at least three underlying pages at each site:

   a. NASA Kids' Club
   b. NOAA Ocean Explorer
   c. AICPA
   d. Jordan's Furniture

2. Review how the site uses images. Do the images add value? Do they match or complement the color scheme? If image maps are used, do the images accurately represent their links' target pages? Do the images contribute to the overall mood of the site and promote the site's message?

3. Write a report that summarizes your review. Be prepared to discuss your report in class.

You can acquire images for your Web site by creating your own image files or, as you learned in Chapter 3 when you researched available stock photographs, by purchasing images from offline or online stores. If you are creating your own images, you will use some combination of these four tools: a digital camera, a scanner, screen capture software, and illustration software.

Digital Cameras

@SOURCE

Digital Photography
For a quick review of digital photography terminology, visit the Web Design 4 Chapter 5 Student Online Companion Web page at **www.cengagebrain.com**, and then click Digital Photography in the @Source links.

Whereas a traditional camera captures images on film that must be processed in a photo lab, a **digital camera** records an image electronically, storing images as digital files. The photographer can review images taken with a digital camera while they are still in the camera, thereby allowing the photographer to reshoot the picture if needed or desired. Because there are no expenses associated with purchasing or developing film, the photographer can take as many shots as necessary to get the perfect one. Digital cameras store images internally or on memory cards or other storage devices; digital images can then be transferred from the camera to your computer. Many smartphones or mobile devices come with a digital camera built-in.

The transfer process from camera to computer varies depending on the camera and the storage method. You can download internally stored images using a connecting cable from the camera to the computer. You can also transfer images stored on memory cards using a wireless or connected reading device. Images on CDs/DVDs can be copied from a computer's CD/DVD drive to an internal hard drive. After the images have been transferred to your computer, you can manipulate and fine-tune them using image-editing software.

The pixel capacity of today's digital cameras typically ranges from 3 to 13 **megapixels** (millions of pixels) per image. Digital cameras with the higher megapixel ratings are often used to produce larger, quality images, such as 8×10 inch and larger prints. Cameras with higher megapixel ratings, such as field cameras and studio cameras, are typically more expensive and are used by photojournalists and professional studios, respectively. Moderately priced cameras in the 7–10 megapixel range, such as the models illustrated in Figure 5-8, will likely produce images suitable for your Web pages.

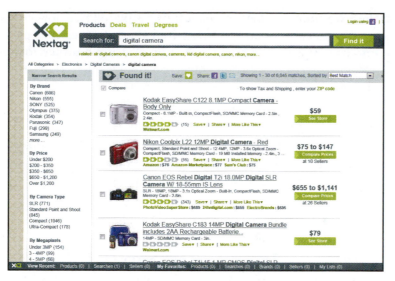

Figure 5-8 An affordable digital camera will produce acceptable images for Web pages.

Megapixel Test
To see the impact variations in megapixels have on digital image quality, visit the Web Design 4 Chapter 5 Student Online Companion Web page at **www .cengagebrain.com**, and then click Megapixel Test in the @Source links.

If purchasing a new digital camera, you should familiarize yourself with your camera's features and modes. Read the manual with your camera in hand to understand all the buttons and switches. Most digital cameras offer auto options for the majority of their settings. If this is your first digital camera, take advantage of the auto options until you have the time to explore the potential advantages and greater control of the customized settings. Remember to transfer your digital images from your camera to your computer's hard drive. Then back up the stored images from your hard drive to a second storage device, such as a CD/DVD or flash drive.

Exploring Digital Cameras

YOUR TURN

1. Visit the Web Design 4 Chapter 5 Student Online Companion Web page at **www .cengagebrain.com**, and then click links in the Your Turn section to the following sites to shop for new digital cameras:

   a. BizRate

   b. Shopzilla

   c. NexTag

2. Review three cameras using information from each site: a low-cost digital camera for less than $200, a medium-priced camera in the range from $200 to $500, and a camera that costs more than $500.

3. Summarize your research in a report. Use a table to compare camera features and cost. Assume that, as a professional Web designer, you often shoot digital images for your Web design projects. Choose one of the three cameras most suitable for your Web design projects. Give the reasons for your choice.

Scanners

A second method to create your own Web page images is to use a scanner to save an electronic copy of a printed image on your computer's hard drive. A **scanner** is a computer input device that reads printed text or images or objects and then translates the results into a file that a computer can use, such as an image file. Three commonly used scanners — flatbed, sheet-fed, and drum — handle the item to be scanned in different ways.

Scanners
For more information about the scanner as a computer input device, visit the Web Design 4 Chapter 5 Student Online Companion Web page at **www .cengagebrain.com**, and then click Scanners in the @Source links.

With a **flatbed scanner**, the image to be scanned is placed face down on a glass surface, and a scanning mechanism passes under it. A **sheet-fed scanner** pulls the object to be scanned into its stationary scanning mechanism. A **drum scanner** rotates the object to be scanned around its stationary scanning mechanism. Drum scanners are typically very expensive and are used primarily by large graphic design and advertising firms. A flatbed scanner is the most commonly used type of scanner.

When you scan images, you should do the following:

- Scan photos and illustrations at approximately the size at which they will be displayed on your Web pages unless you plan to edit them. If so, scan the image a little larger to make it easier to manipulate, and then resize it appropriately when you save it.

- Scan illustrations at 256 colors. Scan photos at higher color settings such as thousands or millions of colors.

- Save scanned images in **Tagged Image File Format (TIFF)**, a standard file format for scanning and storage, which can be edited and saved multiple times without losing quality. When saved in this format, the images are your source files that later must be converted into one of three image file formats for use on the Web. You learn more about image file formats later in this chapter.

Screen Capture Software and Illustration Software

You can use **screen capture software**, such as SnagIt® (Figure 5-9), !Quick Screen Capture®, and FullShot®, to create an image of computer screen contents. Designers use computer screen captures, also called **screen shots**, in print media (like the computer screen illustrations in this text) and online to show the contents of a computer screen at a point in time, for example, on technical blogs, Web page software tutorials, and technical support Web pages. Some screen capture software also contains features for editing the images.

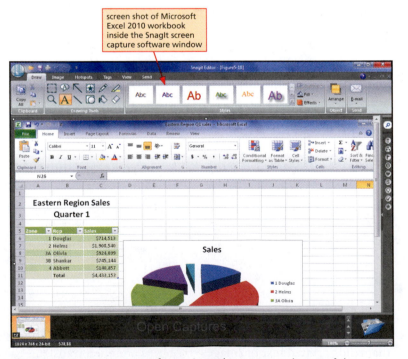

screen shot of Microsoft Excel 2010 workbook inside the SnagIt screen capture software window

Figure 5-9 Screen capture software is used to create an image of the contents of a computer screen.

Illustration software, such as Adobe Illustrator® (Figure 5-10), Xara Xtreme®, and Microsoft Expression Design® 4, is used to create images, such as diagrams and drawings, by drawing shapes, lines, and curves. Images created in illustration software are defined by mathematical statements regarding the drawing and positioning of the shapes, lines, and curves. You learn more about images created using illustration software in the next section.

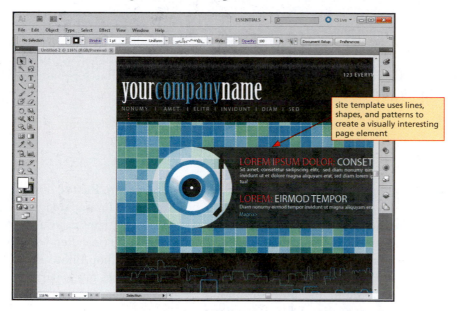

Figure 5-10 Designers use illustration software such as Adobe Illustrator to draw shapes, lines, and curves and then combine them into an image.

If limitations of time, available resources, or expertise prohibit you from creating your own images, various sources for already-created graphics files are readily available. You can search by category, such as sports or medicine, and by photo type (clip art and photography, for example) to purchase digitized images on CD/DVD or from an online store. WYSIWYG editors, image-editing software, or illustration software often provide sample images or drawing templates. You might also be able to download images offered for a fee at some Web sites or download public domain images, such as those found at many U.S. government Web sites. Sites such as morgueFile.com (Figure 5-11) include archives of artist-provided images available for free and with limited copyright restrictions. Always be aware of copyright restrictions when you download images from the Web.

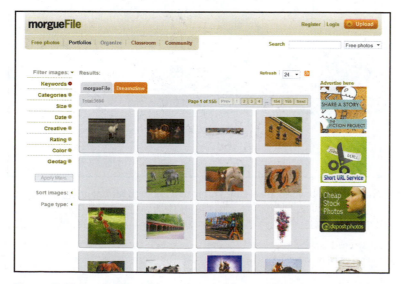

Figure 5-11 Searchable archives of images from multiple artists are available on the Web.

Before downloading photos or illustrations from the Web, ensure that you are not violating copyright restrictions or incurring royalty or licensing fees for the images' use.

Additionally, you should carefully read the Terms and Conditions for Use statement before you download images. You might be required to provide a back link to the page that offers the image, or you might be asked to add a credit line for photographs, even those in the public domain.

Image File Formats

Q&A

Why are raster images called bitmaps?

Raster images are called bitmaps because they are created a bit at a time; one bit equals one screen pixel.

Image files are grouped into two categories: raster and vector. **Raster images**, also called **bitmaps**, are created pixel by pixel. Figure 5-12 illustrates a bitmap image of decorated corks zoomed to show the individual pixels in the image. Bitmaps can be created and edited in **image-editing software**, such as Microsoft Paint® (installed with the Windows operating system), Adobe Photoshop CS5, and Corel PaintShop Photo Pro X3.

A bitmap contains a specific number of pixels measured as pixels per inch (ppi) and is **resolution dependent**, meaning it cannot be resized in image-editing software without losing some image quality. A **file extension** — a period (.) and a file format identifier — is added to a file's name when the file is saved electronically. Bitmap files are commonly referenced by their file extensions, such as GIF or JPEG, as shown in Figure 5-13. You can save an image created originally in one bitmap format in another bitmap format using the Save As command in your image-editing software.

Figure 5-12 Individual pixels are visible in a zoomed bitmap image.

Bitmap Formats and File Extensions

Format	File Extension
Windows Bitmap	.bmp
Graphics Interchange Format	.gif
JPEG File Interchange Format	.jpg or .jpeg
Portable Network Graphics	.png
Macintosh	.pict
PC Paintbrush Exchange	.pcx
Tagged Image File Format	.tiff
Adobe Photoshop	.psd

Figure 5-13 Bitmap images are commonly referenced by their file extensions.

Vector images, also called **vector graphics**, consist of a group of separate drawing objects, such as shapes, curves, and lines, combined to create a single image, as shown in Figure 5-10 on page 137. You can resize a vector image with no loss of image quality; thus, vector images are called **resolution independent**. Illustration software, which you learned about in the previous section, is used to draw vector images. Vector image file extensions are often native to the illustration software, such as *.ai* for Adobe Illustrator.

To use vector images on the Web, you convert them to bitmap images by saving them in a bitmap file format, a process called **rasterizing**. Additionally, some of today's powerful illustration and image-editing software, such as CorelDRAW® Graphics Suite X5 and Adobe Photoshop CS5, contain features for working with both vector and bitmap images. The images you choose for your Web site will likely be in the Graphics Interchange Format, Joint Photographic Experts Group, or Portable Network Graphics bitmap formats supported by popular Web browsers.

Graphics Interchange Format (GIF)

The **Graphics Interchange Format (GIF)** bitmap image file format was created by CompuServe in the late 1980s. The GIF image file format was the original image format used on the Web. All modern browsers support the GIF image format, which contains a compression algorithm that reduces file size. GIF images are 8-bit color images, meaning they are saved with a maximum of 256 colors. This color limitation makes the GIF format inappropriate for complex images, such as photographs. GIFs are most suitable for basic, solid-color images, such as cartoons, diagrams (Figure 5-14), and navigation buttons. A GIF image can be interlaced, transparent, and animated.

Q&A **What type of image is created with screen capture software, digital cameras, and scanners — bitmap or vector?** Images created with screen capture software, digital cameras, or scanners are bitmaps.

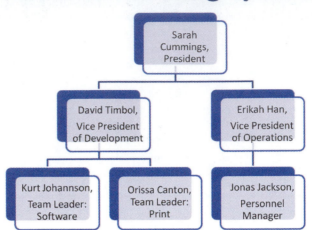

Figure 5-14 GIFs are most suitable for basic, solid-color images, such as cartoons, diagrams, or navigation buttons.

An **interlaced GIF** image appears on the screen in a sequence of passes. Each pass displays the whole image at a higher resolution than the previous pass. Gradually, the image changes from blurry to distinct. An interlaced GIF gives a preview of the image to come without extensively affecting file size. Interlacing, which produces insignificant results when applied to small images, should be reserved only for large images. The benefit of an interlaced GIF is that for visitors with slower dial-up connections, it can provide some idea of what an image looks like as it downloads. For the increasing numbers of visitors with a broadband connection, there is no advantage to interlaced GIF images because of the greatly increased download speed. You can turn on or off a single color in a **transparent GIF** image, such as the image background color, allowing the Web page background color to show through. Image-editing software is used to create both interlaced and transparent GIFs. You will learn about animated GIFs in Chapter 6.

JPEG File Interchange Format (JFIF)

The **Joint Photographic Experts Group (JPEG)**, an international committee sponsored by the International Organization for Standardization (ISO) standards organization, published the **JPEG File Interchange Format (JFIF)** image compression format standard, which today is commonly referred to as the JPEG image format. The JPEG image format is used for digital photographs, photolike paintings, watercolors, and complex illustrations requiring more than 256 colors. JPEG image files, containing millions of colors, are saved in a compressed format, creating smaller files with some loss of quality that is generally not apparent to viewers. Because of smaller file sizes, JPEG images are a good choice for photographs and other high-quality digital images used on Web pages. Figure 5-15 illustrates a JPEG image.

@SOURCE

Image File Formats
For more information about image file formats, visit the Web Design 4 Chapter 5 Student Online Companion Web page at **www .cengagebrain.com**, and then click Image File Formats in the @Source links.

Q&A

What is antialiasing?
Antialiasing of fonts and bitmap images is a technique for smoothing jagged edges by adding shaded pixels that make the image appear to have smooth lines and curves.

Figure 5-15 The JPEG image file format is appropriate for photographs or photo-like art.

Q&A

What are the Camera Raw (RAW) and Scalable Vector Graphics (SVG) image formats?
A RAW image format is the raw data or "digital negative" recorded by a digital camera; RAW image formats might vary by camera manufacturer. Scalable Vector Graphics (SVG) is a vector image format developed by the W3C for XML documents; SVG might play a greater role in Web page images in the future.

A **progressive JPEG** is similar to an interlaced GIF and appears on the screen in a sequence of passes with progressively improved image quality, allowing the viewer a preview of the image. You can specify the number of passes in a progressive JPEG. Like interlaced GIFs, progressive JPEGs might be suitable if your target audience is using slow dial-up Internet access and you want them to be able to preview a lower-quality image before the higher-quality image completely downloads in the browser. However, at broadband access speeds, progressive JPEG images lose their usefulness.

Use the GIF image format for basic, solid-color images that do not require more than 256 colors, such as cartoons, diagrams, and navigation buttons. Use the JPEG image format for photographs or art-like images.

DESIGN TIP

Portable Network Graphics (PNG) Format

As the popularity of GIF images on the Web grew, CompuServe and Unisys, the company that developed the technology used to compress GIFs, announced that anyone using GIF images had to pay a license fee for doing so. The **Portable Network Graphics (PNG)** image format was developed as a free open source image format to replace the GIF format. (Note that the Unisys compression patents expired in 2004; license fees for using GIFs are no longer required.) The PNG format has advantages over the GIF format in two primary ways:

- Greater range of colors than the GIF format; the PNG format supports more than 16 million colors
- Superior transparency capabilities

Whether PNG images will replace GIF images for Web images is still largely undecided. Lack of browser support for PNG was a major reason that designers did not use PNG images in the past; however, current versions of today's most popular browsers do provide support for the PNG format.

YOUR TURN

Exploring Web Image File Formats

1. Using the search tool of your choice and the keywords *image file formats* or similar keywords, search the Web for articles that describe image file formats for the Web.

2. Create a presentation for the class that describes the most commonly used image file formats. Include a discussion of the pros and cons of each format and when, as a Web designer, you would use each format.

@SOURCE

Image Files
For more information about working with image files, especially PNG images, visit the Web Design 4 Chapter 5 Student Online Companion Web page at **www.cengagebrain.com**, and then click Image Files in the @Source links.

Web-Ready Images

Creating **Web-ready images** involves using image-editing software to refine and enhance the images as necessary, selecting the right format for the type of image — for example, selecting the GIF format for a diagram with less than 256 colors or the JPEG format for a photograph with millions of colors — and then optimizing the images to find the balance between the smallest possible image size and the highest possible quality.

Although more and more of your site's visitors are likely connecting with high-speed broadband, it is possible that some of your site's visitors might still be using much slower dial-up or high-speed dial-up connections. Images that are not optimized for size might contribute to excessive Web page download times, leading to frustration on the part of visitors still using slower connections. Additionally, images that are not optimized for size are not an efficient use of server storage space. Finally, images that are not optimized for quality will give your site an unprofessional appearance and will detract from your site's message. You can use image-editing software to optimize your images by achieving a balance between compressing your image files into a smaller size and maintaining the best possible image quality.

Refining Your Images

You can use image-editing software to refine your images to improve their quality. For example, if an image contains more subject matter than you want to include, you can use image-editing software to crop the image. When you **crop** an image, you select the part of the image you want to keep and remove the unwanted portion. Another benefit of cropping an image is reduced file size. Figure 5-16 illustrates cropping an image in Adobe Photoshop CS5.

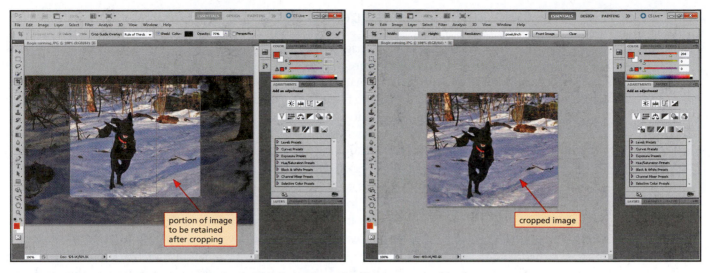

Figure 5-16 Cropping an image creates a focal point and reduces the file size.

> **DESIGN TIP**
>
> Cropping an image can eliminate distracting background elements and establish the focal point. Discarding unwanted portions of an image also results in a smaller file size.

Image-editing software has image-enhancement features ranging from predetermined, automatic settings to very precise, sophisticated, customizable adjustments. For example, you can manipulate the levels of shadows and highlights in an image. Additionally, you can use image-editing software to correct an image that is too dark, blurry, or has unwanted spots or markings. Figure 5-17 illustrates enhancing a photograph using the Smart Photo Fix feature in Corel PaintShop Pro.

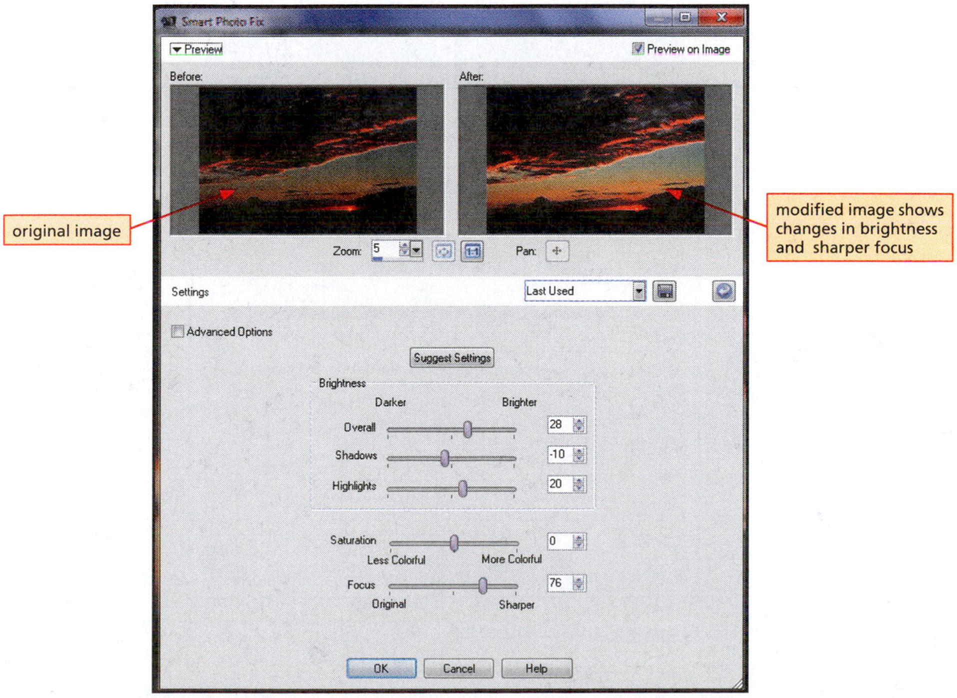

Figure 5-17 Image-editing software offers various image-enhancement features.

Optimizing Your Images for Size and Quality

The three most popular image file formats for Web pages — GIF, JPEG, and PNG — all contain a compression feature that reduces the size of an image file when the file is saved. The GIF and PNG formats offer **lossless compression**, meaning all the image data is retained when the image file is compressed during the save process. Image data retention ensures that the quality of the image is maintained. However, as you have learned, the GIF format is not suitable for photographs or images containing more than 256 colors. The PNG format supports millions of colors, but creates files that might be too large for efficient Web page downloading. Some designers suggest using the PNG format for editing photographs or other images containing millions of colors, but then saving the images in the JPEG format to reduce the file size.

The JPEG format provides **lossy compression**, meaning that some image data is permanently lost during compression. Using a low level of compression results in a loss of data that is undetectable by the human eye; there is no apparent deterioration in the image quality. You can control the level of JPEG compression with digital camera settings or by using the optimizing feature in image-editing software, such as Adobe Photoshop CS5.

JPEG compression values and the resultant image quality have an inverse relationship: the greater the compression value, the smaller the file size — but the poorer the image quality. If you are selecting a JPEG image compression value for your Web page images and your primary concern is image quality, a lower compression value will result in a higher image quality, but at the cost of a larger file size. If, on the other hand, you are more concerned about file size, a higher compression value will result in smaller, faster-loading image files, but at a greater loss of image data, called image degradation or **compression artifacting**. Compression artifacting can result in areas of an image that are blurred or distorted. Figure 5-18 illustrates the "before" and "after" of a JPEG image file with a compression value of 20 percent.

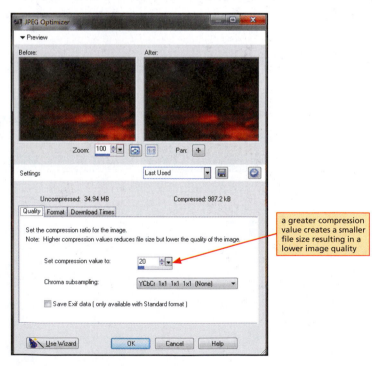

Figure 5-18 The greater the compression value, the poorer the image quality.

Note that each time you reopen, edit, and resave a JPEG image, the compression artifacting or loss of data increases and becomes more visible in the image. To protect image quality in an image that will require multiple edits, some designers suggest saving the image in a lossless compression format, such as TIFF, PSD, PNG, or RAW, until your editing is complete, then saving the image in the JPEG format to reduce its file size. Although it is important to keep a backup copy of all your original unedited images, it is critical to do so for a JPEG image. Because of the progressive compression artifacting that takes place each time a JPEG is saved, you should use a copy of the original unedited JPEG file if you need to start over with your editing.

DESIGN TIP You should make a copy of your unedited original image and consider doing interim edits in a lossless compression format, such as TIFF, PSD, PNG, or RAW. Save your image in a lossy format, such as JPEG, only after you have finished editing.

Many popular image-editing software packages contain features for manually or automatically optimizing images for use on Web pages. You can use these optimization features to help find the best balance between image file size and image quality. Figure 5-19 illustrates the Adobe Photoshop CS5 Save for Web & Devices dialog box with four quality settings of the same JPEG image: Very High, High, Medium, and Low quality settings. Figure 5-20 summarizes the file size, estimated download speed, and quality value for each of the four quality settings.

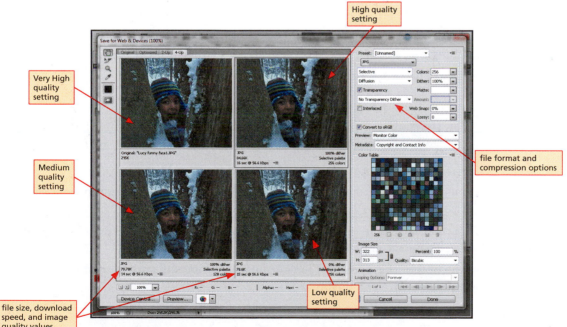

Figure 5-19 Image-editing software packages, such as Adobe Photoshop CS5, contain features to help you optimize your image files for size and quality.

JPEG Compression and Image Quality Comparison

Image #	Quality Setting	File Size	Download Speed @28.8Kbps	Quality Value
1	Very High	116.5K	42 seconds	80 quality
2	High	71.68K	26 seconds	60 quality
3	Medium	37.89K	14 seconds	30 quality
4	Low	23.18K	9 seconds	10 quality

Figure 5-20 The relationship between file size, estimated download speed, and image quality can be previewed in the Adobe Photoshop CS5 Save for Web & Devices dialog box.

Image-editing software provides the capability to refine and optimize any image — whether from a digital camera, scanned from a photograph, created with illustration software, or purchased from a business that sells predesigned images.

YOUR TURN

Exploring Image-Editing Shareware and Freeware

1. Using the search tool of your choice and the keywords *image-editing shareware* or similar keywords, identify at least two image-editing shareware (free to try and then purchase) or freeware (free to use) packages.
2. Compare the features offered in each package and, if possible, find professional reviews of each software package. With permission from your instructor, download and try a shareware or freeware image-editing software package. Explore ways to refine an image and optimize an image for size and for quality.
3. Prepare a presentation for your class that summarizes your research.

Remember to follow these general guidelines when preparing Web-ready images:

- Determine the appropriate image file format for your Web page images.
- Refine your images using enhancement features in your image-editing software.
- Refine and edit your image files in a lossless compression format, such as TIFF or PNG; then save them one time in a lossy compression format, such as JPEG, after all the editing is completed.
- Use the optimization features in your image-editing software to optimize your image files for size and quality.

Chapter Review

Text for Web pages is most effective when you follow the rules of good typography — the appearance and arrangement of the characters that make up text. The features that define type include typeface, type style, and type size. A font comprises the combined features of typeface, style, and size. As a Web designer, you should evaluate potential fonts based on the readability and availability of the font and the mood you want to promote.

If you are creating your own images, you can use these four tools: a digital camera, a scanner, screen capture software, and illustration software. You can also purchase or locate free predesigned images online.

When you select images, be sure you select quality and relevant images that add value to your Web site, match or complement your Web site's color scheme, accurately represent the content to which they link (if used as an image link), contribute to the overall mood you want to set for visitors, and support the site's message. Choose GIF, JPEG, or PNG compression file formats in which to save your images and, if using image-editing software, take advantage of the built-in file optimization features. Creating a Web-ready image involves refining the image, selecting the right format for the type of image, and then optimizing the image for both image size and image quality.

After reading the chapter, you should know each of these Key Terms.

TERMS TO KNOW

absolute font sizes (131)	raster images (138)
bitmaps (138)	rasterizing (139)
bounding box (132)	relative font sizes (131)
compression artifacting (144)	resolution dependent (138)
crop (142)	resolution independent (139)
digital camera (132)	sans serif (129)
drum scanner (136)	scanner (136)
em unit (131)	screen capture software (136)
file extension (138)	screen shots (136)
flatbed scanner (136)	serif (129)
font (138)	sheet-fed scanner (136)
font family (130)	Tagged Image File Format (TIFF) (136)
Graphics Interchange Format (GIF) (139)	transparent GIF (140)
illustration software (137)	type (128)
image-editing software (138)	type size (128)
interlaced GIF (140)	type style (128)
Joint Photographic Experts Group (JPEG) (140)	typeface (128)
JPEG File Interchange Format (JFIF) (140)	typography (128)
lossless compression (144)	vector graphics (139)
lossy compression (144)	vector images (139)
megapixels (134)	Web-ready image (142)
Portable Network Graphics (PNG) (141)	Web-safe font (130)
progressive JPEG (141)	

TEST YOUR KNOWLEDGE

Complete the Test Your Knowledge exercises to solidify what you have learned in the chapter.

Matching Terms

Match each term with the best description.

___ 1. resolution dependent

___ 2. lossy compression

___ 3. rasterizing

___ 4. interlaced GIF

___ 5. relative font sizes

___ 6. PNG

___ 7. JPEG

___ 8. bitmap

___ 9. megapixels

___ 10. bounding box

___ 11. compression artifacting

___ 12. serif

___ 13. crop

___ 14. scanner

___ 15. font family

a. The combined features of a typeface, type size, and type style.

b. A computer input device that reads printed text, images, or objects and then translates the results into a file that a computer can use.

c. A file compression method that results in permanent removal of image data.

d. Images created pixel by pixel; also known as raster images.

e. Where text added to an image appears.

f. A(n) _____ image contains a specific number of pixels and cannot be resized without losing some image quality.

g. A short line extending from the top or bottom of a character.

h. An image that appears on the screen in a sequence of passes.

i. Convert a vector image to a bitmap for use on the Web by saving the image in a bitmap file format.

j. To remove portions of an image in order to focus on certain objects.

k. The font size specified as a percentage in relation to the font size of surrounding text.

l. The image file format most suited for photographs.

m. An image file format originally designed to replace the GIF file format.

n. The loss of image data during file compression that can result in areas of an image that are blurred or distorted.

o. Millions of pixels per digital camera image.

Short Answer Questions

Write a brief answer to each question.

1. Describe typography and define the characteristics that define type.

2. Compare the terms *typeface* and *font* as used in typography.

3. Describe the five generic typeface or font families.

4. Discuss the role of readability when determining Web site fonts.

5. Discuss the role of availability when determining Web site fonts.

6. Describe the three primary image file formats used for the Web.

7. List four factors to be considered when selecting relevant, high-quality images for Web pages.

8. Describe four tools you can use to create your own Web page images.

9. Compare and contrast lossless and lossy compression methods for image files and identify which image file types provide lossless compression and which provide lossy compression.

10. Describe how to optimize your images to create Web-ready images; discuss four ways to help ensure your images are Web ready.

Test your knowledge of chapter content and key terms.

To complete the Learn It Online exercises, start your browser, click the Address bar, and then visit the Web Design 4 Chapter 5 Student Online Companion Web page at **www .cengagebrain.com**. When the Web Design Learn It Online page is displayed, click the link for the exercise you want to complete and then read the instructions.

Chapter Reinforcement TF, MC, and SA

A series of true/false, multiple-choice, and short-answer questions that test your knowledge of the chapter content.

Flash Cards

An interactive learning environment where you identify chapter key terms associated with displayed definitions.

Practice Test

A series of multiple-choice questions that test your knowledge of chapter content and key terms.

Who Wants To Be a Computer Genius?

An interactive game that challenges your knowledge of chapter content in the style of a television quiz show.

Wheel of Terms

An interactive game that challenges your knowledge of chapter key terms in the style of the television show *Wheel of Fortune*.

Crossword Puzzle Challenge

A crossword puzzle that challenges your knowledge of key terms presented in the chapter.

Investigate current Web design developments with the Trends exercises.

Write a brief essay about each of the following trends, using the Web as your research tool. For each trend, identify at least one Web page URL used as a research source. Be prepared to discuss your findings in class.

1 | Digital Cameras

Research the latest digital camera specifications for mobile devices. Compare the highest-quality mobile device cameras to digital cameras available on the market. Choose one mobile device that has a scanner and answer the following questions:

- How would you transfer the images to a computer that has image-editing software?
- Can you make choices such as resolution, zoom, and more with the camera?
- Would the digital camera be sufficient to create Web-ready images?

2 | Typography, Images, and Visual Identity

As you learned in Chapters 2 and 3, using design to establish a visual identity or brand for a corporation or organization can contribute to widespread recognition of the corporation's or organization's products and/or services. Locate a real-world Web site of your choice that has a very well-known visual identity (for example, a recognizable logo, such as Coca Cola, or font, such as Disney). Discuss how typography and image selection contribute to the Web site publisher's visual identity and brand.

Challenge your perspective of Web design and surrounding technology with the @Issue exercises.

Write a brief essay in response to the following issues, using the Web as your research tool. For each issue, identify at least one Web page URL used as a research source. Be prepared to discuss your findings in class.

1 | A Question of Integrity

Image-editing software is constantly evolving, thereby increasing designers' capabilities to apply highly sophisticated techniques. Cloning, editing, blending, and image-correction tools can reconfigure an image so even experts have difficulty perceiving whether the image was altered. The negative aspect to these evolving capabilities is the potential to misrepresent reality. One example is placing an individual in a photo to suggest he or she was present when the photo was taken. This capability to alter images raises the question of integrity. Identify one or two legal and moral issues surrounding misrepresentation using altered images. In addition, discuss the responsibility of Web designers to protect against misrepresentation using altered images.

2 | Optimizing Images for Web Sites

What do you need to consider when optimizing images for use on a Web site? Using your experience with an image-editing software program (such as Adobe Illustrator), or using information gathered from the Web site of an image-editing software program, list the program-specific features and tools that would help you create and edit images for the Web.

Use the World Wide Web to obtain more information about the concepts in the chapter with the Hands On exercises.

1 | Explore and Evaluate: Typographic Principles and Visual Identity

Browse the Web to locate a Web site that has correctly applied typographic principles, and then locate a Web site that has not applied typographic principles. Evaluate each to see how the application of typographic principles helps the site achieve or prevents it from achieving visual identity.

a. Identify the basic typographic principles that have and have not been applied to each Web site.

b. Discuss what, in your opinion, is the potential effect of the two sites' typography on first-time visitors.

c. Describe how the use of typographic principles contributes or does not contribute to the site's visual identity.

d. With your instructor's permission, print the Web pages you review.

2 | Search and Discover: Images in the Public Domain

Use the Bing search engine to identify sources of images in the public domain. Create a list of public domain image sources, including the site name, URL, type of images, and required credit information, if any.

Work collaboratively to reinforce the concepts in the chapter with the Team Approach exercises.

1 | Web-Safe Font Families

Use your favorite search tool to find a list of Web-safe fonts and font families. Join with another student to create a research team whose objective is to create a two- or three-page reference handout for the class. The handout should include the font name, have the font style applied to create a visual reference, and determine the type of font family the font belongs to (serif, sans serif, etc.). In addition, group similar fonts together to create three font families of different types. Each font family should include three similar fonts and a generic font.

2 | Applaud Creativity

The creative use of appropriate Web page images is encouraged in this chapter. Join with two classmates to explore ways to use image-editing software to enhance images in creative ways. Using personal images or sample images provided by your image-editing software, prepare a presentation for class that demonstrates examples of creative image editing.

**CASE
STUDY**

Apply the chapter concepts to the ongoing development process in Web design with the Case Study.

The Case Study is an ongoing development process using the concepts, techniques, and Design Tips presented in each chapter.

Background Information

In this Case Study assignment, you begin to create, gather, and prepare some of the content you have determined in your site plan that will help achieve your Web site's goals and objectives. First, you need to review guidelines and principles presented in this chapter and previous chapters. Specific sections for review are detailed in the assignment.

Chapter 5 Assignment

1. Review the guidelines in Chapter 2 for writing for the Web. Then, use word-processing software to create the text for your Web pages. Remember to check the text's spelling and grammar. If possible, wait at least one day after creating your text before proofing your pages, and have at least one other qualified person proof your pages.

2. Determine the fonts you will use for your Web page text. Select no more than three fonts.

3. Gather or create value-added images for your Web site. Ensure that your images are free of copyright or usage restrictions.

4. Prepare your Web-ready images by using image-editing software to refine the images and then optimize them for size and quality.

5. Save your text and images in the appropriate folders in the directory structure you have created for your Web site on your computer's hard drive.

6. Save a backup copy of your files on an external storage device.

6 Multimedia and Interactivity Elements

Introduction

Now that you know how to develop a site plan and understand the rules of good typography and the methods to prepare and optimize images for your Web site, the next step is to learn how to use multimedia and interactive elements to enhance your Web pages. Multimedia elements, including audio and video, add interest and excitement to a site, whereas interactive elements allow you to connect with your target audience. Multimedia and interactive elements can make an average Web site into a great one by providing a means for collecting feedback from and entertaining your site visitors.

If you choose to include multimedia elements, you can find ready-made elements available for purchase or for free on multimedia e-commerce and sharing sites. With the proper tools and expertise, you can also create your own multimedia elements. You can develop interactive elements in-house or purchase them from vendors.

Objectives

After completing this chapter, you will be able to:

1. Explain Web page multimedia issues

2. Describe types of Web page animation

3. Discuss adding and editing Web page audio and video elements

4. Identify ways to effectively use interactive elements

Multimedia Issues

@SOURCE

Multimedia
For more information about multimedia on the Web, visit the Web Design 4 Chapter 6 Student Online Companion Web page at **www .cengagebrain.com**, and then click Multimedia in the @Source links.

In Chapter 3, you learned that multimedia elements are typically some combination of text, images, animation, audio, and video used to produce stimulating, engaging Web page content, as shown in Figure 6-1. Video clips can play an interview that supports a news story or demonstrate how to use a product correctly. Audio can be used to extend a personal greeting or teach the proper pronunciation of a foreign language. WYSIWYG editors, such as Expression Web and Dreamweaver, include tools for incorporating multimedia with ease; popular browsers support the plug-ins needed to view and play most multimedia elements.

Q&A

What is a podcast?
A podcast is digital audio or video available to listen to remotely. Originally called Webcasts, they are more commonly known as podcasts due to the popularity of the Apple® iPod® player. Examples of podcasts include radio shows, interviews, and classroom lectures. NPR offers a library of podcasts available to download or stream to a remote device or computer.

Figure 6-1 The ABC Web site effectively incorporates multimedia elements: text, images, animation, video, and audio.

Although multimedia is widely used in Web design, it is not essential, and many well-designed Web sites achieve their objectives without it. Drawbacks associated with using multimedia include longer download time for visitors using slower connections, the need for browser plug-ins, and the use of substantial storage space on your site's server. In addition, multimedia elements might not be accessible for visitors with disabilities, such as those who have hearing or visual impairments, and multimedia also might not run successfully on certain mobile devices. Lastly, creating the professional quality multimedia seen on such Web sites as the ABC site often exceeds the expertise and budget of many designers.

Rather than including multimedia in your site, a better option might be to link to multimedia elements in their source program or site. For example, linking to a video on YouTube enables you to show the video while maintaining a link to its original source. Linking to the original source not only maintains a connection to the video's credit information (author, etc.), but also enables the video to play in the Adobe Flash Player, without any additional programming or support from you (Figure 6-2). Other sites such as Flickr (photography) and Rhapsody (music) enable you to add a link to your blog or site to the media they host.

Q&A

What are the Web Accessibility Initiative (WAI) guidelines for multimedia?
Within your Web pages, you should provide a text equivalent for every nontext element, such as animated GIFs, Flash movies, or other audio or video elements.

original site includes
link to YouTube videos

YouTube
window opens
to play videos

Figure 6-2 Linking to a YouTube video opens a window that includes the video player and source information.

Use multimedia sparingly for distinct purposes. Ensure that it adds value, supports your Web site's message, and satisfies target audience expectations for content at your site.

DESIGN TIP

Optimizing multimedia elements for efficient Web delivery is discussed later in this chapter. However, consider these general guidelines for using multimedia at your site:

- Give site visitors a choice of high- or low-bandwidth content, such as audio instead of video.
- List any necessary plug-ins and provide links to locations where they can be acquired.
- Provide text equivalents for all multimedia elements to meet accessibility standards.
- Do not waste bandwidth on an uninteresting video clip with little action when an audio clip alone will convey the real content of value.
- When developing original multimedia, break audio or video files into short segments to create smaller files.

Animation

Web page animation can effectively catch a visitor's attention, demonstrate a simple process, or illustrate change over time, such as the metamorphosis of a butterfly. You can purchase ready-to-use animated elements on CD/DVD or download such content from countless Web sites, such as the two sites shown in Figure 6-3. Be selective when choosing ready-to-use animated elements. Overused, cutesy elements will make your Web site look amateurish. Select only those ready-to-use animations that will promote your site's message and satisfy your target audience's expectation for content at your site.

Figure 6-3 Select ready-to-use animations that promote your site's message and satisfy your target audience's expectation for content.

Web page animation can take many forms, for example, animated GIFs, Flash movies, avatars, and gadgets.

Animated GIFs

You were introduced to animated GIFs in Chapter 3. Animated GIFs are popular and prevalent Web elements. An animated GIF is a single file in which separate images within multiple **animation frames** are stored. Displaying these animation frames in sequence over a specified time interval, usually stated in **frames-per-second** or **fps**, gives the illusion of movement or animation. An individual animated GIF file also contains the instructions and timings to display the image in the browser.

Animated GIFs, like standard GIFs, include up to 256 colors and support transparency. Popular browsers support animated GIFs without requiring a browser plug-in. Conservative, selective use of animated GIFs can add visual appeal to your Web pages. Like other types of animation, animated GIFs should be used only when doing so supports your Web site's message and meets your target audience's expectation for content at your site. If you choose to use animated GIFs, consider limiting them to one per Web page to avoid distracting and annoying your site visitors.

@SOURCE

Animation
For more information about the use of animation on the Web, visit the Web Design 4 Chapter 6 Student Online Companion Web page at **www .cengagebrain.com**, and then click Animation in the @Source links.

You can download inexpensive software specifically designed to create animated GIFs, such as Easy GIF Animator® and GIF Construction Set Professional™, as shareware (try and purchase). You can also use high-end image-editing software, such as Adobe Photoshop CS5, to create animated GIFs. GIF animation software or the animation feature in image-editing software makes creating animated GIFs a quick, simple process. Some GIF animation software contains wizards, which are step-by-step instructions for creating commonly used animated GIFs, such as banners and buttons. Figure 6-4 illustrates the frame-by-frame preview of an animated GIF button created with a button wizard in the Easy GIF Animator software.

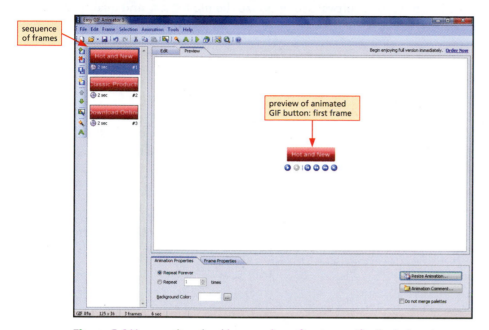

Figure 6-4 You can download inexpensive software specifically designed to create animated GIFs as shareware from vendor Web sites.

In general, when creating animated GIFs, you do the following:

1. Identify in sequential order the GIF images you want to animate. You can use predesigned GIF images or you can create original images using illustration or image-editing software. Some animated GIF software allows **tweening**, in which you only create a beginning and an ending animation frame; the software creates all the animation frames in between.

2. Specify the time interval between frames, typically in seconds or fractions of a second.

3. Specify if the animation should **loop** (repeat). *Remember that endlessly looping animations annoy most visitors.*

4. Set background transparency, if desired.

5. Test the animation and make color, transparency, timing, and looping adjustments as necessary.

Using multiple animated GIFs or an endlessly looping animated GIF can distract and annoy visitors. Follow good design practice and include no more than one animated GIF per Web page, and limit the number of loops.

DESIGN TIP

To optimize your animated GIFs for size and quality, apply the following guidelines:

- Plan ahead to determine the essential animation effects that you want to achieve to limit the number of animation frames.
- Limit image colors for each frame to the same or similar palette of colors selected from the available 256 colors. When possible, decrease the bit depth or number of colors of images. Instead of 8-bit/256 colors, experiment to see if 6-bit/64 colors or 4-bit/16 colors yields satisfactory images.
- Crop unwanted pixels from the image.
- Use GIF animation or image-editing software to optimize the file for size and quality when saving or exporting it.

YOUR TURN

Exploring Animated GIFs

1. Using the search tool of your choice and the keywords *animated GIFs* or similar keywords, locate resource sites for animated GIFs. Identify the URLs of three resource sites that offer royalty-free or low-cost animated GIFs.

2. Identify one royalty-free animated GIF that would be suitable for a C2C auction Web site. With permission from your instructor, download the animated GIF and save the file to your computer's hard drive.

3. Write a report for your instructor discussing your research. Name the source of the animated GIF you chose and describe it. Explain how including the animated GIF on a Web page at a C2C auction site supports the site's message and meets target audience expectations for a C2C auction site.

Q&A

Can Flash movies be created in software other than Adobe Flash CS5?
Yes. A number of software packages, such as SWiSH Max4, SWiSH Video3, and Camtasia Studio®, are available to create Flash movies from scratch or to convert other elements, such as video or Microsoft PowerPoint slide shows, into Flash movies for the Web.

Adobe Flash Professional CS5 and Microsoft Silverlight

In Chapter 3, you were introduced to Flash animation or movies. Adobe Flash Professional CS5 is a powerful, efficient software tool for creating sophisticated Flash movies for use on the Web. Flash movies have wide browser and operating system support and can be used to create an entire Web site or to generate quick-loading, scalable vector animations, which adjust to different browser sizes without degrading quality. Recall from Chapter 3 that visitors must have the Flash media player plug-in installed to view Flash movies. The plug-in is free and widely available.

Flash movies use a fast-paced presentation of changing static images to simulate motion. The changing images are recorded in frames along a timeline, as illustrated in Figure 6-5. The animation process is accomplished in Adobe Flash using either frame-by-frame animation or animation with tweening.

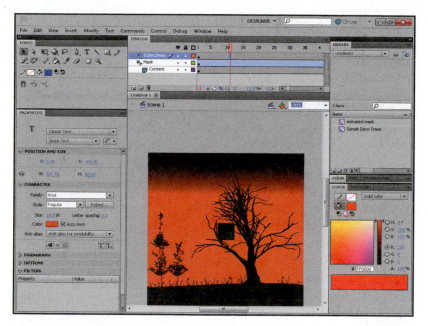

Figure 6-5 Creating sophisticated Flash movies involves placing static images in frames along a timeline.

With **frame-by-frame animation**, the designer must change the image manually, for example, by erasing a portion or increasing the size of the image. With **animation with tweening**, the beginning and ending frames identify the original and final location and/or appearance of an image. Then, the software automatically creates the necessary frames within the changing image in between the beginning and ending frames. Animation with tweening is a more expedient, less-intensive method than frame-by-frame animation.

When deciding whether to incorporate Flash movies at your Web site, consider these guidelines:

- Determine whether you have the necessary expertise and resources to create or maintain a Web site containing Flash movies. The creation of Flash movies is often part of the multimedia producer role discussed in Chapter 1.

- Use Flash movies only if they contribute to your Web site's purpose in a way that other Web site elements cannot.

- Indicate on your Web site the necessary Flash player plug-in version needed for a visitor to experience the Flash components optimally. Provide a link to the plug-in download site.

- If your site has a Flash introduction — a Flash movie entry or splash page — provide an option to skip it and view your site's home page. *Remember! Viewers generally dislike entry or splash pages, even those created as Flash movies.*

@SOURCE

Flash Animation
For more information about working with Flash animation, visit the Web Design 4 Chapter 6 Student Online Companion Web page at **www.cengagebrain.com**, and then click Flash Animation in the @Source links.

Use Flash movies on your Web site or as a splash page only if they add value to the visitor's experience or enhance page content. Provide information about and links to the necessary Flash plug-in so that visitors can ensure that they can play the movie.

DESIGN TIP

Microsoft Silverlight®, illustrated in Figure 6-6 (on the next page), is a browser plug-in technology designed to play the multimedia content found in rich interactive applications. **Rich interactive applications (RIAs)** are Web-based computer applications that contain interactive multimedia elements. Desktop applications, such as word processors, provide users with a window-style interface containing menus, buttons, and so forth while the application's internal instructions are stored on the user's hard drive. RIAs use a browser window for the application's user interface, and the application's internal instructions are stored on an application server. Silverlight is a cross-browser and cross-platform RIA plug-in, which means that you can use it on virtually any personal computer using most popular browsers.

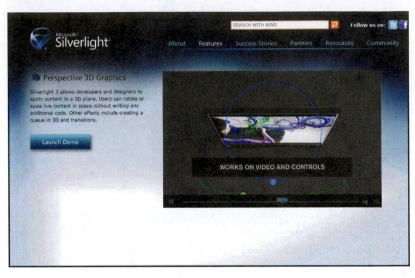

Figure 6-6 Microsoft Silverlight is a plug-in developed for rich interactive applications.

Avatars

In Chapter 1, you learned that millions of gamers interact with each other by playing massively multiplayer online games (MMOGs) or by participating in 3D virtual worlds. These gamers create **avatars — alternative personas** or **virtual identities** for MMOGs or 3D virtual worlds. You might also find avatars used in e-mail marketing campaigns, on business or personal blogs, or at e-commerce Web sites. For example, some B2C clothing retailers, such as Sears and Lands End, provide visitors with avatars, called **virtual models**, which are used to "try on" clothing before purchasing it. MyVirtual Model, shown in Figure 6-7, is a B2B e-commerce company that provides the technology B2C retailers use to enable site visitors to create virtual models and "try on" clothing in virtual dressing rooms.

Figure 6-7 Web site avatars are used by some B2C retailers as virtual models that enable visitors to try on clothing in virtual dressing rooms.

At other e-commerce Web sites, avatars are used to welcome site visitors, provide a "virtual salesperson" to promote products and services, personalize customer support responses, direct visitors to specific Web site pages, provide instructions for Web page tutorials, and so forth. E-commerce avatars might be created as animated GIFs or as Flash movies. Web sites, such as SitePal (Figure 6-8) or Media Semantics, provide low-cost tools you can use to quickly create an avatar and then copy and paste the HTML code for the avatar to your site's pages.

Figure 6-8 Web sites such as SitePal provide low-cost tools to quickly create and maintain e-commerce avatars.

Exploring E-Commerce Avatars

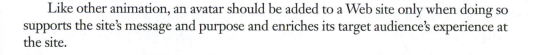

YOUR TURN

1. Using the search tool of your choice and the keywords *Web site avatars* or similar keywords, research designing, creating, and publishing an e-commerce avatar to a Web site. Review online demonstrations, if provided by a vendor.
2. Create a presentation discussing your research for your class. Discuss the pros and cons of using an e-commerce avatar. Assume you are designing a Web site for a B2B company that sells computer programming services. The company's sales manager wants to use an avatar to introduce the site. Explain the process of adding an avatar to the site and discuss the tools you might use to create and maintain the avatar. Lastly, describe the role the avatar has in enhancing the site visitor's experience.

Like other animation, an avatar should be added to a Web site only when doing so supports the site's message and purpose and enriches its target audience's experience at the site.

Gadgets

You were introduced to **gadgets**, also called **widgets**, in Chapter 3. Web site gadgets are small code objects that provide dynamic Web content: clocks, weather reports, breaking news headlines, and so forth. You might be familiar with gadgets that can be added to the Windows 7 computer operating system's desktop using the Windows Desktop Gadgets engine. Where appropriate, for example on a personal Web page or a blog, you might choose to add a gadget to display the current weather or to launch a slide show to add interest or enhance your visitors' Web site experiences. To add a gadget, you can copy and paste HTML code to your page from a source such as Google Gadgets, shown in Figure 6-9.

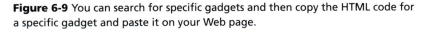

Figure 6-9 You can search for specific gadgets and then copy the HTML code for a specific gadget and paste it on your Web page.

DESIGN TIP
E-commerce avatars and Web page gadgets can add interest to a Web site; however, both should only be used to further the site's message and purpose and enrich its target audience's experience at the site.

The guidelines for when to incorporate gadgets on your Web pages are the same as for the other types of animation discussed in this section.

YOUR TURN

Exploring Web Page Gadgets

1. Using the search tool of your choice and the keywords *Web page gadgets* or similar keywords, research sources for Web page gadgets. Identify different gadgets suitable for personal, organizational/topical, and e-commerce Web sites.

2. Create a presentation of your research for your class. Include a discussion of the gadget resources you reviewed, the types of gadgets suitable for the three types of Web sites, the guidelines for including a gadget on a Web page, and how to add a gadget to a Web page.

Audio and Video Elements

Web audio and video either can be downloadable or streaming. As you learned in an earlier chapter, you must store downloadable media in its entirety on your computer before you can listen to or watch it. In contrast, streaming media begins to play as soon as the data starts to stream, or transfer from the server to the browser. In addition to this distinction, each media type has specific advantages and disadvantages, which are illustrated in Figure 6-10.

Advantages of Downloadable Media	Disadvantages of Downloadable Media	Advantages of Streaming Media	Disadvantages of Streaming Media
Once the file has been downloaded, it can be accessed again and again.	Downloading media can take long periods of time, depending on the speed of the Internet connection and the size of the file.	Users have random access to the data, meaning they can choose the file portion they want to play using the player's control buttons.	Streaming media has very high bandwidth requirements.
Downloadable media utilizes the HTTP protocol to transfer the data, and therefore does not require a specific media server.	Typically, the file is extremely large, resulting in both a long download time and considerable storage space being consumed on the user's computer.	Streaming media consumes RAM only while being played and is purged after viewing.	Streaming media frequently requires a specific media server to transfer the data.

Figure 6-10 Advantages and disadvantages of downloadable and streaming media.

Be careful to avoid copyright infringement when incorporating music at your Web site. For example, including music on your Web site from a music CD without permission violates the artist's copyright.

DESIGN TIP

Audio Elements

Adding audio files to your Web pages — either by providing a Web page link to download an audio file or embedding the audio file in the page's HTML coding — can add sound effects, entertain visitors with background music, deliver a personal message, or sell a product or service with testimonials. Sources of Web-deliverable audio include royalty-free audio files that can be downloaded from the Web or audio files and message creation services you can purchase from vendors. The e-commerce avatars and Flash movies that you learned about in the previous section also often use audio.

@SOURCE

Audio
For more information about including audio files at a Web site, visit the Web Design 4 Chapter 6 Student Online Companion Web page at **www .cengagebrain.com**, and then click Audio in the @Source links.

Many visitors consider Web page background music to be annoying. Only include background music when it supports your site's message and the mood you want to achieve. If you include background music, you should also include a control that turns the music off or on.

DESIGN TIP

You also can create your own audio files. An audio message is an audio file used to deliver specific information. If your personal computer is equipped with an appropriate sound card, a high-quality microphone, and speakers, you can create your own audio messages easily and inexpensively. In addition to the appropriate computer hardware and sound card, you will also need to use audio-recording software, such as RealNetworks' Real-Producer® or Audacity® (freeware) audio-recording and editing software. Ensure that your recordings are high in quality; poor-quality audio is a surefire way to turn off your audience.

YOUR TURN

Exploring Audio Message Products and Services

1. Using the search tool of your choice and the keywords *Web site audio* or similar keywords, research vendors that provide audio message creation and hosting services.

2. Report on your research to your class by comparing and contrasting the products or services offered by at least three vendors. Assume that you are creating an organizational Web site for a client who wants to use an audio introduction on their home page. Select the vendor that, in your opinion, offers products or services appropriate for creating and maintaining the client's audio message.

@SOURCE

Streaming Audio and Video
To learn more about how streaming audio and video work, visit the Web Design 4 Chapter 6 Student Online Companion Web page at **www.cengagebrain.com**, and then click Streaming Audio & Video in the @Source links.

Streaming audio begins playing as the audio is delivered by the server, and is often offered in one of three popular formats: RealAudio, Windows Media, or QuickTime. Visitors must have the RealNetworks' RealPlayer® (Figure 6-11), Windows Media Player®, or Apple QuickTime Player® plug-in installed to listen to audio in these three formats, respectively. To stream audio, your Web page files must be stored on a server that also has streaming software to deliver the audio stream when requested by the browser.

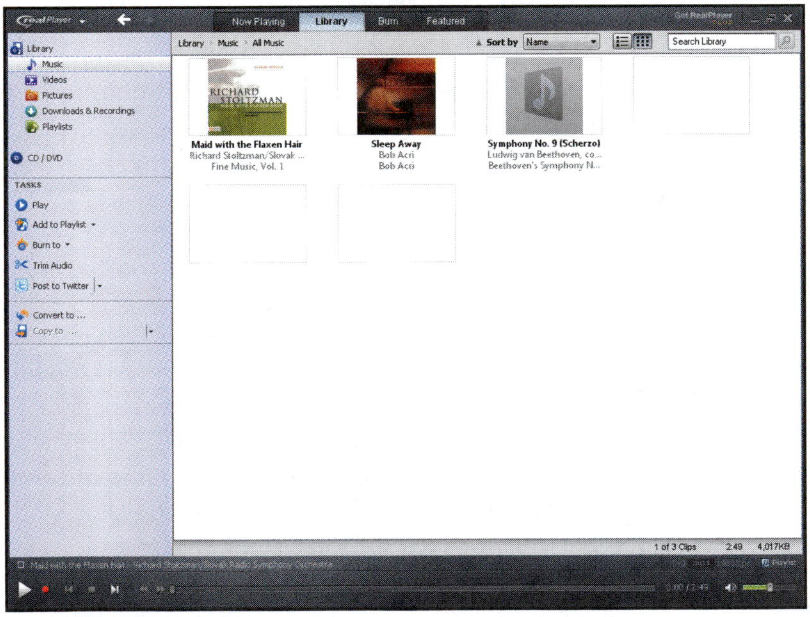

Figure 6-11 RealPlayer is used for playing streaming audio.

EDITING AUDIO FILES　Although you might never edit audio files, understanding certain aspects of audio file editing can help you make better choices when selecting audio files for your Web site. Audio must be in digital format to be used on the Web. Analog audio files can be digitized, or **encoded**, using sound-editing software, such as Audacity or WaveLab 7®. You edit digital audio files by manipulating certain audio aspects, including message size and audio channel selection. Keep in mind these guidelines for creating and editing audio files for the Web:

- Keep recorded audio messages or music clips short; shorter audio messages equal smaller files. Include only necessary content in the audio message.

- Select a mono audio channel to reduce file size; **mono (one-channel)** and **stereo (two-channel)** are the two more well-known audio channels. Selecting a mono audio channel reduces the file size approximately by half over a stereo audio channel. A mono audio channel is also the best choice for an audio message. Whether to choose mono or stereo for a music file depends in part on the desired sound quality and the type of file compression.

- Use an 8 kHz sampling rate for voice-only audio and 22 kHz sampling rate for music audio. The **sampling rate**, measured in kilohertz (kHz), refers to the amount of samples obtained per second during the conversion from analog to digital sound. For example, a sampling rate of 48 kHz yields higher quality audio and also a much bigger file than a sampling rate of 11.127 kHz or 8 kHz.

- Use an 8-bit audio file for voice and 16-bit audio file for music. **Bit depth** is a measure of audio quality; the greater the number of bits, the higher the audio quality level, but the larger the file.

Video Elements

Downloadable or **streaming video** can create a powerful impact, but the efficient delivery of streaming video over the Internet is a challenge. File size is a much greater issue with video than with audio because of the enormous amount of data necessary to describe the dual components of video and audio.

Before you add video to your site, first consider simpler alternatives to video, such as animation or audio. If you decide that only video will best further your Web site's purpose, you can download royalty-free video files from the Web, purchase them from an online store or on CD/DVD, or create your own video files with a good quality **digital camcorder** and video-editing software, such as Adobe® Premiere® Pro CS5, Pinnacle Studio™ Ultimate version 14, or Windows Movie Maker® (Figure 6-12), installed with the Windows 7 operating system.

@SOURCE

Video
For more information about including video files at a Web site, visit the Web Design 4 Chapter 6 Student Online Companion Web page at **www.cengagebrain.com**, and then click Video in the @Source links.

@SOURCE

Streaming Media
For more information about streaming media, visit the Web Design 4 Chapter 6 Student Online Companion Web page at **www.cengagebrain.com**, and then click Streaming Media in the @Source links.

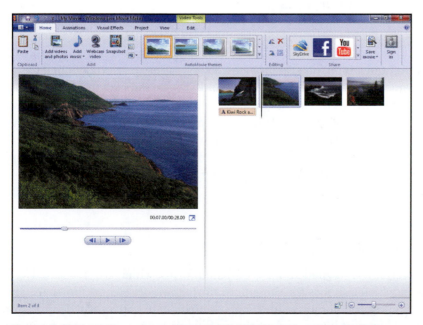

Figure 6-12 You will need a good-quality digital video recorder as well as video-editing software, such as Windows Movie Maker, to create and edit videos.

YOUR TURN

Exploring Video-Editing Software

1. Using the search tool of your choice and the keywords *video-editing software* or similar keywords, research at least three video-editing software packages. Compare the features and cost for each package. Make certain that each software package has features for creating videos for the Web.

2. Write a report for your instructor that discusses the results of your research. Include a recommendation, based on your research, for purchasing a video-editing software package.

Q&A

What is a screencast?
A screencast is a video of a computer screen's changing content over time and is used for Web-based training videos and demonstrations. Software such as Camtasia Studio is used to create a screencast.

@SOURCE

Optimizing Video
For more information about how you can optimize video files, visit the Web Design 4 Chapter 6 Student Online Companion Web page at **www.cengagebrain.com**, and then click Optimizing Video in the @Source links.

EDITING VIDEO FILES   You can manipulate certain aspects of video — frame size, frame rate, bit depth, compression scheme, and overall video quality — to optimize Web videos. Although you might never edit video yourself, understanding these aspects can help you make informed choices about including video at your Web site. You learned about the concept of frames in the previous sections on animation and Flash movies. For Web-based videos, consider the following:

- The common frame sizes are 160×120 or 240×180 pixels; the **frame rate** for Web video ranges from 10 to 15 frames per second (fps).

- As with audio, the greater the number of bits or bit depth, the bigger the file size. If you decrease a video segment from 16-bit to 8-bit, the file size will decrease significantly, as will the quality. Experiment with different settings to find a balance that is acceptable.

- You can define the general quality level of your video, which automatically adjusts the compression. If you define the quality between low and medium, you will achieve a good balance between sufficient compression and video quality that is suitable for the Web.

Interactive Elements

In Chapter 2, you learned that a well-designed Web site should include elements, where appropriate, that enable the site publisher and site visitors to engage in interactive, two-way communication. You also learned about a variety of elements that can be used to promote interactivity, such as contact pages and Web-based forms.

Web-based forms allow visitors to submit information to a site publisher using e-mail or directly to a database. Scripting languages, applets, and servlets play a role in creating interactive elements, such as rollover buttons or games, for Web pages. Enabling your visitors to post comments to an article allows you to get feedback about their opinions about the topic. Many e-commerce sites encourage communication and promote interactivity by using live chat.

Web-Based Form Guidelines

In Chapter 2, you learned about Web-based forms, which are structured Web documents in which a site visitor can enter information or select options. As you also learned in Chapter 2, common form elements include text boxes, check boxes, option buttons, drop-down list boxes, and a Send or Submit button. Forms are frequently used to obtain comments and feedback or to order products or services.

Breaking your form into multiple form pages can help by breaking the information into smaller, screen-sized forms. One benefit is that if a visitor makes an error on one part of the form, he or she only has to go back to that page to find and fix the error. An example of multiple, sequential form pages is an e-commerce site shopping cart. A series of shopping cart form pages allows an online shopper to review purchases, enter shipping information (name, address, and phone number), enter billing information (credit card number, holder's name and address, and an authorization code, if necessary), and, finally, verify entered information and submit the form.

To create attractive, usable Web-based forms, you should:

- Require that visitors complete fields containing essential information before the form can be submitted. Prompt visitors to provide the missing information. Required information might include name, address, telephone number, and e-mail address. Optional information might include position title, income, or marital status.

- Make text boxes large enough to hold the approximate number of characters for a typical response. Restrict responses to characters or numbers or both as appropriate.

- Use check boxes to allow users to submit more than one response to a query.

- Provide space for additional comments or requests for further information.

- Use color to highlight and segment information.

- Include a reset button so that the user can clear the form quickly and reenter the information if necessary.

- Add a button that allows the visitor to confirm the information he or she has entered in the form.

- Send an e-mail confirmation notice assuring the user that the form data was received.

JavaScript, Applets, and Servlets

JavaScript, applets, and servlets are all programming tools that Web designers use to create interactive content elements. JavaScript, which you learned about in Chapter 1, is a scripting language that Web designers can use to create customized interactive Web pages. JavaScript is frequently used to verify form information and to create rollover buttons, advertising banners, and pop-up windows. Programmers insert JavaScript scripts directly into a page's HTML code. *Although a number of Web sites offer free JavaScript scripts for rollover buttons and banners, you should use caution before downloading any type of free dynamic content from an unknown source to prevent downloading malware to your computer.*

Applets are small programs that are designed to execute in a browser and are sent to a browser as a separate file together with the related Web page. Web designers use applets in developing games, flight simulations, specialized audio effects, and calculators. Applets do not require a browser plug-in for viewing. A **servlet** is similar to an applet; however, a servlet executes from the server instead of executing within the visitor's browser. Applets and servlets are created by programming professionals.

Blogs

In Chapters 1 and 2, you learned about blogs — online journals — as a popular way to promote Web site interactivity. Millions of Internet users are now bloggers; and thousands of businesses are learning to harness the power of blogs and blogging to promote their products and services while interacting with their customers.

@SOURCE

Malware
For more information about issues surrounding malware and how to avoid downloading malware to your computer, visit the Web Design 4 Chapter 6 Student Online Companion Web page at **www.cengagebrain.com**, and then click Malware in the @Source links.

@SOURCE

Business Blogs
For more information
about business blogs,
visit the Web Design 4
Chapter 6 Student
Online Companion
Web page at **www
.cengagebrain.com**,
and then click Business
Blogs in the @Source
links.

Sites such as Blogger, Typepad, and WordPress (Figure 6-13) provide tools you can use to quickly create a blog hosted on your own server or on the tool provider's server. Creating a blog using one of these tools can be as simple as entering an e-mail address and password, selecting a layout template for your blog, and specifying where the blog is to be hosted. You are then immediately ready to start posting to the new blog.

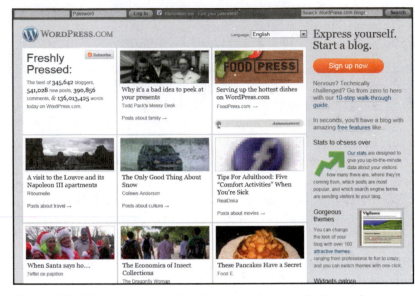

Figure 6-13 A blog is a powerful tool to enhance communication and promote Web site interactivity.

Comments

Adding a comments feature to your site enhances interactivity by enabling visitors to comment on a specific article and by creating a sense of community. News sites use blogs to allow visitors to comment on a specific article. Entertainment news sites that regularly feature recaps or information about a specific television show use the comments feature as a venue in which viewers can discuss characters, story lines, and other aspects of the show. Blogs use comments features extensively to promote interactivity. A blog such as CakeWrecks (Figure 6-14) can receive hundreds of comments per day, helping the site's creators to gauge interest in each day's posting.

Web site designers can add a blog to their site as part of a content management system or through a blog site, such as WordPress.

It is important to monitor comments posted to your Web site for spam or malicious content. Many sites have a disclaimer that anything offensive or that uses foul language will be removed. Some sites permit visitors to rate the comments made by other visitors. Spam often appears in comments as well. Having someone monitor comments before or as they are posted gives you control over any postings that might be offensive or that may contain links to malware or phishing sites. Consider requiring users to create an account before posting comments; doing so helps you keep track of or block users who may violate the code of conduct by introducing spam or using inappropriate language.

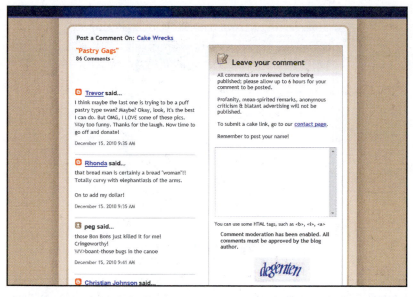

Figure 6-14 Comments features allow site creators to gauge visitors' reactions to postings on a blog or to an article.

Exploring Comment Features

1. Visit the Web Design 4 Chapter 6 Student Online Companion Web page at **www .cengagebrain.com**, and then click links in the Your Turn section to the following sites. On each site, find a recap for a specific episode of a television show and review the comments features on three entertainment sites:
   a. Entertainment Weekly
   b. TV Line
   c. ABC

2. Write a report for your instructor that describes the one show or post for each site that you wrote about. In what way do comment postings promote interactivity between the site publishers and the visitors who read and post comments to the blog? How would a site creator find these to be helpful? How do the three comment features differ and how are they similar?

Live Chat

Another popular tool for interactivity at organizational or e-commerce sites is a live chat feature. **Live chat** allows visitors to ask questions about products or services in real time. Web sites that offer live chat generally allow visitors to click a button to activate the live chat feature and open a browser window in which text messages are exchanged between the visitor and a **chat agent**, a customer service representative who handles the visitor's query. iChat agents can be in-house or they may be outsourced chat agents located in a call center. On some Web sites, the live chat feature automatically engages after a period of time and the chat window automatically opens. Figure 6-15 illustrates the live chat window at the Lands' End e-commerce site.

Q&A

What is Skype?
Skype is a software program that enables users to make voice calls or participate in videoconferences and chats over the Internet. Calls can be made between Skype users for free, or from a Skype user to a landline or mobile device for a fee.

Figure 6-15 Live chat allows site owners to interact with site visitors in real time.

DESIGN TIP   Blogs and live chat are two useful content elements that add interactivity to a Web site. If you do not operate your own servers, you can purchase hosted blog or hosted live chat software or services. You can also purchase outsourced chat agent services.

@SOURCE

Live Chat
For more information about live chat, visit the Web Design 4 Chapter 6 Student Online Companion Web page at **www .cengagebrain.com**, and then click Live Chat in the @Source links.

Businesses, such as Provide Support, CustomerReach, BoldChat (Figure 6-16), and LivePerson, offer chat software that can be installed on your own servers or hosted live chat solutions.

Figure 6-16 A number of businesses offer live chat software for installation on your own servers or hosted live chat solutions.

Exploring Live Chat

1. Using the search tool of your choice and the keywords *live chat* or similar keywords, research live chat options for a B2C e-commerce Web site. Identify at least four live chat solutions: two software solutions and two hosted solutions. Note the features and costs involved with each solution.

2. Write a report for your instructor that describes the live chat solutions you have researched. Include your recommendation for a live chat solution for a B2C Web site that hosts its own servers and a B2C Web site that requires a hosted live chat solution. Be prepared to discuss your research and recommendations in class.

Chapter Review

Multimedia is generally defined as some combination of text, images, animation, audio, and video. Interactive elements promote communication between a site publisher and site visitors. A combination of multimedia and interactive elements can generate exciting, entertaining, and more useful Web pages. Multimedia and interactive elements are not essential for the success of a Web site, and should be included on a Web site if they are used sparingly for distinct purposes, add value, further the Web site's message and purpose, and meet the target audience's expectation for content.

Effective uses of animation can include catching a visitor's attention, demonstrating a simple process, or illustrating change over time, such as the metamorphosis of a butterfly. Animated GIFs are the most popular, widely used form of animation on the Web. Free and shareware software specially designed for creating Web graphics can create animated GIFs. Adobe Flash CS5 is a powerful, efficient tool for creating simple to sophisticated Flash movies.

Web audio and video either can be downloadable or streaming. Both have distinct advantages and disadvantages. Designers should consider alternatives to video that would circumvent issues related to delivering video on the Web. Popular interactive elements include Web-based forms, avatars, gadgets, rollover buttons, and banners created with scripting languages, blogs, comments, and live chat.

TERMS TO KNOW

After reading the chapter, you should know each of these key terms.

alternative personas (160)
animation frames (156)
animation with tweening (159)
applet (167)
avatars (160)
bit depth (165)
chat agent (169)
digital camcorder (165)
encoded (164)
frame rate (166)
frame-by-frame animation (159)
frames-per-second (fps) (156)
gadgets (162)

live chat (169)
loop (157)
mono (one-channel) (165)
rich interactive applications (RIAs) (159)
sampling rate (165)
servlet (167)
stereo (two-channel) (165)
streaming audio (164)
streaming video (165)
tweening (157)
virtual identities (160)
virtual models (160)
widgets (162)

TEST YOUR KNOWLEDGE

Complete the Test Your Knowledge exercises to solidify what you have learned in the chapter.

Matching Terms

Match each term with the best description.

___ 1. WAI guidelines for multimedia

___ 2. animated GIF

___ 3. live chat

___ 4. tweening

___ 5. frame-by-frame animation

___ 6. rich interactive application (RIA)

___ 7. avatar

___ 8. Skype

___ 9. comments

___ 10. sampling rate

___ 11. applet

a. Manually creating a beginning and ending animation frame; the software creates the missing animation frames.

b. Software that enables voice calls or videoconferencing over the Internet.

c. A Web-based computer application containing multimedia elements.

d. A small program that is sent alongside a Web page and executes in the browser when the page loads.

e. A text equivalent for every nontext element.

f. A virtual identity.

g. A feature that enables site creators to gauge visitors' reactions to content.

h. The amount of samples obtained per second during the conversion from analog sound to digital sound.

i. A single file in which separate images in multiple animation frames are stored.

j. A feature that enables interactivity between a site visitor and a customer service or sales representative.

k. A Flash movie in which the image in each animation frame is manually edited.

Short Answer Questions

Write a brief answer to each question.

1. List the general guidelines for adding multimedia to a Web site.
2. Define tweening and how it is used to create objects. In your definition, include the type of object that can be created and software programs that enable tweening.
3. Discuss the guidelines for using Flash movies at a Web site.
4. Describe the roles avatars can play at e-commerce sites.
5. Discuss guidelines for adding and monitoring comments for a Web site.
6. Discuss the guidelines for creating and editing audio for the Web.
7. Write a paragraph describing how an e-commerce site would use live chat.
8. Describe how to optimize video for the Web in terms of frame size, frame rate, bit depth, compression scheme, and overall video quality.
9. Explain the design guidelines for creating attractive and usable Web-based forms.
10. Discuss how JavaScript, applets, and servlets are used to add interactivity to a Web site.

Test your knowledge of chapter content and key terms.

Instructions: To complete the Learn It Online exercises, start your browser, click the Address bar, and then visit the Web Design 4 Chapter 6 Student Online Companion Web page at **www.cengagebrain.com**. When the Web Design Learn It Online page is displayed, click the link for the exercise you want to complete and then read the instructions.

Chapter Reinforcement TF, MC, and SA

A series of true/false, multiple-choice, and short-answer questions that test your knowledge of the chapter content.

Flash Cards

An interactive learning environment where you identify chapter key terms associated with displayed definitions.

Practice Test

A series of multiple-choice questions that test your knowledge of chapter content and key terms.

Who Wants To Be a Computer Genius?

An interactive game that challenges your knowledge of chapter content in the style of a television quiz show.

Wheel of Terms

An interactive game that challenges your knowledge of chapter key terms in the style of the television show *Wheel of Fortune*.

Crossword Puzzle Challenge

A crossword puzzle that challenges your knowledge of key terms presented in the chapter.

TRENDS

Investigate current Web design developments with the Trends exercises.

Write a brief essay about each of the following trends, using the Web as your research tool. For each trend, identify at least one Web page URL used as a research source. Be prepared to discuss your findings in class.

1 | Web Site Design Trends Blogs

Find two blogs that discuss Web site design trends. On each site, find blog entries on a specific interactive feature, such as comments or gadgets. On each of the two design trends blogs, read a few entries on the subject to get information about current trends. Evaluate the blogs' interactive and site features, such as comments and multimedia. Write a report for your instructor that evaluates the blogs' interactive features. List three things that you learned from the blog's content. What does each blog do well? What changes might you make to the layout or features? Evaluate each blog as a source of information.

2 | Applets and Servlets

Research the types of JavaScript, applets, and servlets site designers can download or create to add to their site. Find two sources for reputable, safe dynamic content. List the concerns site designers and site visitors have regarding JavaScript, applets, and servlets. Discuss the advantages of including this type of dynamic content to a Web site.

AT ISSUE

Challenge your perspective of Web design and surrounding technology with the @Issue exercises.

Write a brief essay in response to the following issues, using the Web as your research tool. For each issue, identify at least one Web page URL used as a research source. Be prepared to discuss your findings in class.

1 | Viewing Multimedia on Mobile Devices

Some multimedia can be difficult to view on a mobile device due to screen size or bandwidth limitations. Find two articles that discuss considerations and new developments that will enable multimedia on a site to be viewed effectively on a mobile device. What advice would you give a site designer considering what multimedia elements to use and how to prioritize them? Be specific, including size limitations or tools to use.

2 | Broadband Availability and Impact

Recall that high-speed, always-on broadband connections include cable modem, DSL, ISDN, and satellite. Businesses and homes with broadband services find streaming media over a broadband connection to be very practical. Research and discuss the availability of broadband services across the United States and around the world. Discuss the impact that the availability of broadband services has on Web design.

Use the World Wide Web to obtain more information about the concepts in the chapter with the Hands On exercises.

1 | Explore and Evaluate: Embedding Video or Audio Content from Other Sources

Browse the Web and locate three Web sites that effectively include links to video, audio, or images from YouTube or other original sources.

a. Describe the multimedia element and explain how the element is used by a visitor.

b. Describe the advantages and disadvantages of including this type of content on your site.

c. Which of the three sites does the best job of incorporating multimedia?

d. What might you change about how any of the sites link to external multimedia sources?

2 | Search and Discover: Microsoft Silverlight and Rich Interactive Applications

Search the Web using the Google search tool to research rich interactive applications and Microsoft Silverlight or other plug-ins used to display multimedia elements in RIAs. Create a presentation for your class on rich interactive applications and RIA plug-ins. Discuss the effect of RIAs on the future of Web design.

Work collaboratively to reinforce the concepts in the chapter with the Team Approach exercises.

1 | Evaluate Forms

Join with another student to evaluate the use of multiple forms at two e-commerce Web sites.

a. Fill out the forms using fake information, but do not submit the forms. Skip information, such as your name or e-mail address, which should be required to see what kind of response is generated.

b. Describe how the forms are broken into multiple parts and what information is required.

c. Create a presentation for the class that describes the steps needed to complete the form and a review of your experience.

2 | Apply Your Knowledge

Join with two other students to form a team to identify a list of interactive elements that you should add to the Regifting sample Web site discussed in previous chapters.

a. As a team, write a report for your instructor that lists five interactive elements in the order of priority (from most to least effective).

b. For each element, briefly describe the technical skills you would need to employ to add the element.

c. For each element, describe what its purpose would be as part of your site.

CASE STUDY

Apply the chapter concepts to the ongoing development process in Web design with the Case Study.

The Case Study is an ongoing development process using the concepts, techniques, and Design Tips presented in each chapter.

Background Information

In the Case Study assignments in the previous five chapters, you have created your Web site plan, generated the text content for your Web pages, and created or gathered and optimized the images for your site.

Chapter 6 Assignment

In this chapter's Case Study, you will create your Web site. In the final part of the process, you will apply the concepts presented in this chapter and gather or create any multimedia and/or interactive elements that will help achieve your Web site's purpose. Remember that multimedia and/or interactive elements are not required elements for a successful Web site. Using the site plan you created in Chapters 3 and 4, and the guidelines in Chapters 2, 5, and 6, complete the following steps to create your Web site.

1. Choose whether you will generate your pages with HTML code and a text editor such as Notepad or with WYSIWYG software, such as Expression Web or Dreamweaver. You may use a WYSIWYG template, if desired.

2. Begin to create your Web pages. As you add your text and position your optimized images, remember the following:

   a. Apply the rules of good typography.

   b. Include alternative text descriptions for images; consider using thumbnails when appropriate.

   c. Develop your home page and underlying pages according to the defined Web site structure.

   d. To achieve unity, establish and apply a consistent page layout and color scheme for all pages at your site. Limit the color scheme to no more than three complementary colors. Most WYSIWYG software offers predefined themes. Use them if desired, but ensure that the color scheme is no more than three colors.

3. Download from the Web, purchase, link to, or create any multimedia you want to include on your Web pages. Insert the elements into your pages following the guidelines for multimedia.

4. Develop any Web-based forms you want to include on your Web pages following this chapter's guidelines for creating usable forms.

5. Download from the Web, purchase, or create interactive elements. Incorporate the interactive element(s) into your Web site.

6. Save your completed Web site files to your hard drive and save a copy of the files to an external storage device.

7 Promoting and Maintaining a Web Site

Introduction

In Chapter 1, you learned about Internet and Web fundamentals and why the Web is a powerful tool for communication and commerce. In Chapters 2 through 6, you learned about fundamental design guidelines for creating a Web site's structure and adding page content such as text, links, images, and multimedia. You also learned how to effectively use color and layout to promote unity and visual identity at your Web site. Along the way, you created a site plan and, at the end of Chapter 6, you followed your site plan to create the pages for your site. Beyond the initial work of designing and developing a site, the work of creating the site is still not finished.

Next, you must test your Web site to make certain that all elements work as intended, that your site accomplishes the site plan's stated goals and objectives, and that the site's content satisfies your target audience's needs and expectations. After your site is thoroughly tested, you are ready to publish it to a Web server to make it available to your audience. Once your Web site is published, you then start the ongoing processes of promoting and maintaining your site.

Objectives

After completing this chapter, you will be able to:

1. Explain how to test a Web site before it is published

2. Describe how to publish a Web site to a Web server

3. Identify ways to promote a published Web site

4. Discuss the importance of maintaining and evaluating a published Web site

Web Site Testing

In Chapter 4, you learned why it is important to perform usability testing during the Web site development process. Usability testing during development helps to ensure that your site's navigation system is both user based and user controlled. The testing process does not stop when the original site development is completed. Before publishing your site to a Web server, you must test the site to identify and fix any undetected problems with navigation. Testing also identifies any problems with structure and content. Failure to thoroughly test your site might lead to loss of credibility with your site's visitors, which would be embarrassing at best and could lead to your site's failure at worst.

Many organizations and businesses publish their Web sites to a temporary Web server, called a **staging server**, to enable testing in an environment similar to that of a live Web server. Thoroughly testing a Web site prior to publishing incorporates both self-testing and testing by interested parties not involved with the site's design and development.

Self-Testing

The first phase of prepublication Web site testing is **self-testing**. During this phase, you test your site's structure and page layout, color scheme, and other elements to ensure the Web site's pages look and function as designed and to confirm that all aspects of the design plan are satisfied. If you have been performing usability testing during your Web site's development and creation, you should find few problems during the self-testing process. If you are using a WYSIWYG editor, use the program-specific tools to test links, browser versions, spelling, and accessibility.

As part of the self-testing process, you should do the following:

1. Ensure that images appear in the page layout as designed and that alternative text appears when the display of images is turned off in the browser. If images do not appear, verify that the page code does not contain misspellings of the image file name or link to an invalid folder location.

2. Test all internal and external links to make certain they work properly and none are broken links. A **broken link** is one that no longer works. Verify that the link text clearly identifies its target and that the correct page opens when clicked; if relevant, make sure that the new page opens in the same browser window, a new tab, or a new window as specified.

3. Make certain you include a text equivalent for all nontext elements to satisfy WAI guidelines for images and multimedia.

4. Correct any problems that arose during testing, and retest to verify your corrections solved the issues.

5. Use different browsers and different browser versions running on different operating system platforms, including mobile devices if relevant, to perform Steps 1 to 4. Pages may appear in different browsers or browser versions with slight variations, including exact color tone and object placement. You should accept a reasonable range of variances as long as the page appears legible and looks well laid out in each instance.

Target Audience Testing

The second testing phase involves recruiting a small group of testers, including colleagues not involved in the site development, people who represent your target audience, and other interested parties, to review your Web site and test its navigation, links, and other features. For an e-commerce site, for example, other interested parties might include employees, vendors, and other business partners.

Using an outside group of testers to evaluate your Web site can help provide insight about how potential visitors will respond to your Web site and use its pages. Additionally, the testers might find problems that you, as the designer, could not identify because you were too close to the process. If possible, you and others in a designated observation team should watch some (preferably all) of the testers to record their experiences as they explore your Web site. Observe the testers to determine the following:

- Which pages appear to appeal to them?
- Which pages appear to disinterest them?
- How much time do they spend on various pages?
- Which links do they visit or ignore?
- How easily do they navigate the Web site?
- Do they at any time demonstrate any confusion or impatience?

After observing the testing, ask the testers to complete a survey in which they can express their candid opinions about their experience at your Web site. In addition to identifying specific settings (such as browser version, screen resolution, and operating system) being used by the tester, your survey should include questions such as the following:

- Did the site's content satisfy your needs, wants, and expectations for content at the site?
- Was the site's content interesting and valuable?
- Was it easy or difficult to navigate the site?
- What improvements, if any, would you suggest for the site?
- Would you return to the Web site and recommend the site to others?

You should also provide the same survey for testers who cannot be observed by you or your observation team.

@SOURCE

Testing
For more information about conducting thorough Web site testing, visit the Web Design 4 Chapter 7 Student Online Companion Web page at **www.cengagebrain.com**, and then click Testing in the @Source links.

Exploring How to Organize a Test Group

YOUR TURN

1. Review the audience profile you developed for your Web site; the profile should include age range, gender, educational background, geographic location, careers, income levels, and lifestyles. Review the identified target audience needs, wants, and expectations for site content.

2. Identify individuals you know who match your target audience's profile. Ask the identified individuals and other interested parties, such as friends, family members, and fellow students, to participate in the testing of your Web site.

3. Develop a questionnaire for the testers in which they can express their candid opinions about their experiences at your Web site.

After testing your Web site, seriously consider all comments and suggestions, both negative and positive. Implement those comments and suggestions that will further the original purpose, goals, and objectives, meet the audience's needs, and generally improve the Web site's value, functionality, and usability. Consider a second round of testing if the comments required considerable changes. File away for future consideration all appropriate suggestions that cannot, for some valid reason such as time or money, be implemented at this time. After all corrections and adjustments are made to your site, you are ready to publish it to a live server.

> **DESIGN TIP**
> Perform both a self-test and target audience testing on your Web site before publishing it to a live server. Fix any necessary issues that impede visitors' experiences.

Web Site Publishing

Once your Web site has been thoroughly tested and any identified problems corrected, you can make it available to your audience by publishing it to a live Web server. Publishing your site to a live server involves acquiring server space and uploading all of your site files — HTML and CSS documents, images, multimedia, and other related files — to the server. Before you begin your research into Web server and hosting options, you should know the approximate server space needed and determine the frequency of updates you will be making and any tools or capabilities necessary to display your content or support interactive and multimedia features of your site.

Q&A

What is client/server computing?
Client/server computing involves a client, such as a Web browser, requesting services from a server. A browser's request for a Web page is a client-side function. Server-side functions refer to those actions happening on the remote server, such as serving up Web pages or executing scripts.

@SOURCE

Web Hosting
For more information about Web hosting companies, visit the Web Design 4 Chapter 7 Student Online Companion Web page at **www .cengagebrain.com**, and then click Web Hosting in the @Source links.

Server Space

In Chapter 1, you learned that a Web server is an Internet-connected computer used to store Web pages. A Web server runs server software that allows it to "serve up" Web pages and their related files upon request from a browser. Thousands of **Web hosting companies**, such as those shown in Figure 7-1, offer personal or small business server space for a modest monthly fee. Some accredited registrars that you learned about in Chapter 1, such as register.com and Network Solutions, also offer low-cost Web hosting services. Your Internet service provider (ISP) might also provide a limited amount of server space as part of your monthly Internet access fee, which might suit your needs for a personal or small business site. If you are a student, staff, or faculty member, server space might also be available on your university's or college's Web server, although there might be restrictions, such as the site content must be related to your research, school organization, or classes. Other Web hosting companies, such as those illustrated in Figure 7-2, cater to midsized to large e-commerce sites requiring a more sophisticated level of server support. With a higher level of support might come tools such as shopping carts, comments features, and more to meet your site's needs.

Figure 7-1 Thousands of Web hosting companies offer personal or small business server space for a modest monthly fee.

Figure 7-2 Some Web hosting companies offer a more sophisticated level of server support to midsized to large e-commerce companies.

To find the right Web hosting service, you can ask business associates for recommendations. Ask them which hosting service they use, how long they have used the hosting service, and how they would rate the quality of the customer support provided. You can also research the Web to learn about more Web hosting service options. After you narrow your choices, evaluate each potential Web hosting service by learning about the cost, level of customer support, and technical requirements for the service level you require. One way to do that is to get answers to questions similar to the following:

1. What is the monthly fee to host a personal or commercial Web site?

2. How much server space is allotted for the monthly fee? What does additional space cost?

3. What technical support is offered, and when is it available?

4. Does the server on which the Web site will reside experience frequent nonscheduled outages? How long do the outages last?

5. What is the longest scheduled downtime on a monthly basis for maintenance and backup procedures?

Q&A

How do I get a domain name for my site?
In Chapter 1, you learned about selecting and registering a domain name for your Web site. You can go to an accredited registrar's site, such as register.com or GoDaddy, identify an available domain name, and register it at the site for a fee. Alternatively, some Web hosting services might assist with acquiring a domain name for an additional fee or as part of the original setup fee for the hosting services.

6. Does the Web hosting service offer support for e-commerce, multimedia, scripting languages, applets, servlets, or other elements related to your site and its pages? Does the Web hosting service support the Secure Sockets Layer (SSL) protocol for encrypting confidential data? Are additional fees required for these capabilities?

7. How are your Web site files uploaded to the server? What is the procedure for updating and republishing pages to your site? Does the Web hosting service limit the number, size, or type of files that you can upload?

YOUR TURN

Exploring Web Site Hosting Companies

1. Search the Web using the search tool of your choice and the keywords *Web hosting* or similar keywords to identify at least 10 Web hosting services. Evaluate a mix of accredited registrars that offer hosting services, ISPs, and Web hosting companies.

2. Create a report that summarizes your research. Include a table that lists the Web hosting source, services offered, and cost. Select one service appropriate for hosting a personal Web site, one service appropriate for hosting a small business Web site, and one service appropriate for hosting a midsized to large e-commerce site. Give the reasons for your choices in terms of cost and services offered.

These questions can help you eliminate options and narrow down your choices to one or two that fit your needs. Once you choose the best option, you need to finalize and upload your Web site files.

DESIGN TIP　Carefully evaluate potential Web site hosting services from accredited registrars, ISPs, and Web hosting companies to make the best choice for the level of hosting services your site requires.

Q&A

What is an anonymous FTP site?

Private servers, such as an ISP or Web hosting company server, require a unique user name and password for access. File servers that are open to anyone, such as some college or university file servers, are called anonymous servers or sites because anyone can log on using the word *anonymous* as their user name with no password required.

Uploading Web Site Folders and Files

A Web site is published when the files that make up your site are uploaded to the server specified by your Web hosting service. In the initial publication, you should upload the folders and folder contents (HTML and CSS documents, images, multimedia files, and so forth) for all pages at your site; going forward, you will only need to upload and overwrite any changed files. Before uploading your Web folders and files, review the contents of your Web folders, and move any unnecessary files to another location, such as original image or word-processing files or backup files to save space on the server and to limit any extra time in loading pages in your site.

To upload your files, you might use FTP client software or the publishing feature included in your WYSIWYG editor. If you are using a Windows operating system, such as Windows 7, you also have access to FTP through a command-line interface.

FTP CLIENT   File Transfer Protocol (FTP) is the standard protocol, or set of rules, for uploading or downloading files over the Internet. FTP is commonly used to upload files to a Web server. FTP client software is one option for uploading your Web site folders and files. An **FTP client** is a software program that provides a user interface for transferring files using the FTP protocol, such as CuteFTP®, SmartFTP®, or the free, open source program FileZilla© (Figure 7-3). Typically, the FTP client user interface provides a split view of the folders and files on a local computer, such as the user's hard drive, and on a remote computer, such as the Web server. An FTP client offers a familiar graphical user interface in which you click menu commands and toolbar buttons, or use drag and drop to transfer files from a local computer to a remote computer or vice versa. After the site is published, you can **sync** the files, which makes sure that any changed files are the same on both servers.

FTP
For information about transferring files using FTP, visit the Web Design 4 Chapter 7 Student Online Companion Web page at **www.cengagebrain.com**, and then click FTP in the @Source links.

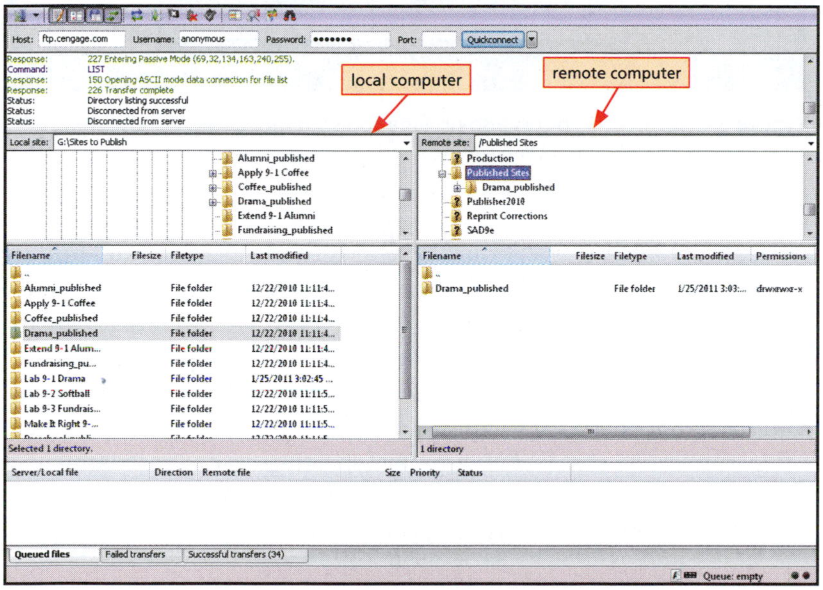

Figure 7-3 An FTP client transfers files between a local computer and a remote computer.

Before using an FTP client, you must add the name and URL of the remote computer plus enter your assigned user name and password to the FTP client interface. This information is available from the hosting service provider. Next, you establish a connection between your computer and the remote computer using the FTP client. Then, you are ready to upload your Web folders and their contents to the remote computer.

WYSIWYG EDITOR   If you are using a WYSIWYG editor, such as Microsoft Expression Web (Figure 7-4 on the next page), you can publish and update your site from within the program. As with other uploading methods, you need to arrange for server space and provide access information — name and URL of the remote server and your assigned username and password — before uploading your Web folders and files.

Figure 7-4 WYSIWYG editors also provide tools for uploading or publishing Web folders and files to a Web server.

@SOURCE

Command-Line Interface

For information about using the Windows 7 command-line interface window to transfer files using FTP, visit the Web Design 4 Chapter 7 Student Online Companion Web page at **www .cengagebrain.com**, and then click Command-Line Interface in the @Source links.

COMMAND-LINE INTERFACE   A third option is to use a **command-line interface**, a DOS-based or nongraphical window (Figure 7-5) opened by typing the cmd command in the Search box on the Windows 7 Start menu. You can type the ftp command in the command-line interface window to log on to a remote computer, and then type commands to view the file and folder structure on the server and to upload your files. Using the command-line interface to upload and download files is more difficult than using an FTP client or a WYSIWYG editor, which provide the more familiar graphical user interface. However, if you are not using a WYSIWYG editor and have not downloaded an FTP client, you can use this option.

Figure 7-5 A nongraphical command-line interface window and FTP are used to upload and download files to or from a remote computer.

DESIGN TIP   FTP clients and WYSIWYG editors are two easy tools you can use to upload your Web site files to a live server.

Retesting Published Pages

After your files have been uploaded or published to the live server, you must continually monitor your site to ensure that it is always functioning correctly and does not contain outdated information. Conduct a testing process similar to your prepublishing testing. Check the following elements when your Web site "goes live" and periodically over the life of the site:

- Confirm that all images are displayed properly.
- Make certain that no broken links exist.
- Ensure all interactive elements, such as forms, are functioning properly.
- If any changes are necessary, correct the page file(s) on your local computer and then upload the corrected page file to the server.
- Skim the content, especially when it contains schedule or date information that may be time sensitive.

Remember to retest your Web site periodically after it is published to ensure that all features are functioning properly.   **DESIGN TIP**

Web Site Promotion

Once the site is published, it is time to announce your Web site's presence to its target audience. The amount of traffic you want or need to generate depends on the type of Web site. Attracting numerous visitors might or might not be a top-level concern for a personal Web site or blog. For an organizational/topical or e-commerce Web site, a large number of visitors are a factor in the site's success or failure.

To generate a high volume of traffic to your Web site, launch a full-scale campaign using both online and traditional promotional techniques. If you have a limited budget for Web site promotion, consider using manual search tool submission, search tool optimization techniques, free link exchange, awards, and traditional word of mouth as ways to get your site noticed. If you are publishing an e-commerce site, you should consider increasing your promotion budget to add other paid online promotional tools to the mix: search engine paid or sponsored placement, a search tool submission service, an affiliate program, Web site advertising using an online advertising network, and opt-in e-mail advertising.

Online Promotional Techniques

You can capitalize on the power of the Internet and the Web for enhanced communication by using online tools to announce your Web site and drive visitors to it. For example, in previous chapters you learned about the increasing importance of business blogs in promoting e-commerce sites. Other online tools for Web site promotion include search tool advertising methods (search tool submissions, search engine optimization, and search tool paid or sponsored placement), search tool submission services, affiliate programs, link exchanges, online advertising networks, RSS feeds, Web-industry awards, and opt-in e-mail advertising. You can also take advantage of technologies such as blogs, Twitter, and Facebook to establish a presence and generate a following.

SEARCH TOOLS   In Chapter 1, you learned about search tools — search engines and search directories — and how search tools build their Web page databases or indexes. When your site is included in search engines' indexes, you gain the obvious advantage of allowing searchers to locate your Web pages that relate to specific keywords. Not being listed in search engines' indexes is like not having a business telephone number or address listed in the Yellow Pages. You can wait for search engines' spiders to find your pages and add them to their indexes, which might take days or weeks. Alternatively, you can take the initiative and register your site's URL with major search engines and directories (Figure 7-6). Depending on the search engine, a fee may be required to expedite your submission; other search engines allow you to register for free.

Figure 7-6 Registering a URL with search engines adds the site's pages to the search engines' indexes.

@SOURCE

SEO
For more information about search engine optimization, visit the Web Design 4 Chapter 7 Student Online Companion Web page at **www .cengagebrain.com**, and then click SEO in the @Source links.

In Chapter 1, you also learned about the concept of search engine optimization (SEO): applying design and development techniques to your Web pages to increase the possibility that they will appear near the top of a search results list for specific keywords. For example, you can increase the possibility of your Web pages appearing in some search results lists by including meta tags and carefully crafting each page's title. Clearly worded Web page text, the density of specific keywords in your page text, and an impressive number of incoming links to your Web pages are also part of SEO. You can search the Web for more SEO techniques, which might vary depending on the individual search engines to which you are directing your SEO efforts. For medium to large e-commerce sites, it might be helpful to hire an SEO consultant to help direct SEO efforts.

YOUR TURN

Exploring SEO Techniques and Consultants

1. Using the search tool of your choice and the keyword *SEO* or similar keywords, learn more about SEO techniques and SEO consultants.

2. Create a list of SEO techniques that you, as a Web designer, should incorporate in the design and development of the B2C Web site you are creating for the recycling site scenario that you worked on in earlier chapters of this book.

3. Research at least four SEO consultants. Create a summary of your research, including the name, services offered, and costs for each consultant.

4. Create a presentation for your recycling site team that summarizes the steps you are taking to optimize the Web site pages for search engine indexing. Include a recommendation of whether to hire an SEO consultant.

In Chapter 1, you were also introduced to the concept of paid or sponsored search results placement as an online advertising tool. Search tool advertising programs, such as Google AdWords (Figure 7-7), Yahoo! Small Business sponsored search, and Microsoft Digital Advertising Solutions Search Advertising allow you to add a paid placement or sponsored listing for specific keywords to a search results page. You pay for the advertising on a **pay-per-click** basis — each time a visitor clicks on your paid or sponsored listing, you pay a small fee to the search tool.

@SOURCE

Paid Placement
For more information about search engine paid placement, visit the Web Design 4 Chapter 7 Student Online Companion Web page at **www .cengagebrain.com**, and then click Paid Placement in the @Source links.

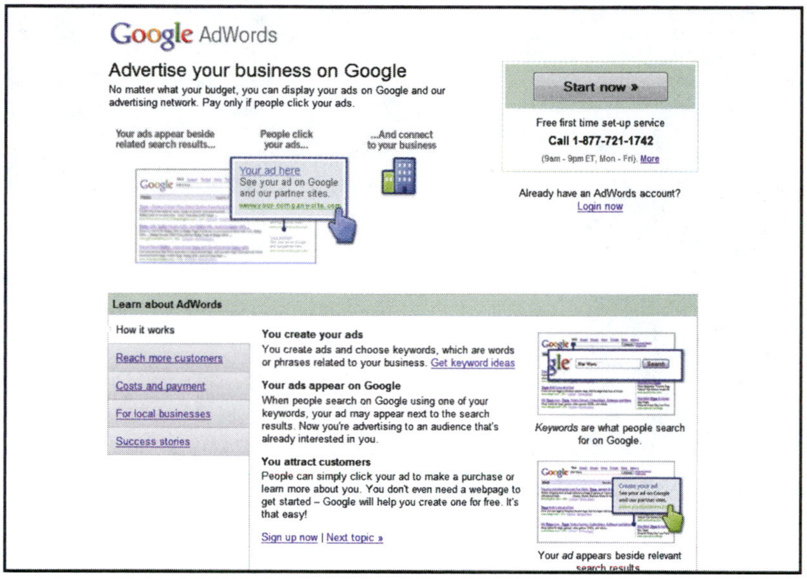

Figure 7-7 Search tool paid or sponsored placements allow Web site owners to advertise their sites based on a keyword search and then pay for the advertising on a pay-per-click basis.

Exploring Paid or Sponsored Placement Online Advertising

YOUR TURN

1. Visit the Web Design 4 Chapter 7 Student Online Companion Web page at **www .cengagebrain.com**, and then click links in the Your Turn section to the following sites to review three paid or sponsored placement advertising programs:
   a. Google AdWords
   b. Yahoo! Small Business Search Advertising
   c. Microsoft Digital Advertising Solutions

2. Assume that you are part of the design and development team for a midsized e-commerce company. Your manager instructs you to recommend a paid or sponsored placement program for the company. Using your research, draft a recommendation based on price, services offered, and other significant program features and submit it to your instructor.

SEARCH TOOL SUBMISSION SERVICES   Using a search tool submission service is an alternative to waiting for search engines to find and index your site or spending your own time registering your Web pages with multiple search tools. A **search tool submission service** (Figure 7-8 on the next page) is a business that registers Web sites with multiple search tools for you. Some SEO consultants offer submission services as a way to promote their SEO consulting services. To use a submission service, you typically provide information about your site, such as its URL, a brief description of the site, and keywords to associate with the site. If you choose to use a submission service, take care to pick one that registers your site with the most frequently used search tools.

Figure 7-8 A search tool submission service is a business that registers Web sites with multiple search tools.

DESIGN TIP

Manual search engine submission, search engine optimization of your pages, free link exchange, awards, and tools such as Twitter and Facebook are inexpensive techniques to promote your published Web site.

@SOURCE

Affiliate Programs
For more information about the benefits of participating in an affiliate program, visit the Web Design 4 Chapter 7 Student Online Companion Web page at **www.cengagebrain.com**, and then click Affiliate Programs in the @Source links.

AFFILIATE PROGRAMS   An **affiliate program** is an e-commerce online advertising program in which a Web site, called the **advertiser**, pays a fee or commission on sales generated by visitors driven to the site by links on other Web sites, called **publishers**. One of the most well-known and oldest affiliate programs is the Amazon.com Associates program; a more recent example is the iTunes Affiliate Program (Figure 7-9). Affiliate program publishers place specially formatted links to advertisers' sites on their Web pages. A visitor who clicks one of these affiliate links is directed to an advertiser's Web site. If the visitor makes a purchase at the advertiser's Web site, the publisher receives a commission on the sale or a flat fee, depending on the affiliate agreement. Sponsoring an affiliate program is a good way to drive traffic to an e-commerce site; participating in an affiliate program is a useful revenue source for other Web sites. An **affiliate management network**, such as Google Affiliate Network, is a business that manages affiliate programs by helping to establish the relationship between advertisers and publishers, by monitoring visitors' click-throughs, and by processing commission or fee payments.

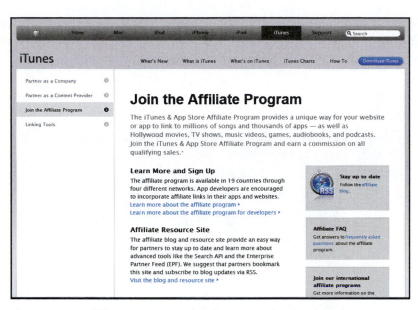

Figure 7-9 An affiliate program is an online promotional tool for site advertisers and a revenue-generating tool for site publishers.

The criteria and rewards for becoming an affiliate program publisher vary. Although most affiliate programs accept applications from a variety of Web sites, even personal Web sites, only those sites that meet the affiliate program's criteria are accepted into the program.

Exploring Affiliate Programs

1. Search the Web using the search tool of your choice and the keywords *affiliate programs* or similar keywords to research affiliate programs from two points of view: as an advertiser and as a publisher.
2. Write a report for your instructor that summarizes your research. Discuss the advantages and disadvantages of being an affiliate program advertiser and a publisher. Discuss the role of an affiliate management network. Assume you are part of the Web design team for a large B2C site; what advice would you give the site's owner on participation in an affiliate program as an advertiser or as a publisher?

LINK EXCHANGE PROGRAMS   A **reciprocal link** is a link between two Web site owners who agree informally to put a respective link to the other's site on their Web pages. Reciprocal links work well when the companies are in related fields, but are not direct competitors. For example, a fashion accessories Web site might exchange links with catering, clothing, home design, jewelry, and other upscale vendor sites that attract a similar audience. Some sites, such as those shown in Figure 7-10 on the next page, provide **link exchange programs** that use reciprocal links in a more formal manner and on a much larger scale. Some link exchange programs offer reciprocal links free to members; others charge a fee to establish reciprocal links. By becoming a member of a link exchange program, you can choose other member Web sites with which you want to exchange

@SOURCE

Link Exchange
For more information about the beneficial arrangement of using reciprocal links, visit the Web Design 4 Chapter 7 Student Online Companion Web page at **www.cengagebrain.com**, and then click Link Exchange in the @Source links.

reciprocal links. The benefits of membership include increased targeted traffic to your Web site. You also can gain a higher ranking of your site's pages by search engines that rank pages in a search results list based on the number of incoming links to the pages.

Figure 7-10 Link exchange involves exchanging reciprocal links with other Web sites.

@SOURCE

Online Advertising Networks
For more information about the use of banner advertising on the Web, visit the Web Design 4 Chapter 7 Student Online Companion Web page at **www .cengagebrain.com**, and then click Online Advertising Networks in the @Source links.

ONLINE ADVERTISING NETWORKS   An **online advertising network**, such as Advertising.com, Batanga Network (Figure 7-11), and ValueClick Media, brings together companies that want to purchase online advertising with companies that want to sell ads on their sites.

Figure 7-11 An online advertising network brings together Web site advertisers and publishers.

As with affiliate programs, the Web site that wants to place online ads is the advertiser; the Web site that has space to display the ads is the publisher. When a visitor clicks an ad on a publisher's site, the visitor's browser goes to the ad's link target, which is usually a Web site for the advertised product or service. Ads provided by an online advertising network are stored on an ad server and "served up" when added to a search results page or when a visitor requests a publisher's pages.

TYPES OF ONLINE ADS   The types of ads typically offered by an online advertising network include banner ads, pop-up and pop-under ads, and rich media ads. A **banner ad** is a horizontal rectangular Web page advertisement that links to the advertiser's Web site. Figure 7-12 illustrates a banner ad on the Boston.com home page and its target — the Boston College ticket site. When a banner ad is a vertical rectangle, it is sometimes called a **sidebar ad**. The purpose of a banner or sidebar ad is to motivate visitors to click the ad, thereby driving traffic to the advertiser's site, in a process called a **click-through**.

Figure 7-12 Clicking a banner ad on the Boston.com home page takes the visitor to the Boston College ticket page.

Q&A

What is a banner exchange site?
Similar to link exchange sites, banner exchange sites facilitate an exchange of banner ads among members.

DESIGN TIP

Joining an online advertising network as an advertiser is a good way to ensure that your online advertising appears on a variety of appropriate Web sites; joining as a publisher is a way to generate revenue at your site.

Other types of online ads include pop-up, pop-under, and rich media ads. A **pop-up ad** (Figure 7-13 on the next page) opens in its own window on top of the page a visitor is currently viewing; a **pop-under ad** opens in its own window underneath the browser and the page currently being viewed. A visitor might not even be aware of the pop-under ad window until he or she closes the browser window. Pop-up and pop-under ads contain links that visitors can click to jump to the advertiser's site. Pop-up and pop-under ads are so unpopular with visitors that today's Web browsers contain pop-up window blocking features, which are mostly effective at blocking these types of ads.

Q&A

Do browser pop-up window blocking features block all pop-ups?
In some instances, a visitor might want to view pop-up windows from specific Web sites. Browser pop-up window blocking settings generally allow users to specify exceptions to pop-up window blocking.

Figure 7-13 A pop-up ad opens in its own window on top of the current page being viewed in the browser.

Rich media ads contain multimedia elements. This category of online ads includes **floating ads** (Figure 7-14), ads that seem to float across the screen for a few seconds, **expandable banner ads** that grow larger when clicked (Figure 7-14), and multimedia **Flash movie ads**. Rich media ads are growing in popularity among advertisers as more and more Web visitors use broadband Internet connections.

Publishers base the amount of money they charge advertisers for a banner, pop-up, pop-under, or rich media ad on **impressions**, the number of times the ad is viewed, or on the number of click-throughs to the advertiser's site. Your Web site hosting service might offer analytical tools that help you measure the success of your ads.

Figure 7-14 Floating and expandable banner ads are called rich media ads.

Exploring Rich Media Ads

1. Search the Web using the search tool of your choice and the keywords *rich media ads* or similar keywords. Search for information on media ads related to a specific angle, such as the technology used to create them, articles rating good or bad ads, or online advertising networks that provide this type of ad.

2. Assume that you are a midsized to large B2C advertiser with a national audience, such as a home pickup dry cleaning service or custom stationery printing. Which type of rich media ad do you think is a good choice to target your current audience? What type of online ad would you choose, and why? What type of publication(s) would you choose?

3. Assume that you are a small C2C publisher interested in selling ad space on your site. Which types of rich media ads would you allow and why?

4. Write a report for your instructor that summarizes your research and discusses your recommendations as both an advertiser and as a publisher.

WEB-INDUSTRY AWARDS   Receiving an award for your Web site can help promote your site. Winners' pages are featured on the sponsoring site, and depending on the award, press coverage can feature your site and attract a new audience. Figure 7-15 illustrates one of the more popular Web award sites, the Webby Award. Industry organizations such as the Web Marketing Association and business magazines such as Forbes also recognize exemplary Web sites. Be selective in the awards you pursue. If you decide to compete for an award, ensure that the award is relative to your Web site's content and objectives.

Q&A

What are the criteria for being designated as an award-winning site? The criteria for being designated as an award-winning site vary depending on the award contest sponsor. Many award sites recognize characteristics related to design, creativity, usability, and functionality. Some award sites focus on a specific industry or type of business.

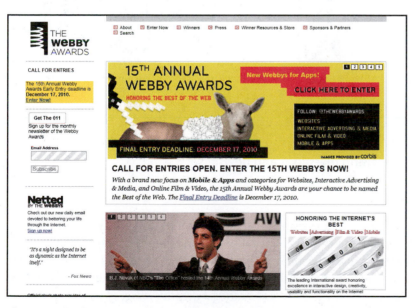

Figure 7-15 Winning a prestigious award can help promote a Web site.

An award will benefit your Web site only if it comes from a respected, credible source. Avoid the numerous trivial award sites that unfortunately populate the Web.

DESIGN TIP

OPT-IN E-MAIL ADVERTISING   E-mail messages can be a cost-effective way to promote a Web site and, in the case of an e-commerce site, its products and services. If you choose to use e-mail advertising, take care to ensure that you use only opt-in e-mail advertising. **Opt-in e-mail advertising** is also called **permission-based e-mail advertising**; opt-in e-mail advertising requires that the message recipient "opt-in" or formally agree to receive the e-mail advertising. This advertising consists of e-mail messages sent to recipients who have granted permission to the advertiser to send the ad. This arrangement is doubly beneficial — the recipient gets information he or she wants, and the advertiser can send a targeted message to a receptive audience. Opt-in e-mail advertising begins with a visitor submitting his or her e-mail address and other required information at your site and agreeing to receive e-mail messages. Although you hate to lose customers, always provide an option to unsubscribe to your e-mail newsletter; many people dislike receiving e-mail, even from sites they visit frequently. Figure 7-16 illustrates an opt-in form at the GameStop Web site and an opt-in e-mail advertising message from GameStop.

Figure 7-16 Opt-in e-mail advertising requires that the message recipient formally agree to receive e-mail advertising.

DESIGN TIP   Be considerate and always provide a way for recipients to unsubscribe from opt-in e-mail advertising messages and newsletters.

Unsolicited e-mail advertising is called **spam**. You have likely experienced spam messages clogging your e-mail client Inbox folder. Spam is so unpopular that many Internet service providers (ISPs) offer their customers a feature to block spam messages from ever reaching their e-mail Inboxes. Additionally, as a result of the federal CAN-SPAM Act of 2003, sending spam is illegal. *To avoid creating a negative image of your Web site or violating the CAN-SPAM Act, never use spam to promote your site!*

An effectively written, free permission-based **e-mail newsletter** can entice visitors to revisit your Web site to learn about new products or services and upcoming events, participate in contests, or take advantage of special promotions. When creating a permission-based e-mail newsletter, devote the time to ensure that your newsletter is personable, engaging, relevant, and free of grammatical and spelling errors. Be realistic when determining a schedule for your newsletter. One well-written, motivating monthly newsletter will have more impact than four hastily written, dull, weekly newsletters.

DESIGN TIP
Effective promotional techniques for an e-commerce site include the inexpensive techniques used for a noncommercial site, plus paid or sponsored search engine placement, affiliate programs, online advertising networks, opt-in e-mail advertising, and promotional giveaways.

Traditional Promotional Techniques

Traditional techniques can also be used successfully to promote your Web site. These traditional methods include word of mouth, print materials, and promotional giveaways.

WORD OF MOUTH   Simply telling people about your Web site is an easy, free way to market your Web site. To get the word out, announce the creation of your Web site to family, friends, colleagues, and business associates. Inform them of your Web site's URL and encourage them to check out the site. If you belong to an organization or company, encourage other members or coworkers to use their personal networks to publicize your Web site. Setting up a Facebook fan page or Twitter feed, or creating a blog visitors can subscribe to, are other free ways to grow your audience. Similar to word of mouth, a person can recommend a fan page on Facebook to their friends, retweet posts from your Twitter feed to his or her followers, or forward the link to your blog to their friends.

PRINT MATERIAL   If your Web site is organizational/topical or commercial, it is likely that you publish and use various print materials. Your Web site's URL should appear prominently on every print publication you use, including stationery, business cards, brochures, reports, print media ads, signage, and magazines. Visitors interested in learning more details about your site's content, products, or services can enter the URL into their browser to find the information they need.

PROMOTIONAL GIVEAWAYS   **Promotional giveaways** include such items as magnets, coffee mugs, coasters, T-shirts, caps, pens, memo pads, and calendars. Promotional giveaways that are boldly inscribed with your Web site name and URL add an element of fun to promoting your Web site. You can hand out promotional giveaways when meeting new customers or distribute them at trade shows, conferences, or other events.

Web Site Maintenance and Evaluation

The Web is a dynamic environment where rapid changes in technology and visitors' expectations can cause sites to quickly look out of date. A savvy Web designer understands that Web design is a continuing process and that the work of developing, creating, and maintaining a Web site is never really finished.

@SOURCE

Web Site Promotion
For more information about promoting a new Web site, visit the Web Design 4 Chapter 7 Student Online Companion Web page at **www.cengagebrain.com**, and then click Web Site Promotion in the @Source links.

@SOURCE

The Wayback Machine
To see how popular Web sites have evolved, visit the Web Design 4 Chapter 7 Student Online Companion Web page at **www.cengagebrain.com**, and then click The Wayback Machine in the @Source links.

Ongoing Maintenance, Updating, and Retesting

It is important to maintain, update, and retest your Web site elements on a regular basis. In addition to checking for problems, such maintenance keeps your site fresh and keeps your audience coming back by offering something new. As part of an ongoing maintenance plan, you should do the following:

- Add timely content. For example, change photographs, add to/substitute text, publicize upcoming events, and offer timely tips or create a frequently updated blog. Fresh, appealing content will encourage visitors to return to your Web site.
- Check for broken links and add new links. Prevent frustration for your site visitors by maintaining a functional navigational system that includes links to the primary pages in your site.
- Include a way to get user feedback, and then act on that feedback. Visitors' suggestions and criticisms can help you improve your Web site.
- Evaluate and implement new technologies when they can further your site's objectives and increase its accessibility and usability, as well as fit into your site budget and meet your audience's expectations.
- Retest site features periodically.

Although some WYSIWYG editors include the capability to update pages residing on the live server, generally, it is recommended that you avoid this practice. Updating live pages carries the risk that your audience will see incomplete or undesired changes. Follow these steps for maintaining and updating your Web site:

1. Download the desired Web page from the Web server to your computer, if necessary, to work with the most current version of the page.
2. Update the Web page.
3. Open the Web page in a browser and check the changes and the page display.
4. If the changes and the page display are acceptable, then upload the updated page to the server, replacing the existing page.

Evaluating Web Site Performance

When you created your original design plan, you first created a purpose statement and listed your site's primary and secondary goals and the necessary objectives. After publishing your site, you must then begin the ongoing process of evaluating your site's performance toward achieving its stated goals and purpose. Evaluating the performance of a simple personal or topical site with one or two goals should not be too difficult. In most cases, getting feedback from family, friends, classmates, and other members of the site's target audience is sufficient to ensure that the site is accomplishing its goals and purpose.

Web site performance evaluation is much more complicated for large, complex organizational or commercial sites with multiple goals and broadly defined purposes. Typically, these types of sites follow a formal evaluation plan that, in addition to ongoing testing and visitor feedback, might include benchmarking, Web server log transaction analysis, and a review of other performance measures, often by third-party marketing professionals.

BENCHMARKING A **benchmark** is a measurement standard with which actual performance can be compared. For example, a benchmark for an organizational or e-commerce site might be to increase the number of visitors by 10 percent per month over the next 12 months. Comparing the benchmark with the actual growth in the number of site visitors each month can help a site's owner determine what, if any, changes to make at the site. A performance benchmark is not static; after evaluation against actual performance, you might need to adjust a benchmark to make it more realistic.

WEB SERVER LOG ANALYSIS   In Chapter 2, you learned that each time a browser requests a Web page from a Web server, that request for a page is recorded in the server's transaction log. Web server log transactions provide a wealth of information, such as the following:

- The requesting computer's IP address
- The browser making the request
- The date and time of the request
- The URL of a referring link (the link the visitor clicked to jump to the site's page)
- The path a visitor takes from page to page through a Web site

From the raw data contained in a Web server transaction log, additional measures of visitors' behaviors can be evaluated using **Web server log analysis software**. Web server log analysis software can be installed on your own servers or might be provided by your hosting company. However, many large organizations and e-commerce companies contract with professional marketers that focus on Web site performance evaluation. Professional marketers, such as VisiStat and Webtrends (Figure 7-17), often provide a complete analysis package that combines a variety of data-gathering techniques, including Web server log transaction analysis, with software that measures and reports on Web site performance. These performance measurements are called Web analytics.

Figure 7-17 Professional marketers that focus on Web site performance offer products and services used to develop Web site performance measurements.

WEB ANALYTICS   Developing **Web analytics**, sometimes called **Web metrics**, involves combining various types of visitor data — server log analysis, eye-tracking studies, tracking cookies, page tagging, sales data, and so forth — and then analyzing that data to discover how visitors act at a Web site. Typical Web analytics reports contain a variety of measurements, such as unique visitors, repeat visitors, page views, click-stream analysis, and, for e-commerce sites, conversion rate.

A **unique visitor** is an individual visitor to a site; the unique visitor measurement can help determine the success of your Web site promotional efforts at driving visitors to your site. A **repeat visitor** is a unique visitor who visits your site more than one time

Q&A

What are tracking cookies?
Tracking cookies are small text files stored on a Web page visitor's hard drive, usually without the visitor's knowledge. Tracking cookies installed by Web marketers are used to monitor which sites the visitor visited and other visitor behaviors. Many visitors consider tracking cookies an invasion of privacy and most popular computer security software packages, such as Norton, locate and remove tracking cookies.

Q&A

What is page tagging?
Page tagging is a technique used by Web marketers to track visitors' behaviors, similar to tracking cookies. A site publisher adds JavaScript tags to its Web pages. When a visitor views a page containing a tag, information about the visitor, similar to that recorded in a server log, is gathered and transferred to a database. The information is analyzed later by the professional Web marketers and the site's publisher.

@SOURCE

Web Analytics
For more information about measuring Web site activity using Web analytics, visit the Web Design 4 Chapter 7 Student Online Companion Web page at **www.cengagebrain.com**, and then click Web Analytics in the @Source links.

during a specific time period. A small number of repeat visitors might indicate those who are visiting your site are not finding useful information or helpful features. The **page views** measurement is used to determine page popularity. For example, if you have a page that is seldom viewed, you might consider evaluating the page's content and retesting all the links to the page to see if there is a problem with the page. A **click-stream analysis** identifies how a visitor moves through your site by clicking from link to link and might also indicate how long the visitor stayed at each page. Finally, an important measurement for an e-commerce site is the **conversion rate** — the rate at which a visitor who is shopping at the site becomes a buyer of the site's products or services. The conversion rate is calculated by dividing the number of completed shopping cart transactions by the number of unique visitors.

One factor in an e-commerce site's success is the number of sales made and the overall profit generated. However, it is also important to measure the number of visitors, the percentage of visitors who initiate a transaction, and the percentage of visitors who complete a transaction. Having a large number of visitors who do not initiate a purchase could mean that your advertising dollars are attracting the wrong audience or that there is something wrong with either the products themselves or the way they are displayed. Although it is normal to experience a small number of visitors who initiate but do not complete a transaction, if many customers are abandoning the purchase in the middle, it could indicate issues with the usability of your site. Prepublishing testing typically identifies this type of issue; if they are occurring on your site, you must address them, determine the cause, and solve the problems.

Taken alone, none of these individual measurements can tell you how a site is performing against stated goals. But by combining benchmarking, server log analysis, and other Web analytics with management expertise, the owners and managers of a complex organizational or e-commerce Web site can better understand the site's overall performance and take steps, if needed, to correct any problems or make necessary improvements.

Chapter Review

This chapter introduced you to testing, publishing, promoting, maintaining, and evaluating a Web site. You learned that prepublishing testing, perhaps on a staging server, is an important step that Web designers must take before publishing a site to a live server. To publish your Web site, you first must acquire server space from an ISP, Web hosting company, accredited registrar, or other source. Then, you are ready to upload all your Web site files to a server using an FTP client or WYSIWYG editor. After publishing your Web site to a live server, you should continue to test your pages for appearance and functionality on an ongoing basis.

You can use both online and traditional promotional techniques to make your target audience aware of your site. Online promotional techniques include business blogs, getting your site's pages indexed by search tools, using search tool paid or sponsored placement, using an affiliate program, creating a presence using social media tools, exchanging reciprocal links, participating in an online advertising network, securing Web-industry awards, and sending opt-in e-mail advertising. Traditional methods include old-fashioned word of mouth, inclusion of your site's name and URL on all printed materials, and promotional giveaways.

After your site is published, the work continues as you update your site with current content, check for broken links, and implement new technologies. You also must continue to evaluate your site's ongoing performance against your stated goals and purpose using techniques such as benchmarking or Web server log analysis, or contracting with third-party marketing professionals to develop your site's Web analytics.

After reading the chapter, you should know each of these key terms.

advertiser (188)
affiliate management network (188)
affiliate program (188)
banner ad (191)
benchmark (196)
broken link (178)
click-stream analysis (198)
click-through (191)
command-line interface (184)
conversion rate (198)
e-mail newsletter (195)
expandable banner ads (192)
File Transfer Protocol (FTP) (183)
Flash movie ad (192)
floating ad (192)
FTP client (183)
impression (192)
link exchange program (189)
online advertising network (190)
opt-in e-mail advertising (194)
page views (198)

pay-per-click (187)
permission-based e-mail advertising (194)
pop-under ad (191)
pop-up ad (191)
promotional giveaways (195)
publisher (188)
reciprocal link (189)
repeat visitor (197)
rich media ad (192)
search tool submission service (187)
self-testing (178)
sidebar ad (191)
spam (194)
staging server (178)
sync (183)
unique visitor (197)
Web analytics (197)
Web hosting companies (180)
Web metrics (197)
Web server log analysis software (197)

Complete the Test Your Knowledge exercises to solidify what you have learned in the chapter.

Matching Terms

Match each term with the best description.

____ 1. staging server

____ 2. sync

____ 3. click-stream analysis

____ 4. impression

____ 5. benchmark

____ 6. FTP client

____ 7. pay-per-click

____ 8. affiliate program

____ 9. expandable banner ad

____ 10. sidebar ad

____ 11. reciprocal links

____ 12. Web analytics

a. A vertical banner ad.

b. A type of rich media ad that adjusts its size when clicked.

c. An e-commerce online advertising program in which a Web site, called the advertiser, pays a fee or commission on sales generated by visitors driven to the site by links on other Web sites.

d. Identifies how a visitor moves through your site by clicking from link to link and might also indicate how long the visitor stayed at each page.

e. A temporary Web server used for prepublishing testing.

f. Software with a graphical user interface that is used to transfer files over the Internet.

g. Links exchanged between two Web sites.

h. The measurement and analysis of visitors' actions at a Web site.

i. A measure of the number of times an online ad is viewed.

j. The process of updating remote and local site pages so that they match.

k. A payment method for online advertising in which a small fee is paid each time a visitor clicks on your ad.

l. A measurement standard with which actual performance can be compared.

Short Answer Questions

Write a brief answer to each question.

1. Discuss the processes of self-testing and target audience testing a prepublished Web site.

2. Identify at least three options for acquiring Web server space.

3. Define FTP and compare the use of an FTP client, a WYSIWYG editor, and a command-line interface for uploading Web site files.

4. Briefly discuss why it is necessary to retest the pages at a published Web site and how to perform retesting.

5. Discuss at least three ways to get your Web site pages added to major search tool indexes.

6. Explain how an affiliate program works as both an advertising program and a revenue generation program; give two real-world affiliate program examples.

7. Explain the role of an online advertising network.

8. Define the following: floating ad, sidebar ad, expandable banner ad, pop-under ad, and rich media ad.

9. Explain why unsolicited e-mail advertising (spam) is an inappropriate method for promoting a Web site. What other free methods could you employ instead?

10. Explain the purpose of benchmarking and Web analytics in evaluating Web site performance.

LEARN IT ONLINE

Test your knowledge of chapter content and key terms.

Instructions: To complete the Learn It Online exercises, start your browser, click the Address bar, and then visit the Web Design 4 Chapter 7 Student Online Companion Web page at **www.cengagebrain.com**. When the Web Design Learn It Online page is displayed, click the link for the exercise you want to complete and then read the instructions.

Chapter Reinforcement TF, MC, and SA

A series of true/false, multiple-choice, and short-answer questions that test your knowledge of the chapter content.

Flash Cards

An interactive learning environment where you identify chapter key terms associated with displayed definitions.

Practice Test

A series of multiple-choice questions that test your knowledge of chapter content and key terms.

Who Wants To Be a Computer Genius?

An interactive game that challenges your knowledge of chapter content in the style of a television quiz show.

Wheel of Terms

An interactive game that challenges your knowledge of chapter key terms in the style of the television show *Wheel of Fortune*.

Crossword Puzzle Challenge

A crossword puzzle that challenges your knowledge of key terms presented in the chapter.

Investigate current Web design developments with the Trends exercises.

Write a brief essay about each of the following trends, using the Web as your research tool. For each trend, identify at least one Web page URL used as a research source. Be prepared to discuss your findings in class.

1 | Making Money Using Advertising

As a Web site designer, you can use advertising to earn money to support your site. Research one of the methods described in this chapter, and write a report evaluating its methods and effectiveness. How would you use this approach as a site designer?

2 | Using Social Media to Build a Customer Base

Find two examples of companies who are using social media and interactive Web tools such as Twitter, Facebook, or blogging to reach customers. Write a report that describes the methods being used and the type of information they are sharing. Include any personal experiences you have had interacting with a business using these methods.

Challenge your perspective of Web design and surrounding technology with the @Issue exercises.

Write a brief essay in response to the following issues, using the Web as your research tool. For each issue, identify at least one Web page URL used as a research source. Be prepared to discuss your findings in class.

1 | Web Analytics

Web marketers use a variety of techniques, from server logs to tracking cookies and page tagging, to identify Web site visitors' actions and then analyze these actions to develop the Web metrics or analytics necessary to evaluate Web site performance. Some of these data-gathering techniques might be considered an invasion of privacy by many site visitors. Research the ways in which Web analytics data is gathered and analyzed. Then create a presentation for your class that describes data-gathering and analysis methods. Discuss the effect of visitors' data gathering from two perspectives: as a site visitor and as a site owner.

2 | Security Issues

Search the Internet for articles that deal with security issues surrounding rich media ads and other online ads. Find recommendations for your browser settings. Check the settings in your browser. Write a report for your instructor that summarizes security concerns and recommendations and lists the steps you took, if any, to protect yourself.

HANDS ON

Use the World Wide Web to obtain more information about the concepts in the chapter with the Hands On exercises.

1 | Explore and Evaluate: Site Hosting Options

Browse the Web to identify at least two high-cost Web site hosting packages that are geared toward medium to large e-commerce sites. Create a report for your instructor that summarizes the packages' features and costs. Choose a package that you would like to use. Explain the reasons for your choice.

2 | Search and Discover: Search Tool Submission Programs

Search the Web using the Bing search engine to identify at least five search tool submission programs. Create a presentation for your class that summarizes your research. Recommend a search tool submission program to your classmates; give the reasons for your recommendation.

TEAM APPROACH

Work collaboratively to reinforce the concepts in the chapter with the Team Approach exercises.

1 | Recommend Promotional Techniques for a New Entertainment Site

Join with two other students to create a team. Assume the team is charged with the responsibility of identifying free or low-cost promotional techniques for a new entertainment Web site whose audience will be parents with young children interested in finding information on family-friendly movie and TV options. Create a presentation for the site's owner that summarizes at least three techniques the team recommends. Give reasons for your recommendations.

2 | Web Site Evaluation

Create three teams of students according to the type of Web site they designed: personal, organizational/topical, or commercial. Within each team, each member should present his or her Web site to the team for evaluation, explaining how he or she developed and implemented his or her Web site plan. Each team then chooses the top two sites in their group according to overall design and the degree to which each site achieves its stated goals and purpose. Next, have the entire class evaluate the top two sites from each team and select the one site whose design and implementation best fits its stated goals and purpose.

Apply the chapter concepts to the ongoing development process in Web design with the Case Study.

The Case Study is an ongoing development process using the concepts, techniques, and Design Tips presented in each chapter.

Background Information

You are now ready to test, publish, and promote your own Web site. You will apply what you have learned about self-testing, target audience testing, online and traditional promotion techniques, and ongoing site maintenance and evaluation.

Chapter 7 Assignment

Create an outline that describes exactly how you will complete the following steps. If possible, actually test and publish your Web site.

1. Self-test your prepublished Web site. Create a team of testers and have them test your site. If necessary, have your testing team members simulate target audience members.

2. Select an appropriate Web hosting service. Determine exactly how you will upload your files to the hosting service's Web server. If possible, actually upload your Web site files to a Web server using information provided by your instructor.

3. Identify the online and traditional promotional techniques you will use to promote your site. Create a mock-up of at least one method — an ad, an opt-in e-mail, or a flyer announcing your site.

4. Develop a regular schedule for site maintenance, updating, and, when necessary, retesting.

5. Identify the methods you will use to evaluate your site's performance against its stated goals and purpose.

A | Design Tips

Summary of Design Tips

This appendix lists in chapter sequence the Design Tips presented throughout this book. The first column contains a general tip description, the second column contains the page number on which the Design Tip is found, and the third column contains the tip text.

Description	Page	Tip Overview
	Chapter 1	
Hyperlinks	Page 3	Whether you choose to indicate hyperlinks in text by color, bold, or underline, be consistent throughout your site.
Communication	Page 4	Design your Web site so that it communicates trustworthiness, timeliness, and value.
Educational site content	Page 8	Any formal or informal educational Web site should contain content that is timely, accurate, and appealing. Such sites also should include elements to provide feedback, maintain records, and assess learning.
Connectivity	Page 8	Include methods to share your site's content by providing links to send content using e-mail; post to the user's Facebook page, RSS feed, or Twitter account; as well as link to related content that site users would find interesting and relevant.
E-commerce products and technologies	Page 10	To develop an e-commerce Web site, you must determine the potential customers for your products or services. Categorize your items or provide a search feature so customers can easily find what they need. Additionally, you must decide which e-commerce technologies, such as shopping cart and credit card processing technologies, are best suited for your e-commerce site.
Images and multimedia	Page 12	Although large images and multimedia elements on Web pages can degrade the audience's viewing experiences at slower Internet access speeds, most sites assume users have high-speed dial-up, cable, or wireless connectivity.
Browser variations	Page 14	A Web page might appear differently depending on the browser type or version, so you should test your pages with different browsers as you develop your Web site. For example, features of your site that work within the Internet Explorer 9 browser might not work in earlier versions, such as Internet Explorer 6.

Description	Page	Tip Overview
Domain names	Page 15	Select a short, easy-to-remember domain name that ties directly to a site's purpose or publisher's name or is hard to forget. Examples of effective domain names include webkinz.com (social network for kids), business.com (business-oriented search directory), and ask.com (search tool).
Microbrowsers	Page 16	Some of your site visitors might be viewing your pages using a microbrowser on a handheld computer or smartphone. Limiting site graphics and keeping text brief and to the point can enhance their viewing experience. You can also create a version of your Web site specifically for smartphones or mobile devices.
Personally identifiable information (PII)	Page 17	Do not include personally identifiable information that can be misused, such as a Social Security number, on a personal Web site. Be careful what you put online, whether it is a personal Web site or a social networking site. Employers, college recruiters, and anyone with an Internet connection can find information, posts, or photos quite easily, even with privacy settings enabled.
Value-added content	Page 18	Take care to ensure that your Web pages contain accurate, current, objective, and authoritative content.
Search engine optimization (SEO)	Page 20	Adding meta tags to your Web pages and carefully crafting each Web page title can increase the probability that your pages will be included in many search engines' indexes and that your pages will appear in search results lists for important keywords and phrases.
Integrating new technologies	Page 23	Make sure to integrate any new technologies with the design, features, and content of your site. Only add the new technology if it will enhance the browsing experience for site visitors.
Markup languages	Page 23	Even if you are designing a Web site using a content management system or WYSIWYG editor that does not require the use of markup codes, it is important to understand the basic principles of markup languages to understand how Web pages are coded.
Cascading Style Sheets (CSS)	Page 24	Apply Cascading Style Sheets (CSS) to ensure that all the pages at a site have the same look.
Scripts	Page 25	A Web designer might choose to purchase ready-made scripts to perform routine or common functions, such as e-commerce shopping carts, FAQs (frequently asked questions) lists, and banner ad management. Such scripts are available on CDs or by download from commercial Web sites.

Description	Page	Tip Overview
	Chapter 2	
Updating content	Page 41	Although your Web site might not need as frequent updating as a news-oriented or B2C site, you still must take care to keep the site's content up to date.
Content review and interactivity	Page 43	After your Web site is published, plan to review the site's content for credibility, accuracy, and timeliness on a regular basis and update the content as necessary.
Interactivity	Page 44	Build into your site appropriate ways to promote interactivity, such as a contact page, Web-based form, or blog.
Cost and delivery advantage	Page 45	Use your Web site to expand on your printed content. For example, if you have a large event to promote, send a less-expensive postcard directing users to the Web site for the event. Provide minimal details on the postcard, but save on printing and mailing costs by having registration for the event online.
White space	Page 47	You can create white space by adding line breaks, paragraph returns, paragraph indents, and space around tables and images.
Slide shows	Page 47	Using a slide show enables you to have one central focal point whose content changes automatically or as a result of user intervention. You can feature several articles at once in a small amount of space.
Web page layout concepts	Page 48	Use balance, proximity, and white space to create effective, organized Web pages. Use contrast to stimulate interest and establish a focal point for your Web pages.
Unity and visual identity	Page 49	Generate a sense of unity, maintain visual identity, and promote your brand at your Web site by using consistent alignment, branding elements, and a common color scheme across all pages at the site.
Search engine optimization (SEO)	Page 50	To help Web users more easily find your site, carefully consider the text that you place in headings to use search engine optimization techniques to their best advantage. Search engine optimization (SEO) was introduced in Chapter 1 and is discussed in more detail in Chapter 7.
Scannability	Page 50	To keep Web page text succinct, place information that is not crucial, such as historical backgrounds or related topics, on linked subsidiary pages, both within the content as linked text, or as a separate link or list of links at the bottom or side of an article. For example, in a business news article about a company, you can link to the company's Web site, the NASDAQ site to show the company's current stock price, and a related story from a previous day.

Description	Page	Tip Overview
Credibility	Page 51	Establish credibility for your Web site by providing accurate, verifiable content. Show content currency by including the date the content was last updated.
Writing style	Page 51	Site visitors typically scan online text looking for useful information instead of reading the text word for word. Chunking text allows your site visitors to quickly scan your Web pages and improves usability, as well as makes your page content more easily readable on a mobile device.
Scannability	Page 53	When writing in the inverted pyramid style, summary text should include the "who, what, when, why, where, and how" of the topic. Avoid transitional words or phrases, such as "similarly," "as a result," or "as stated previously."
Color scheme	Page 54	Before making color choices for your Web site, it is a good idea to visit several commercial and noncommercial Web sites, including sites similar to yours, and review each site's color scheme.
Image loading	Page 55	Create faster-loading Web pages by limiting the number and file size of images or using thumbnail images.
Browser variations	Page 56	Web pages might appear quite differently when viewed with different browsers and browser versions. For this reason, test your Web pages with different browsers and browser versions before publishing your site.
Bandwidth and monitor resolution	Page 57	Web design standards for bandwidth and monitor resolution change over time with advances in Web technologies. Consider designing your Web site to accommodate the current most commonly used Internet access speeds and monitor resolutions.
Connectivity	Page 59	Using connectivity tools to allow site visitors to share your content helps to protect you from copyright concerns. These tools direct the visitor back to your site, which allows you to share your content or connect to other sites' content while clearly crediting the source.
Privacy and security policies	Page 61	Establish privacy and data security policies for your Web site operations. Make certain everyone associated with designing, maintaining, and operating the site is aware of the policies. Then explain your policies to site visitors by publishing a privacy and security policy statement.
Web site accessibility	Page 62	Design your Web site to be accessible by people with various types of special needs, such as lost or impaired vision or color blindness, by following the WAI and Section 508 guidelines for Web accessibility. If using a WYSIWYG editor, use the tools provided by the program to check for potential accessibility issues.

Description	Page	Tip Overview
	Chapter 3	
Design plan	Page 70	When creating a design plan, make sure to get the plan reviewed by colleagues, managers, or others with a stake in the outcome of your Web site. Although you might think that visual design would be the most important aspect of a Web site, you need to first determine the purpose, audience, content, and structure to come up with a visual design that meets the needs of your site.
Goals and objectives	Page 72	You will constantly refer back to your goals and objectives as you complete the site plan. Before publishing the Web site, you should evaluate how well the site's content, structure, and design help to meet the site's goals and objectives.
Purpose statement	Page 73	Formulating a well-written purpose statement requires a clear understanding of a site's goals and objectives.
Audience expectations	Page 75	To create a successful Web site, you should assess your target audience's wants, needs, and expectations and then design your site to satisfy them.
Target audience	Page 75	The content elements you choose for your Web site must support the site's purpose and satisfy your target audience's needs and expectations.
Home page	Page 77	A Web site's home page should contain elements that draw the visitor in and encourage further exploration. The home page should also be different enough to stand out as the primary page, but still connect visually with other pages at the site.
Splash page	Page 79	If you must include a splash page, be sure to add a link that jumps to the site's home page for those visitors who do not want to view the splash page.
Repurposed content	Page 80	Do not reuse content created for print on Web pages. Repurpose the content so that it will add value.
Images	Page 82	Web page images can powerfully communicate and motivate. Select relevant, high-quality images that can support the Web site's purpose.
Copyright adherence	Page 82	Remember to ensure that content elements you use at your Web site are free of copyright restrictions.
Audio	Page 83	Inform visitors when a site link launches an audio file so that they can use a headset or turn off their speakers so as not to disturb those around them. Repetitive sounds can be irritating to frequent site visitors, so use sound sparingly.

Description	Page	Tip Overview
Bandwidth concerns	Page 83	Consider how your target audience will be accessing your site when adding video clips to your site. Most Internet connections can present video without causing delays or problems, but if a large portion of your audience uses lower bandwidth connection methods, consider reducing the size or number of video files.
Animation and multimedia	Page 84	Limit the use of animation and multimedia on your Web pages. Animation and multimedia elements should be used only when doing so supports your site's purpose and satisfies your target audience's expectations for content at your site.
Ready-made multimedia	Page 84	Web designers without the necessary programming resources and expertise can purchase ready-made multimedia elements from professional multimedia developers.
File organization and backup	Page 87	Plan an organized file system for your Web site files. You will work more effectively, minimize the risk of losing or misplacing content elements, and facilitate the publishing of your Web site if you are organized. Back up your files on a regular basis.
Site structure	Page 91	Plan the structure of your Web site to support the site's purpose and make it easy for visitors to meet their needs and expectations at the site. Formalize the structure plan using a text outline, storyboard, or flowchart.
Chapter 4		
Content placement	Page 98	You have no control over visitors' monitor resolution or scrolling habits. To increase usability, take care to place important content, such as logos, names, and major links, above and to the left of potential scroll lines.
Scrolling	Page 99	If vertical scrolling is necessary, ensure a logical flow of information. Avoid horizontal scrolling on all pages. Add "top of page" links at logical positions within a page that flows beyond two screens and is not intended to be printed and read offline.
Layout	Page 100	Consider the needs of your likely site visitors when deciding on a fixed-width or liquid layout, and make sure to test your pages at different resolutions.
Visual consistency	Page 101	Repeating design features, such as the color scheme, and content, such as a logo, name, and major links, across all pages at a site is one technique for creating visual consistency.
Color scheme	Page 103	Limit your Web site color scheme to three major colors. Choose a text color for titles, headlines, and so forth to attract the appropriate amount of attention. Test the background and text colors in your color scheme to ensure both on-screen readability and print legibility.

Description	Page	Tip Overview
Images	Page 104	Images that you include on Web pages, such as clip art, illustrations, and photos, will add more color to your pages. Choose images with colors that match or complement your site's color scheme.
Cascading Style Sheets (CSS)	Page 104	Because no current browser supports all CSS specifications, be sure to test how the Web pages you format using CSS appear in different browsers.
Layout grids	Page 107	Use a layout grid to position page content that consistently appears on all pages, for example, the logo, site publisher's name, images, and major links. Then carefully add other page content that generates interest and variety while maintaining visual consistency.
Usability	Page 111	Create a user-based navigation system to match the way visitors actually move from page to page at your site. Consider conducting usability testing as you develop your site's navigation system to ensure navigation is user based.
Link colors	Page 112	Consider using the traditional blue text link color for fresh links and purple text link color for followed links. Avoid using color alone to specify a text link; add underlining in addition to color to meet accessibility standards.
Hidden links	Page 112	Avoid hidden mouseover or rollover text links unless their inclusion satisfies your target audiences' expectations for text links and there is no adverse effect on the usability and accessibility of your site's pages.
Image maps	Page 114	Follow WAI guidelines for image maps. Remember to choose an image that accurately represents the target pages and follows design guidelines for visual consistency.
Navigation design	Page 115	Basic design rules apply to navigation menus, bars, and tabs. Use these design elements consistently across all pages at a site, use color scheme colors, and make certain the target page is clearly indicated.
Breadcrumb trail	Page 116	A breadcrumb trail displays the relationship between the home page and the current page. Use a breadcrumb trail in combination with other navigation elements, such as navigation menus or bars.
Site maps	Page 117	Provide a text link-based site map for large Web sites with many pages. Organize a site map's text links in a logical way, such as alphabetically or by topic.
User-controlled navigation	Page 118	Create a user-controlled navigation system by combining in your navigation system text links; image links; navigation menus, bars, and tabs; a breadcrumb trail; a site map; and search capability as appropriate for your target audiences.

Description	Page	Tip Overview
	Chapter 5	
Fonts	Page 131	Specify commonly used fonts for your Web pages to increase your chances of overriding default browser font settings. Before publishing your Web pages, test your font and font sizes in different browsers and on different operating systems.
Accessibility	Page 133	Keep Web accessibility in mind as you select images for your Web pages. Include redundant text links for image maps and add an alternative text description for each image.
Copyrighted images	Page 138	Before downloading photos or illustrations from the Web, ensure that you are not violating copyright restrictions or incurring royalty or licensing fees for the images' use.
Image file formats	Page 141	Use the GIF image format for basic, solid-color images that do not require more than 256 colors, such as cartoons, diagrams, and navigation buttons. Use the JPEG image format for photographs or art-like images.
Image editing	Page 143	Cropping an image can eliminate distracting background elements and establish the focal point. Discarding unwanted portions of an image also results in a smaller file size.
Image compression	Page 145	You should make a copy of your unedited original image and consider doing interim edits in a lossless compression format, such as TIFF, PSD, PNG, or RAW. Save your image in a lossy format, such as JPEG, only after you have finished editing.
	Chapter 6	
Multimedia	Page 155	Use multimedia sparingly for distinct purposes. Ensure that it adds value, supports your Web site's message, and satisfies target audience expectations for content at your site.
Animation	Page 157	Using multiple animated GIFs or an endlessly looping animated GIF can distract and annoy visitors. Follow good design practice and include no more than one animated GIF per Web page, and limit the number of loops.
Flash usage	Page 159	Use Flash movies on your Web site or as a splash page only if they add value to the visitor's experience or enhance page content. Provide information about and links to the necessary Flash plug-in so that visitors can ensure that they can play the plug-in.
Avatars and gadgets	Page 162	E-commerce avatars and Web page gadgets can add interest to a Web site; however, both should only be used to further the site's message and purpose and enrich its target audience's experience at the site.
Copyrighted music	Page 163	Be careful to avoid copyright infringement when incorporating music at your Web site. For example, including music on your Web site from a music CD without permission violates the artist's copyright.

Description	Page	Tip Overview
Background music	Page 163	Many visitors consider Web page background music to be annoying. Only include background music when it supports your site's message and the mood you want to achieve. If you include background music, you should also include a control that turns the music off or on.
Blogs, live chat	Page 170	Blogs and live chat are two useful content elements that add interactivity to a Web site. If you do not operate your own servers, you can purchase hosted blog or hosted live chat software or services. You can also purchase outsourced chat agent services.
	Chapter 7	
Testing	Page 180	Perform both a self-test and target audience testing on your Web site before publishing it to a live server. Fix any necessary corrections that impede visitors' experiences.
Hosting services	Page 182	Carefully evaluate potential Web site hosting services from accredited registrars, ISPs, and Web hosting companies to make the best choice for the level of hosting services your site requires.
Uploading to a server	Page 184	FTP clients and WYSIWYG editors are two easy tools you can use to upload your Web site files to a live server.
Testing	Page 185	Remember to retest your Web site periodically after it is published to ensure that all features are functioning properly.
Site promotion	Page 188	Manual search engine submission, search engine optimization of your pages, free link exchange, awards, and tools such as Twitter and Facebook are inexpensive techniques to promote your published Web site.
Online advertising networks	Page 191	Joining an online advertising network as an advertiser is a good way to ensure that your online advertising appears on a variety of appropriate Web sites; joining as a publisher is a way to generate revenue at your site.
Awards	Page 193	An award will benefit your Web site only if it comes from a respected, credible source. Avoid the numerous trivial award sites that unfortunately populate the Web.
Unsubscribing	Page 194	Be considerate and always provide a way for recipients to unsubscribe from opt-in e-mail advertising messages and newsletters.
Site promotion	Page 195	Effective promotional techniques for an e-commerce site include the inexpensive techniques used for a noncommercial site, plus paid or sponsored search engine placement, affiliate programs, online advertising networks, opt-in e-mail advertising, and promotional giveaways.

HTML 4.01 Quick Reference

HTML Tags and Attributes

HTML is the original language used for publishing hypertext on the World Wide Web. It is a nonproprietary format based on Standard Generalized Markup Language (SGML). HTML documents can be created with a wide variety of tools, from simple plain text editors, such as Notepad, to sophisticated WYSIWYG editors, such as Expression Web or Dreamweaver. HTML uses tags such as <h1> and <p> to structure text into headings, paragraphs, lists, hypertext links, and so on. Many of the same tags are used in XHTML 1.0, although the usage could vary, such as whether an end tag is required.

Many HTML tags have **attributes** that can be defined in different ways to further modify the look of the Web page. The table on the following pages lists HTML tags and associated required, standard, and optional attributes. The list provides a brief description of each tag and its attributes. Many tags also could be further modified by specifying **event attributes**, which indicate the trigger to tag, such as onkeypress or onclick; these are not included in the list. In the right column, the default value for each attribute is indicated by bold text, where applicable. For a comprehensive list, more thorough descriptions, and examples of all HTML tags, visit the World Wide Web Consortium Web site at www.w3.org.

As the World Wide Web Consortium updates the HTML specifications, HTML tags constantly are being added to, deleted, and replaced by newer tags. In the list below and on the following pages, **deprecated elements**—tags that can be replaced with newer elements—are indicated with an asterisk in the right column. Deprecated elements still are available for use, and most browsers still support them. An element is deprecated when it is widely replaced with another method of completing the same task, such as using CSS. Obsolete elements are no longer in use and are not supported by common browsers. This appendix does not list obsolete elements. As a Web site designer, you should keep up to date with current standards and trends.

@SOURCE

HTML Tags and Attributes
For more information about the HTML tags and attributes listed here, visit the Web Design 4 Appendix B Student Online Companion Web page at **www .cengagebrain.com**, and then click HTML Tags and Attributes in the @Source links.

HTML Tags and Attributes

HTML Tag and Attributes	Description
<a>....</a>	Identifies the anchor; creates a hyperlink or fragment identifier
charset=*character set*	Specifies the character encoding of the linked resource
href=*url*	Specifies the target URL of a hyperlink reference
name=*text*	Specifies a name for enclosed text, allowing it to be the target of a hyperlink
rel=*relationship*	Indicates the relationship going from the current page to the target
rev=*relationship*	Indicates the relationship going from the target to the current page
target=*name*	Defines the name of the window or frame in which the linked resource will appear

HTML Tag and Attributes	Description
<address>....</address>	Defines information such as authorship, e-mail addresses, or addresses; enclosed text appears italicized and indented in some browsers
class=*classname*	Specifies an element's classname
dir=*rtl, ltr*	Sets the text direction for content
id=*id*	Specifies an element's unique id
lang=*language_code*	Specifies language code
style=*style_definition*	Specifies an element's inline style
title=*text*	Specifies extra information about an element
xml:lang=*language_code*	Specifies an element's content's language code, in XHTML documents
<area>....</area>	Creates a clickable area, or hot spot, on a client-side image map
coords=*value1, value2*	Specifies the coordinates that define the edges of the hot spot; a comma-delimited list of values
href=*url*	Specifies the target URL of a hyperlink reference
nohref	Indicates that no link is associated with the area
shape=*shape*	Identifies the shape of the area (poly, rect, circle)
target=*name*	Defines the name of the window or frame in which the linked resource will appear
<b>....</b>	Specifies text to appear in bold
<base/>	Identifies the base in all relative URLs in the document
href=*url*	Specifies the absolute URL used to resolve all relative URLs in the document
target=*name*	Defines the name for the default window or frame in which the hyperlinked pages are displayed
<big>....</big>	Increases the size of the enclosed text to a type size bigger than the surrounding text; exact display size depends on the browser and default font
<blockquote>....</blockquote>	Sets enclosed text to appear as a quotation, indented on the right and left
cite=*URL*	
<body>....</body>	Defines the start and end of a Web page
alink=*color**	Defines the color of an active link
background=*url**	Identifies the image to be used as a background
bgcolor=*color**	Sets the document's background color
link=*color**	Defines the color of links not yet visited
vlink=*color**	Defines the color of visited links

HTML Tag and Attributes	Description
** **	Inserts a line break
clear=*margin*	Sets the next line to start in a spot where the requested margin is clear (left, right, all, none); used to stop text wrap
<caption>....</caption>	Creates a caption for a table
align=*position* *	Sets caption position (top, bottom, left, right)
<center>....</center>*	Centers the enclosed text horizontally on the page
<cite>....</cite>	Indicates that the enclosed text is a citation; text usually is displayed in italic
<code>....</code>	Indicates that the enclosed text is a code sample from a program; text usually is displayed in a fixed-width font such as Courier
<col>....</col>	Organizes columns in a table into column groups to share attribute values
align=*position*	Sets horizontal alignment of text within the column (char, center, top, bottom, left, right)
span=*value*	Sets the number of columns that span the <col> element
valign=*position*	Specifies vertical alignment of text within the column (top, middle, bottom)
width=*value*	Sets the width of each column in the column group
<colgroup>....</colgroup>	Encloses a group of <col> tags and groups the columns to set properties
align=*position*	Specifies horizontal alignment of text within the column (char, center, top, bottom, left, right)
char=*character*	Specifies a character on which to align column values (for example, a period is used to align monetary values)
charoff=*value*	Specifies a number of characters to offset data aligned with the character specified in the char property
span=*number*	Sets the number of columns the <col> element spans
valign=*position*	Specifies vertical alignment of text within the column (top, middle, bottom)
width=*value*	Sets the width of each column spanned by the colgroup statement
<dd>....</dd>	Indicates that the enclosed text is a definition in the definition list
<div>....</div>	Defines block-level structure or division in the HTML document
align=*position* *	Specifies alignment of the content block (center, left, right)
class=*name*	Assigns the class name to each class of divisions
id=*name*	Assigns a unique name to a specific content block
<dl>....</dl>	Creates a definition list
<dt>....</dt>	Indicates that the enclosed text is a term in the definition list

HTML Tag and Attributes	Description
\<em\>....\</em\>	Indicates that the enclosed text should be emphasized; usually appears in italic
\<fieldset\>....\</fieldset\>	Groups related form controls and labels
align=*position**	Specifies alignment of a legend as related to the fieldset (top, bottom, middle, left, right)
\<font\>....\</font\>*	Defines the appearance of enclosed text
size=*value**	Sets the font size in absolute terms (1 through 7) or as a relative value (for example, +2)
color=*color**	Sets the font color; can be a hexadecimal value (#rrggbb) or a word for a predefined color value (for example, navy)
face=*list**	Identifies the font face; multiple entries should be separated by commas
\<form\>....\</form\>	Marks the start and end of a Web page form
action=*url*	Specifies the URL of the application that will process the form; required attribute
enctype=*encoding*	Specifies how the form element values will be encoded
method=*method*	Specifies the method used to pass form parameters (data) to the server
target=*text*	Specifies the frame or window that displays the form's results
\<frame\>....\</frame\>	Delimits a frame within a frameset
frameborder=*option*	Specifies whether the frame border is displayed (yes, no)
marginheight=*value*	Adds *n* pixels of space above and below the frame contents
marginwidth=*value*	Adds *n* pixels of space to the left and the right of the frame contents
name=*text*	Specifies the name of the frame
noresize	Prevents the user from resizing the frame
scrolling=*option*	Adds scroll bars or not—always (yes), never (no), or add when needed (**auto**)
src=*url*	Defines the URL of the source document that is displayed in the frame
\<frameset\>....\</frameset\>	Defines a collection of frames in a frameset
cols=*value1, value2,...*	Defines the number and width of frames within a frameset
rows=*value1, value2,...*	Defines the number and height of frames within a frameset
frameborder=*option*	Specifies whether the frame border is displayed (yes, no)
\<hn\>....\</hn\>	Defines a header level *n*, ranging from the largest (h1) to the smallest (h6)
align=*position*	Specifies the header alignment (**left**, center, right)
\<head\>....\</head\>	Delimits the start and end of the HTML document's head

HTML Tag and Attributes	Description
<hr>	Inserts a horizontal rule
align=*type**	Specifies the alignment of the horizontal rule (left, **center**, right)
noshade*	Specifies to not use 3D shading and to round the ends of the rule
size=*value**	Sets the thickness of the rule to a value in pixels
width=*value or %**	Sets the width of the rule to a value in pixels or a percentage of the page width; percentage is preferred
<html>....</html>	Indicates the start and the end of the HTML document
version=*data**	Indicates the HTML version used; not usually used
<i>....</i>	Sets enclosed text to appear in italic
<iframe>....</iframe>	Creates an inline frame, also called a floating frame or subwindow, within an HTML document
align=*position**	Aligns the frame with respect to context (top, middle, **bottom**, left, right)
frameborder=*option*	Specifies whether a frame border is displayed (1=yes; 0=no)
height=*value*	Sets the frame height to a value in pixels
marginheight=*value*	Sets the margin between the contents of the frame and its top and bottom borders to a value in pixels
marginwidth=*value*	Sets the margin between the contents of the frame and its left and right borders to a value in pixels
name=*text*	Assigns a name to the current frame
src=*url*	Defines the URL of the source document that is displayed in the frame
scrolling=option	Adds scroll bars or not—always (yes), never (no), or add when needed (auto)
width=value	Sets the frame width to a value in pixels
<img>....</img>	Inserts an image into the current Web page
align=*type**	Defines image alignment in relation to the text or the page margin (top, middle, bottom, right, left)
alt=*text*	Provides a text description of an image if the browser cannot display the image; always should be used
border=*value**	Sets the thickness of the border around the image to a value in pixels; default size is 3
height=*value*	Sets the height of the image to a value in pixels; always should be used
src=*url*	Specifies the URL of the image to be displayed; required
usemap=*url*	Specifies the map of coordinates and links that defines the href within this image
width=*value*	Sets the width of the image to a value in pixels; always should be used

HTML Tag and Attributes	Description
<input>....</input>	Defines controls used in forms
alt=*text*	Provides a short description of the control or image button; for browsers that do not support inline images
checked	Sets option buttons and check boxes to the checked state
disabled	Disables the control
maxlength=*value*	Sets a value for the maximum number of characters allowed as input for a text or password control
name=*text*	Assigns a name to the control
readonly	Prevents changes to the control
size=*value*	Sets the initial size of the control to a value in characters
src=*url*	Identifies the location of the image if the control is set to an image
tabindex=*value*	Specifies the tab order between elements in the form, with 1 as the first element
type=*type*	Defines the type of control (**text**, password, check box, radio, submit, reset, file, hidden, image, button)
value=*data*	Sets the initial value of the control
<ins>....</ins>	Identifies and displays text as having been inserted in the document in relation to a previous version
cite=*url*	Specifies the URL of a document that has more information on the inserted text
datetime=*datetime*	Specifies the date and time of a change
<kbd>....</kbd>	Sets enclosed text to display as keyboard-like input
<label>....</label>	Creates a label for a form control
for=*data*	Indicates the name or ID of the element to which the label is applied
<legend>....</legend>	Assigns a caption to a fieldset element, as defined by the <fieldset> tags
<li>....</li>	Defines the enclosed text as a list item in a list
value=*value1* *	Inserts or restarts counting with value1
<link>....</link>	Establishes a link between the HTML document and another document, such as an external style sheet
charset=*character set*	Specifies the character encoding of the linked resource
href=*url*	Defines the URL of the linked document
rel=*relationship*	Indicates the relationship going from the current page to the target
rev=*relationship*	Indicates the relationship going from the target to the current page

HTML Tag and Attributes	Description
target=*name*	Defines the name of the frame into which the linked resource will appear
type=*MIME-type*	Indicates the data or media type of the linked document (for example, text/CSS for linked style sheets)
<map>....</map>	Specifies a client-side image map; must enclose <area> tags
name=*text*	Assigns a name to the image map
<meta>	Provides additional data (metadata) about an HTML document
content=*text*	Specifies the value for the <meta> information; required
http-equiv=*text*	Specifies the HTTP-equivalent name for metadata; tells the server to include that name and content in the HTTP header when the HTML document is sent to the client
name=*text*	Assigns a name to metadata
scheme=text	Provides additional context for interpreting the information in the content attribute
<noframes>....</noframes>	Defines content to be displayed in browsers that do not support frames; very important to include
<object>....</object>	Includes an external object in the HTML document such as an image, a Java applet, or other external object, not well-supported by most browsers
archive=*url*	Specifies the URL of the archive containing classes and other resources that will be preloaded for use by the object
classid=*url*	Specifies the URL of the embedded object
codebase=*url*	Sets the base URL for the object; helps resolve relative references
codetype=*type*	Identifies the content type of the data in the object
data=*url*	Identifies the location of the object's data
declare	Indicates the object will be declared only, not installed in the page
height=*value*	Sets the height of the object to a value in pixels
name=*text*	Assigns a control name to the object for use in forms
standby=*text*	Defines the message to display while the object loads
tabindex=*value*	Specifies the tab order between elements, with 1 as the first element
type=*type*	Specifies the content or media type of the object
usemap=*url*	Associates an image map as defined by the <map> element
width=*value*	Sets the width of the object to a value in pixels
<ol>....</ol>	Defines an ordered list that contains numbered list item elements (<li>)
type=*option* *	Sets or resets the numbering format for the list; options include: A=capital letters, a=lowercase letters, I=capital Roman numerals, i=lowercase Roman numerals, or **1**=Arabic numerals

HTML Tag and Attributes	Description
\<option\>....\</option\>	Defines individual options in a selection list, as defined by the \<select\> element
label=*text*	Provides a shorter label for the option than that specified in its content
selected	Sets the option to be the default or the selected option in a list
value=*value*	Sets a value returned to the server when the user selects the option
disabled	Disables the option items
\<p\>....\</p\>	Delimits a paragraph; automatically inserts a blank line between text
align=*position**	Aligns text within the paragraph (left, center, right)
\<param\>....\</param\>	Passes a parameter to an object or applet, as defined by the \<object\> or \<applet\> element
id=*text*	Assigns an identifier to the element
name=*text*	Defines the name of the parameter required by an object
type=*type*	Specifies the content or media type of the object
value=*data*	Sets the value of the parameter
valuetype=*data*	Identifies the type of parameter used in the value attribute (data, ref, object)
\<pre\>....\</pre\>	Preserves the original format of the enclosed text; keeps line breaks and spacing the same as the original
\<q\>....\</q\>	Sets enclosed text as a short quotation
lang=*option*	Defines the language in which the quotation will appear
\<samp\>....\</samp\>	Sets enclosed text to appear as sample output from a computer program or script; usually appears in a monospace font
\<script\>....\</script\>	Inserts a client-side script into an HTML document
defer	Indicates that the browser should defer executing the script
src=*url*	Identifies the location of an external script
type=*MIME-type*	Indicates the data or media type of the script language (for example, text/javascript for JavaScript commands)
\<select\>....\</select\>	Defines a form control to create a multiple-choice menu or scrolling list; encloses a set of \<option\> tags to define one or more options
disabled	Disables the selection list
multiple	Sets the list to allow multiple selections
name=*text*	Assigns a name to the selection list

HTML Tag and Attributes	Description
size=*value*	Sets the number of visible options in the list
tabindex=*value*	Specifies the tab order between list items, with 1 as the first element
<small>....</small>	Sets enclosed text to appear in a smaller typeface
....	Creates a user-defined container to add inline structure to the HTML document
....	Sets enclosed text to appear with strong emphasis; usually displayed as bold text
<style>....</style>	Encloses embedded style sheet rules for use in the HTML document
media=*data*	Identifies the intended medium of the style (**screen**, tty, tv, projection, handheld, print, braille, aural, all)
title=*data*	Indicates the title of the style sheet
type=*data*	Specifies the content or media type of the style language (for example, text/CSS for linked style sheets)
_{....}	Sets enclosed text to appear in subscript
^{....}	Sets enclosed text to appear in superscript
<table>....</table>	Marks the start and end of a table
align=*position**	Aligns the table text (left, right, center)
border=*value*	Sets the border around a table to a value in pixels
cellpadding=*value*	Sets padding around each cell's contents to a value in pixels
cellspacing=*value*	Sets spacing between cells to a value in pixels
frame=*option*	Defines which parts of the outer border (frame) to display (void, above, below, hsides, lhs, rhs, vsides, box, border)
rules=*option*	Specifies which inner borders are to appear between the table cells (none, groups, rows, cols, all)
summary=*text*	Provides a summary of the table's purpose and structure
width=*value or %*	Sets table width in pixels or a percentage of the window
<tbody>....</tbody>	Defines a group of rows in a table body
align=*option*	Aligns text (left, center, right, justify, char)
char=*character*	Specifies a character on which to align column values (for example, a period is used to align monetary values)
charoff=*value*	Specifies a number of characters to offset data aligned with the character specified in the char property
valign=*position*	Sets vertical alignment of cells in a group (top, middle, bottom, baseline)

HTML Tag and Attributes	Description
<td>....</td>	Defines a data cell in a table; contents are left-aligned and normal text by default
abbr=*text*	Provides an abbreviated version of the cell's contents that browsers can use if space is limited
align=*position*	Specifies horizontal alignment (left, center, right, justify, char)
bgcolor=*color**	Defines the background color for the cell
char=*character*	Specifies a character on which to align column values (for example, a period is used to align monetary values)
charoff=*value*	Specifies a number of characters to offset data aligned with the character specified in the char property
colspan=*value*	Defines the number of adjacent columns spanned by the cell
headers=*idrefs*	Defines the list of header cells for the current cell
rowspan=*value*	Defines the number of adjacent rows spanned by the cell
scope=*option*	Specifies cells for which the element defines header cells (row, col, rowgroup, colgroup)
valign=*position*	Sets vertical alignment of cells in the group (top, middle, bottom, baseline)
width=*n* or %	Sets the width of the cell in either pixels or a percentage of the whole table width
<textarea>....</textarea>	Creates a multiline text input area within a form
cols=*value*	Defines the number of columns in the text input area
disabled	Disables the element
name=*data*	Assigns a name to the text area
readonly	Prevents the user from editing content in the text area
rows=*value*	Defines the number of rows in the text input area
tabindex=*value*	Specifies the tab order between elements, with 1 as the first element
<tfoot>....</tfoot>	Identifies and groups rows into a table footer
align=*position*	Specifies horizontal alignment (left, center, right, justify, char)
char=*character*	Specifies a character on which to align column values (for example, a period is used to align monetary values)
charoff=*value*	Specifies a number of characters to offset data aligned with the character specified in the char property
valign=*position*	Sets vertical alignment of cells in a group (top, middle, bottom, baseline)
<th>....</th>	Defines a table header cell; contents are bold and center-aligned by default
bgcolor=*color**	Defines the background color for the cell
colspan=*value*	Defines the number of adjacent columns spanned by the cell

HTML Tag and Attributes	Description
rowspan=*value*	Defines the number of adjacent rows spanned by the cell
width=*n* or %*	Sets the width of the cell in either pixels or a percentage of the whole table width
<thead>....</thead>	Identifies and groups rows into a table header
align=*position*	Specifies horizontal alignment (left, center, right, justify, char)
char=*character*	Specifies a character on which to align column values (for example, a period is used to align monetary values)
charoff=*value*	Specifies a number of characters to offset data aligned with the character specified in the char property
valign=*position*	Sets vertical alignment of cells in a group (top, middle, bottom, baseline)
<title>....</title>	Defines the title for the HTML document; always should be used
<tr>....</tr>	Defines a row of cells within a table
align=*position*	Specifies horizontal alignment (left, center, right, justify, char)
bgcolor=*color**	Defines the background color for the cell
char=*character*	Specifies a character on which to align column values (for example, a period is used to align monetary values)
charoff=*value*	Specifies a number of characters to offset data aligned with the character specified in the char property
valign=*position*	Sets vertical alignment of cells in a group (top, middle, bottom, baseline)
<tt>....</tt>	Formats the enclosed text in teletype- or computer-style monospace font
<u>....</u>*	Sets enclosed text to appear with an underline
<ul>....</ul>	Defines an unordered list that contains bulleted list item elements (<li>)
type=*option**	Sets or resets the bullet format for the list; options include circle, **disc**, square
<var>....</var>	Indicates the enclosed text is a variable's name; used to mark up variables or program arguments

C Cascading Style Sheets (CSS)

Introduction

Appendix C discusses Cascading Style Sheets (CSS), which is a multifeatured specification for HTML 4.01 and XHTML. CSS also meets the current Web Accessibility Initiative (WAI) standard for Web page element formatting and page layout. Before reviewing this appendix, you should study the information on CSS and text formatting, typography, and page layout in Chapters 4 and 5 in this text. As you review this appendix, be sure to check out the @Source references to the Student Online Companion Web page links for additional information about using CSS. Finally, keep in mind that the information presented in this appendix is a brief overview. An in-depth review of using CSS to layout and format Web page elements is beyond the scope of this appendix.

CSS Benefits

The specific benefits of using CSS include the following:

- **Significant control over typography and page layout** — CSS allows for the specification of font formatting, leading (space between lines), tracking (space between words), and kerning (space between letters). Additionally, you can control margins, indents, and element positioning through CSS.
- **Ability to make global changes to a Web site** — With CSS, you can control the appearance of hundreds of Web pages using a single style sheet. Therefore, you can quickly and consistently apply changes to all the pages in a site simply by editing the style sheet.
- **Separation of structure and presentation** — The original purpose of HTML was to define the structure of a Web document rather than the presentation of content. Using CSS to determine the presentation of the content allows for a document's appearance to be changed without impacting the document's structure.

In the past, lack of support for CSS by older browser versions deterred many Web designers from wholeheartedly adopting and using CSS. Although modern browsers offer greater levels of support for CSS, as of this writing, none offer total support for all CSS standards. Despite this limitation, most professional Web designers use at least some elements of CSS when developing Web pages to promote accessibility and usability, and to comply with industry standards.

@SOURCE

CSS Benefits
For more information about the benefits of using CSS, visit the Web Design 4 Appendix C Student Online Companion Web page at **www .cengagebrain.com**, and then click CSS Benefits: Accessibility or CSS Benefits: SEO in the @Source links.

Style Rule Syntax, Properties, and Values

Using CSS to format Web page elements is similar to formatting text using styles in word-processing software; you can apply multiple formatting instructions to page elements at one time. CSS formatting uses style rules to define the appearance or location of Web page elements. A style rule consists of a *selector*, the element affected by the rule, and a *declaration*, the property: value pairs that provide the actual formatting instructions contained within a pair of brackets { }. Figure C-1 illustrates two style rule examples.

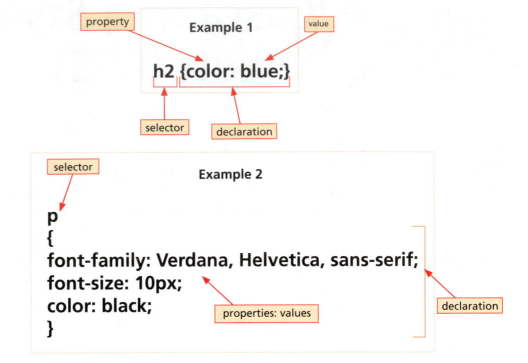

Figure C-1 A style rule consists of a selector and a declaration containing properties and their values.

@SOURCE

Syntax
For more information about style rule syntax, visit the Web Design 4 Appendix C Student Online Companion Web page at **www .cengagebrain.com**, and then click Syntax in the @Source links.

In style rule Example 1, the *selector* is the h2 heading style element and the *declaration* contains the color property and the blue value. This style rule specifies that all heading style 2 text be formatted with the blue color. The style rule in Example 2 is more complex and uses a line-by-line arrangement of the style rule elements to improve readability.

In Example 2, the *selector* is the p element (paragraph text) and the *declaration* contains multiple property: value pairs. Note that multiple values, as shown in Example 2, are separated by a comma and multiple property: value pairs are separated by a semicolon. The first property, *font-family*, specifies three values indicating three font choices for paragraph text:

- The Verdana Web font — The preferred choice
- The Helvetica sans-serif font — An alternate choice if the Verdana Web font is not available
- An available sans-serif font — A default choice if neither the preferred nor alternate font choice is available

The second property, *font-size*, specifies the paragraph text font size as 10 pixels; the third property, *color*, specifies the paragraph text font color as black.

Each CSS property has its own rule about acceptable values, such as colors, numbers, percentages, predefined values, and so forth. For example, the *font-size* property in Example 2 could have an absolute size value stated in the number of points, inches, or centimeters; a size value stated in pixels, which is relative to the screen; a size value stated as a percentage of the base font size; or a size value stated as an em value. See the CSS Property Quick Reference (Figure C-5) at the end of this appendix for a list of frequently used CSS properties.

@SOURCE

Properties and Values
For more information about CSS properties and values, visit the Web Design 4 Appendix C Student Online Companion Web page at **www .cengagebrain.com**, and then click Properties and Values in the @Source links.

Inline Styles, Internal Style Sheets, and External Style Sheets

CSS style rules are applied to a Web page in one of three ways:

- As an *inline style* inserted within the individual HTML tags on a page
- As part of an *internal style sheet* inserted within a page's HTML heading tags
- As part of an *external style sheet* linked to Web pages with an HTML tag

Inline styles involve inserting the style rule within an element's HTML tag. You should use this method sparingly because inline styles have a number of disadvantages, including failure to separate content from design (which is the primary goal of CSS), increased Web page maintenance issues, and accessibility issues. Figure C-2 provides an example of an inline style as part of the <h2> </h2> tag pair. External style sheets are the most flexible because you can use them to apply formatting rules to multiple site pages.

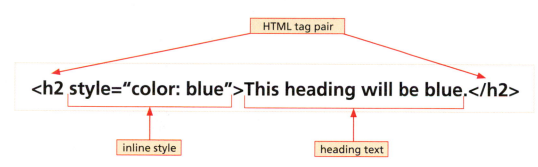

Figure C-2 Inline styles are inserted within an element's HTML tag.

Internal style sheets, also called embedded style sheets, are included within a page's HTML <head> and </head> tag pairs along with other heading information, such as a page's title. Style rules in an internal style sheet only modify elements on the page in which the rules are embedded. Figure C-3 illustrates an internal style sheet.

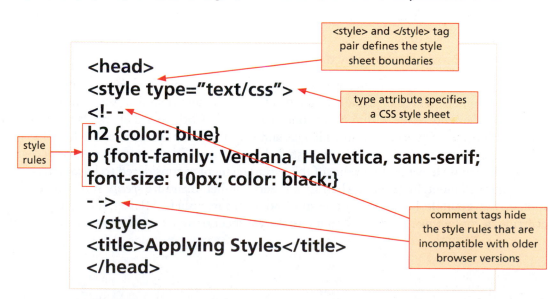

Figure C-3 Style rules in an internal style sheet only affect elements on the page in which the rules are embedded.

@SOURCE

Inline Styles
For more information about advantages and disadvantages of using inline styles, visit the Web Design 4 Appendix C Student Online Companion Web page at **www.cengagebrain.com**, and then click Inline Styles in the @Source links.

@SOURCE

Internal Style Sheets
For more information about using internal style sheets, visit the Web Design 4 Appendix C Student Online Companion Web page at **www.cengagebrain.com**, and then click Internal Style Sheets in the @Source links.

@SOURCE

External Style Sheets
For more information about using external style sheets, visit the Web Design 4 Appendix C Student Online Companion Web page at **www.cengagebrain.com**, and then click External Style Sheets in the @Source links.

An external style sheet, sometimes called a linked style sheet, is a separate text document that contains style rules. Unlike an internal style sheet, the style rules in an external style sheet can be applied to one or more Web pages by linking the pages to the external style sheet. External style sheets are a powerful tool for changing the formatting or layout of multiple pages at a site at one time simply by editing the style sheet. Figure C-4 illustrates the link to an external style sheet within a Web page's heading tags.

```
<head>
<title>My Document</title>
<link rel="stylesheet" type="text/css"
href="fundamental.css" />
</head>
```

link relationship and document type information

external style sheet URL for style sheet saved with the related Web pages

Figure C-4 The style rules in an external style sheet can be applied to one or more Web pages by linking the pages to the external style sheet.

@SOURCE

Order of Precedence
For more information about style sheet conflict resolution, visit the Web Design 4 Appendix C Student Online Companion Web page at **www.cengagebrain.com**, and then click Order of Precedence in the @Source links.

Style Sheet Conflicts

A conflict might occur when more than one style sheet applies to a Web page element. For example, a site designer could use both an inline style and an external style sheet, both of which could contain different style rules for the same page element. To resolve style sheet conflicts, browsers follow an order of precedence for applying the style sheets based on location, sometimes called a cascading order. In general, the order of precedence for a browser's application of style sheets from highest to lowest order is as follows:

1. Inline styles
2. Internal style sheet
3. External style sheet
4. Default browser styles set by the user

@SOURCE

Cascading and Inheritance
For more information about style sheet conflict resolution, visit the Web Design 4 Appendix C Student Online Companion Web page at **www.cengagebrain.com**, and then click Cascading and Inheritance in the @Source links.

In addition to the location of the style sheet, two other factors play a role in resolving style rule conflicts: inheritance and specificity. HTML elements can be nested, meaning some code elements reside within other code elements. In CSS, nested elements have a parent-child type of relationship in which certain parent element properties, such as the color property, can force their value on nested child elements when no style rule is specified for the child elements. The value of the parent element is considered to be *inherited* by the child element. In general, when style sheets conflict, the more *specific* style rule is applied. For example, because an inline style modifies a *specific* HTML tag, the inline style overrides a conflicting style rule in an internal style sheet or an external style sheet.

Figure C-5 provides a quick reference for CSS properties.

CSS Properties Quick Reference

Property	Description
Background	
background-color	Specifies the background color in hex or word codes, as in body {background-color: #ffffff}
background-image	Specifies the background image
background-attachment	Specifies whether a background image scrolls with the page or is fixed
background-position	Sets the position of a background image
Font	
font-family	Specifies typeface
font-style	Specifies the normal or italic style
font-size	Specifies the size of the text as absolute, relative, a percentage, or by length
font-weight	Specifies normal or bold
font-variant	Specifies normal or small caps
Margin	
margin-left, margin-right, margin-top, margin-bottom	Specifies the amount of space around an element
Position	
position	Specifies the placement of an image; absolute for specific placement or relative for placement in relation to other images
Text	
text-align	Aligns text horizontally
text-decoration	Adds underline, line-through, or other text decoration
text-indent	Specifies the amount of the first-line indent from a paragraph's left margin
word-spacing	Controls the amount of spaces between words
text-transform	Specifies uppercase or lowercase
color	Specifies text color

Figure C-5 Commonly used CSS properties.

@SOURCE

Tips and Tricks
For tips about using CSS to insert figures with captions, create different types of menus, select font families, align text and images, and more, visit the Web Design 4 Appendix C Student Online Companion Web page at **www .cengagebrain.com**, and then click Tips and Tricks in the @Source links.

D Designing for Mobile Devices

Introduction

Appendix D introduces topics related to creating a separate version of your site for mobile device users. As the number of people using phones and other mobile devices to access the Internet increases, many companies are concerned with providing these visitors with site versions that work better with a mobile device. The decision to create a mobile-friendly site depends on several factors, including your audience's needs, your current site's structure and features, and the cost and time restrictions you have.

First, consider the demographic and psychographic profile of your typical site visitor (included in your target audience profile), and determine how many visitors might be accessing the Internet through a mobile device. Next, determine how important a mobile version of your site would be to site visitors. For example, visitors checking on train schedules or driving directions are more likely to need easily viewable content through their mobile device than visitors who are doing research into retirement plans.

If you determine that your site's typical visitors have a need to frequently access your site using mobile devices, next evaluate your current site setup. Do you use long paragraphs of text, many high-resolution images, or Flash or JavaScript elements that might not work with a mobile device? If so, you will need to make a separate mobile site.

Once you decide to create a mobile site version, identify the amount of time and resources you can devote to this endeavor. Depending on the conclusions you reach, there are free and low-cost options to consider as well as more expensive methods. Whatever method you choose, you will need to create a site that fits your audience's needs as well as meets W3C standards.

Technical Requirements

To create a mobile site or evaluate your site for its adaptability, you must understand the following technical aspects of mobile sites:

@SOURCE

Mobile Web Standards

For more information about W3C standards, visit the Web Design 4 Appendix D Student Online Companion Web page at **www .cengagebrain.com**, and then click Mobile Web Standards in the @Source links.

- **Protocols** — Wireless Access Protocol (WAP) is a protocol developed for use by mobile Web browsers, based on HTTP standards. WAP 2.0 was followed by other Wireless Internet Protocols, including later versions of WAP, XHTML Basic, and Nokia's HXTML Mobile Profile. Wireless Internet Protocols enable Web pages to display in Web browsers and mobile browsers without requiring the creation of separate versions of the same page.

- **W3C standards** — The W3C guidelines for mobile site development include tips such as using HTTP transfer compression and using CSS to speed page loading and minimize battery usage, as well as user-oriented features such as making phone numbers "Click-to-call," meaning that the user simply has to click or touch it to initiate a voice call.

- **Wireless markup language (WML)** — Wireless markup language is like a limited version of HTML. To create a WML document, you need to indicate in the header of the HTML document that the document uses WML. In WML, pages are called cards. A card is the amount of content shown within a screen at a time.

- **CSS usage** — Use CSS for layout to make sure your pages load faster and are more compatible with mobile browsers. Using HTML tables for layout will cause problems with the display.

- **Differing screen sizes** — Just as you consider screen resolution when designing your site, screen size can also differ greatly in mobile devices. Use a liquid layout to minimize scrolling, and place the most important information at the top of the page.

- **Navigation and input methods** — Consider providing Back buttons and links in case the visitor's mobile browser doesn't include navigation methods. Include features such as radio buttons and lists for user input to avoid the visitor needing to type data.

- **Limit media and animated content** — Flash, JavaScript, and even static images can cause a slowdown of the mobile browser, take up space on the visitor's screen, and might be incompatible with the visitor's browser, causing errors.

@SOURCE

Mobile Site Adaptors
For more information about mobile site adaptors, visit the Web Design 4 Appendix D Student Online Companion Web page at **www.cengagebrain.com**, and then click Mobile Site Adaptors in the @Source links.

Creating and Publishing a Mobile Site

With a certain amount of know-how, you can adapt your site for mobile purposes or create a mobile version from scratch using familiar Web site creation software, such as Adobe Dreamweaver. If you are creating or adapting your mobile site using programming tools or a WYSIWYG editor, you can test it either within the WYSIWYG editor or by using mobile site emulators, such as iphonetester.com.

Depending on your resources, experience, and time, you can also create and publish a mobile site in very little time using free and low-cost mobile device site adaptors from sites such as Zinadoo, Winksite, MobiSiteGalore, or MoFuse or using Google's conversion utility. Figure D-1 shows a site in a traditional browser and the same site adapted by Google's conversion tool.

Figure D-1 Mobile device site adaptors help streamline content and adjust page width.

When your site is complete, you will need to publish it. Using a domain such as .mobi indicates to search engines that the site is specifically created or adapted for mobile users. You can also publish your mobile site as a subdomain of your main site and redirect users with mobile devices automatically.

Once your site is published, you should register it with multiple mobile-only Web directories to make sure visitors can find it quickly. Examples of mobile-only Web directories include the MobileWeb Directory, Mobile Mammoth, W3Moz, Click4Wap, and JumpTap.

Index

Credits